YOU TURN

A Family Devotional

Written by
Fountainview Academy Students

Fountainview Academy
Box 500, Lillooet, BC, V0K-1V0
Canada

Fountainview Academy
P.O. Box 500
Lillooet, British Columbia V0K1V0
CANADA
Web Address: www.fountainview.ca
E-mail: info@fountainviewacademy.ca

Copyright © 2009 by
Fountainview Academy
All rights reserved

Introductory quotations from the *Holy Bible* or from *Sketches from the Life of Paul,* Copyright © 1974 by The Ellen G. White Estate, Inc.

Scripture quotations marked KJV are from the King James Version.
Bible verses credited to NKJV are from the New King James Version. Copyright © 1979, 1980, 1982 by Thomas Nelson, Inc. Used by permission. All rights reserved.
Scripture quotations marked NIV are from the *Holy Bible, New International Version.* Copyright © 1973, 1978, 1984, International Bible Society. Used by permission of Zondervan Bible Publishers.
Texts credited to NET are from The NET ® Bible, New English Translation, Copyright © 1996 by Biblical Studies Press, L.L.C. All rights reserved.
Scripture quotations marked NASB taken from the NEW AMERICAN STANDARD BIBLE®, Copyright © 1960, 1962, 1963, 1968, 1971, 1972, 1973, 1975, 1977, 1995 by The Lockman Foundation. Used by permission.
Texts credited to ESV are from the The Holy Bible, English Standard Version, which is adapted from the Revised Standard Version of the Bible, copyright Division of Christian Education of the National Council of the Churches of Christ in the U.S.A. All rights reserved.
Scripture quotations marked NLT are taken from the Holy Bible, New Living Translation, Copyright © 1996, 2004. Used by permission of Tyndale House Publishers, Inc., Wheaton, Illinois 60189. All rights reserved.

This book was
Edited by Mike Lemon, Cara Dewsberry and Donna Brown
Cover Design by Robert Richards, Leighton Sjoren and Vanessa Richards
Cover Photo by Robert Richards of Leighton Sjoren
Authors' Pages by Brad Donesky
Electronic Makeup by D. Luke Gonzalez
Typeset: 10/12 Liberation Sans, 11 Liberation Serif

PRINTED IN U.S.A.

ISBN 10: 0615288111
ISBN 13: 9780615288116

Introduction

YOU TURN zooms in on the 180-degree turnaround that took the bitter, malice-filled heart of Saul of Tarsus and produced a complete metamorphosis. The proud, passionate nature of Saul had been so transformed by the grace of Christ that "the communion with Christ which Paul now enjoyed, was more intimate and more enduring than a mere earthly and human companionship" (*Sketches from the Life of Paul*, pg. 277).

The Fountainview Academy, Grade 11, English class (Graduating Class of 2010) wrote this FAMILY DEVOTIONAL, *YOU TURN*. I gave them the assignment of reading the book *Sketches from the Life of Paul*, by Ellen G. White, and then writing twenty-three devotional readings each, based on Bible verses or quotes from *Sketches*. After marking and editing their work, I had the assistance of two students, Cara Dewsberry and Donna Brown, to format, to organize the order of the devotional readings, and to help make corrections to the book prior to its publication. It was truly a labor of love!

It is our prayer that, as you read daily from these pages, you will grow "to apprehend Christ by faith, to have a spiritual knowledge of him... [which is] more to be desired than a personal acquaintance with him as he appeared on earth" (*Sketches from the Life of Paul*, pg. 277).

Mike Lemon
English Teacher
Fountainview Academy
British Columbia, CANADA

About
the
Authors

Jennifer Atkins, 19
Washington, USA
Interests/Goals: music, journaling, being with friends, biking, camping, traveling, reading, and spending time alone to think or daydream.

Rebecca Brousson, 17
British Columbia, Canada
Interests/Goals: spending time with God and family and friends, music, shopping, animals, cooking/baking, trying new things, being adventurous, reading, hiking, running, swimming, snowboarding; become a registered nurse, massage therapist, fitness trainer, or something that has to do with nutrition.

Melissa Butler, 16
Oregon, USA
Interests/Goals: music, reading, writing, cooking, eating, gardening, biking, camping, kayaking; interior design, business, being a missionary.

David Chang, 18
Gyeonggi-Do, South Korea
Interests/Goals: music, hanging out with friends; to be like Jesus.

Cara Dewsberry, 17
California, USA
Interests/Goals: reading, writing, music, hanging out with friends, traveling, horseback riding, talking, daydreaming, interior design; to grow closer to God, maybe be an editor, travel Europe.

Brad Donesky, 18
Tennessee, USA
Interests/Goals: Computers, traveling, sports, cooking, building things, and of course, spending time with friends, to grow closer to God every day.

Jon Fink, 18
Montana, USA
Interests/Goals: aviation, skiing, working/playing with electronics, playing guitar and bass; get into professional aeronautics, run a ranch for troubled boys, have a Christian band, be more like Jesus.

Robby Folkenberg, 17
Washington, USA
Interests/Goals: playing cello, soccer, mountain biking, mountaineering, reading biographies, backpacking; get a double major in music and theology, backpack Europe, become a pastor and missionary.

Ryo Fusamae, 17
Japan
Interests/Goals: music, traveling; become a music producer, have my own recording label.

D. Luke Gonzalez, 17
California, USA
Interests/Goals: theology, psychology, reading, book collecting, canoeing, computers/Linux; become a professor of theology, get an article in the Journal of Adventist Theological Society, get a Ph.D. in the Philosophy of Religious Education.

Jeremy Grabiner, 16
Tennessee, USA
Interests/Goals: sports, music, hanging out with friends; do mission work.

Michael Hamel, 17
Oregon, USA
Interests/Goals: reading, drawing, playing viola and classical guitar, baking and cooking, horseback riding; become a pilot and a better worker for God.

Joseph Heagy, 17
Washington, USA
Interests/Goals: snowmobiling, snowboarding, mountain biking, backpacking, the outdoors, music, friends, God, computers, electronics; to get into business, construction.

Melody Hyde, 16
Michigan, USA
Interests/Goals: spending time with God and family and friends, sewing, knitting, crocheting, reading, singing, talking; to be joyful, to serve the Lord and be open to His leading in my life.

Sharon Jeon, 16
South Korea
Interests/Goals: bright colors, home design, psychology, writing music, photography; become a naturopathic pediatrician, become a medical missionary.

Rebecca Luchak, 17
British Columbia, Canada
Interests/Goals: God, family, friends, snowboarding, horseback riding, music, cooking, dirt-biking, camping, swimming, shopping, fashion design/interior design; go to Southern Adventist University, eventually become a nurse/homemaker/overseas missionary.

Jenny McCluskey, 17
Washington, USA
Interests/Goals: reading, knitting, cooking, missions, writing poems; to be like Jesus, to become a doctor or ophthalmologist.

Veronica Nudd, 17
Tennessee, USA
Interests/Goals: animals, reading, friends, singing, 3-wheeling, trucks/cars; go to Southern University, join medical field, be a friend forever.

David Ortiz, 17
Montemorelos, Mexico
Interests/Goals: God, family, reading, listening to classical music, walking in nature, spending time with friends, playing with my pets, shopping, biking, canoeing, hiking; go to Southern University, study music.

Douglas Schappert, 17
Wisconsin, USA
Interests/Goals: mountain biking, 4-wheeling, horseback riding, blogging; become a mechanic or heavy equipment operator.

Jonathan Sharley, 17
Washington, USA
Interests/Goals: music, art, mountaineering, yodeling; live life to the fullest, truly make a difference in other's lives, herd goats in the Swiss alps.

Leighton Sjoren, 17
Oregon, USA
Interests/Goal: I'd like to be either a chiropractor, or a sports doctor, because I really enjoy learning about how the body works. Other things I am interseted in include computer technology, skiing, weightlifting, and hanging out with friends.

Jourdain Smith, 16
Maryland, USA
Interests/Goals: playing cello, audio/video editing, soccer, football, biking, snowboarding, hanging out with friends and family, spending time with God, eating, having fun; to become a mechanical engineer, pilot, musician, counselor.

Buddy Taylor, 16
Tennessee, USA
Interests/Goals: animation, architecture, computers, cooking, swimming, rollerblading.

Dave White, 17
West Virginia, USA
Interests/Goals: playing the piano, music, hanging out with friends, soccer;
to show Jesus to someone.

Amy Windels, 18
Alberta, Canada
Interests/Goals: nature photography, reading,
hanging out with friends.

Mike Lemon, English Teacher
British Columbia, Canada
Interests/Goals: Jesus, My Wife, My children,
Teaching, Preaching, Reading, Writing, Horseback
riding, Gardening, Learning new things,
and Getting lost in the mountains.

Donna Brown, Senior Student/Editor, 18
Alabama, USA
Interests/Goals: Camping, backpacking,
hanging out with friends, photography, writing,
reading, cooking, and health. Be a blessing
wherever I am, travel, go to college and be a true
christian music.

January 1

From the Days of Old

The Lord hath appeared of old unto me, saying, Yea, I have loved thee with an everlasting love: therefore with loving kindness have I drawn thee. – Jeremiah 31:3 KJV

How would you classify the story of Paul? With all the murder plots, shipwrecks, and narrow escapes from danger, maybe it could be a mystery or action/adventure story. Or, because the majority of Paul's life was devoted to sharing Christ, it could be a mission story. But have you ever thought of it as being a love story? It really is, you know, but not in a romantic sense. It's a story about the immeasurable transforming love of God for a wretched sinner.

John 3:16, one of the most famous Bible verses, describes this thrilling love in a simple yet profound way: "For God so loved the world, that he gave his only begotten Son, that whosoever believeth in him should not perish, but have everlasting life" (KJV). From the very beginning, God knew what He would do if man chose to rebel. In His amazing love, He formulated the plan of salvation—the plan that would send Jesus to our doomed planet to live and suffer and die for you and me. This sacrifice of love was made so that it would be possible for sinners to find forgiveness and victory; so that Saul of Tarsus could become Paul the Apostle; so that when, two thousand years later, a little girl named Cara was born, she would have a chance at eternal life.

From the days of old, God has loved you and me. Will you follow the example of Paul and let Him save you? He yearns for the day when He can meet with you face to face.

~ Cara Dewsberry

January 2

Shhhhh!

He had no personal knowledge of Jesus of Nazareth or of his mission, but he readily imbibed the scorn and hatred of the rabbis toward one who was so far from fulfilling their ambitious hopes; and after the death of Christ, he eagerly joined with priests and rulers in the persecution of his followers as a proscribed and hated sect.
– Sketches from the Life of Paul, pg. 10

Gossip pervades our society like the plague. It's everywhere you go—plastering magazine covers in the grocery store; dominating your best friend's conversations; even slipping into prayer meetings and churches. You hear a snippet of interesting news, and you pass it on. You hardly ever stop to find out whether it's true or not, but simply join in no matter how it might make the person feel.

Saul didn't personally know Jesus, but he respected his fellow rabbis who absolutely hated Christ. They spread lies about Him and were ever seeking to destroy His followers. Saul didn't study out the facts for himself to see if this Jesus was the Messiah. Instead he studied for evidence to support the lies of the rabbis. Because this "gossip" blinded Saul, he took a very influential part in the trial and execution of Stephen; and Jesus literally had to knock him off his high horse before Saul realized that he was the one in error.

If you hear gossip knocking at your door today, remember the trouble it caused Saul and resist the urge to let it in. The information may or may not be true; so instead of spreading it around, say something nice about the person or change the subject. Just think of how you would feel if someone were spreading a rumor about you.

~ Melissa Butler

January 3

God of the Past and the Future

The disciples, endowed with a power and energy hitherto unknown, preached Christ... Signs and wonders confirmed their words...thousands openly declared their faith in Jesus of Nazareth. – Sketches from the Life of Paul, pg. 11

The disciples preached with great enthusiasm after the Holy Spirit fell on them. They were on fire for God, even willing to stand up and suffer persecution for His sake. They were met with many hardships and endured imprisonment and beatings for preaching Christ; but their work wasn't futile. Converts were daily added to the church, and countless miracles were performed. Nothing could stop the disciples from preaching, and God's mighty hand was with them constantly.

When Peter and John were imprisoned by the murderous Jews, God miraculously opened the prison doors and delivered them because His plan for them wasn't finished yet. God provided for the needs of all who were being persecuted or separated from their families. God never forgot about His faithful few.

Over the years, we have heard many times that we are living in the last days. I used to be scared of the last days with their persecution and danger. But the stories of the apostles and their deliverance from trials are very encouraging. We will encounter similar persecution and hardships; but God will be with us and pour out the Holy Spirit again. Many will be converted and miracles will be performed. When we are in distress, God will provide as He has in the past. Read this out loud: Although I might be afraid of persecution and trials ahead, I know that God will help me as He has helped His people in the past.

~ Sharon Jeon

January 4

Forsaken—but not by God

Most of the early believers were cut off from family and friends by the zealous bigotry of the Jews. Many of the converts had been thrown out of business and exiled from their homes, because they had espoused the cause of Christ. – Sketches from the Life of Paul, pg. 14

In a mountain village of northern Rwanda, there lived a little girl whose name was Christine. She always wore a torn red dress, for it was all she had. With excitement and interest, she attended every youth Bible study held by the Seventh-day Adventists. But the pastor refused to baptize her because he thought she was too young to be serious about Jesus. However, she kept going to the Bible studies and learning all she could.

Christine's alcoholic mother beat her and told her never again to attend the Seventh-day Adventist meetings on the hill. Her new Bible was taken from her and sold, and she was beaten so severely that she fled to another village to live with her older sister. Despite the beatings, little Christine still loved Jesus. Though she was forsaken by her mother, God did not leave her alone.

Jesus warns us that we will be hated for His name's sake. But through the Bible He gives us the comforting message: "He that endureth to the end shall be saved" (Mathew 10:22 KJV). Jesus also tells us to rejoice when we are suffering for His sake, for suffering is heaven's highest honor, and we will receive our reward. Revelation 2:10 says, "Fear none of those things which thou shalt suffer: behold the devil shall cast some of you into prison, that ye may be tried…Be thou faithful unto death, and I will give thee a crown of life" (KJV).

~ Jenny McCluskey

January 5

Stuck

My brethren, count it all joy when ye fall into divers temptations; Knowing this, that the trying of your faith worketh patience. But let patience have her perfect work, that ye may be perfect and entire, wanting nothing. – James 1:2-4 KJV

There I was with my dean, stuck in a small car, in a foot of snow, five miles from the nearest house. What started out as a routine trip to the doctor turned into a faith-trying experience. The main road was blocked because of a forest fire, and the only way around led us through this undesirable, snowy place. As we assessed the situation, our prospects appeared dim. Help seemed far away; yet it was really right there. Our heavenly Father was with us, and He helped us get out. He sent an angel to give us the extra push that got us unstuck. When we needed that added strength, both physical and spiritual, God sent it.

The apostles fell into the same predicament that we were in. They were cast into prison for persistently sharing Jesus with others—they were stuck! This was surely not in their plans, and their faith was severely tried. But though the situation was out of their hands, they depended fully on the Lord, and He helped them through.

In life, problems beset us, and we get stuck. But we have the comfort that God will be there to lead us. Circumstances sometimes do not go the way we've planned, but God allows this that our characters may be perfected. He will give us the extra strength to overcome.

~ Jourdain Smith

January 6

Life of Love

Wherefore, brethren, look ye out among you seven men of honest report, full of the Holy Spirit and wisdom, whom we may appoint over this business. – Acts 6:3 KJV

God called for the appointing of seven upright men to take over the work of distributing charity to the poor. To accomplish this work, the Holy Spirit filled the men, and Christ became the theme of their daily lives. Stephen, the most well known of the seven, understood and explained the Bible so clearly that not even the priests could argue against him. The seven deacons ministered to people in their own communities, and many were added to God's kingdom because of their work.

We also are to be actively proclaiming the truth. To do this, we need not leave our home or workplace, for it is often those nearest us who need the Savior's love the most. Simple acts of kindness, such as offering a glass of lemonade to a thirsty passer-by, can show the love of Jesus. I remember a particular time when I was shown Christ's love by a friend. That day, sickness plagued me; I felt delirious and was in much pain. My friend saw me in agony and demonstrated his love and concern by taking time out of work to care for me and help me regain my health. I cannot forget that day; my friend was so Christ-like, and I so undeserving. Through my friend, I could see Jesus caring for me.

How often are there people around us, whose day could be brightened by one small act of kindness? By helping someone in need, you are showing him the love of our Savior. Today, take the time to reach out to someone who is hurting. In doing so, God's purpose will be fulfilled through you.

~ Buddy Taylor

January 7

Ignoring the Evidence

Many who beheld the lighted countenance of Stephen trembled and veiled their faces; but stubborn unbelief and prejudice never faltered.
– Sketches from the Life of Paul, pg. 17

    The Pharisees ignored the evidence in favor of Christ and were blinded by their stubborn pride. When Stephen was tried for preaching Jesus, the priests and rulers beheld a holy radiance all about him. But they still refused to accept Christ and chose to cling to their prejudices. Their persistent unbelief turned to satanic rage, and dragging Stephen out of the judgment hall, they stoned him. The Pharisees didn't realize that they were being controlled by the devil, for they had convinced themselves that they were doing God's will.

    Although Christ's power was revealed many times, the religious leaders remained unmoved. Even when the priests witnessed the miraculous healing of the cripple by Peter and John, they would not believe in Jesus. Soon after, the disciples were imprisoned for their faith. The next morning, the prison doors were found securely bolted with the guards standing at their posts. But the apostles' cell was empty; they had been released by an angel and were again preaching in the temple. Despite all this God-given evidence, the leaders still would not abandon the stubborn bias that was blocking their way to Christ.

    When I was younger, my little brother and I would argue for fun. Even when I knew I was losing an argument, my pride would refuse to admit defeat. In situations like this, the Holy Spirit speaks to our hearts, and we can choose to listen to Him and give up our selfish inclinations. If, like the priests and rulers, we ignore the evidence and let unbelief and pride take over, our salvation will be jeopardized. Remember, the reward of heaven is for those who *surrender* to Jesus.

~ Joey Heagy

January 8

Holy Radiance

And all that sat in the council, looking steadfastly on him, saw his face as it had been the face of an angel. – Acts 6:15 KJV

Stephen was one of the first deacons of the early church. He helped the poor and widowed and taught in the synagogues of the Greek Jews. It was in these synagogues that his trouble began. The priests would often engage him in public discussions where he would, with the help of the Holy Spirit, defend the truths he taught.

Over time, the priests and rulers developed a bitter hatred for Stephen. Finally they called a trial and summoned scholarly Jews from the countries round about Israel. Saul was among those called, and when he met Stephen, he found in him a man of equal intelligence and spiritual understanding. The priests tried to prove that Stephen was teaching dangerous and blasphemous doctrines. But they were no match against this man of God and his wisdom from above. Stephen's face shone with a holy radiance as he answered the charges against him.

As we look at the world around us, we see that we are in the end times. It may not be long until we are called before a judge to answer for our faith. Do you want to be so close to God that, when you are called to give an answer, your face shines as the face of an angel? I hope that is your prayer and goal.

~ Amy Windels

January 9

Do You Shine?

His face [Stephen's]... shone with an angelic light.
– Sketches from the Life of Paul, pg. 19

    Darkness fell earlier than we expected. The sudden blackness of night penetrated the whole mountain. Thankfully, a few members of our team of hikers had remembered their headlamps. The beams of light illuminated the trail that led down to camp.

    In this same manner, the face of Stephen shone through the intense darkness that surrounded him at his trial. During the final moments of his life, Stephen addressed the Sanhedrin and told about his best friend Jesus. What a contrast this scene portrayed! In the midst of Satan's helpers, who were bursting with diabolic rage, the calm, Spirit-filled Stephen radiated the light of Heaven. This light sent a message to all present: Stephen had been with Jesus.

    This same light was seen on the face of Moses after he had spent time with God on Mount Sinai. Exodus 34:29 says, "His face glowed because he had spoken to the Lord face to face" (NLT). After Moses had personally talked with God, his countenance was noticeably different. It was obvious that he had been in the presence of divinity.

    During His time on earth, Jesus emphasized the importance of "light." He told His disciples, "You are the light of the world" (Matthew 5:14 NKJV). Our job as Christians is to illuminate the darkness of Planet Earth. If you will spend time with the Savior, He will "make His face shine upon you..." (Numbers 6:25 NKJV). As a result, your face will glow with the light of Heaven, and others will be able to recognize that you have been with Jesus. Will your face shine today?

~ Jonathan Sharley

January 10

The Nightmare

The martyrdom of Stephen made a deep impression upon all who witnessed it...The signet of God upon his face, his words that reached to the very soul of those who heard them, remained in the memory of the beholders... – Sketches from the Life of Paul, pg. 19

Kneeling there with the face of an angel, young Stephen seemed to ignore the stone that had found its mark. His voice, filled with love, rang out pleadingly, "Lord, lay not this sin to their charge." Silence filled the air while the love and peace radiating off Stephen's face pierced the cold hearts of his murderers, warming them for a few moments. Then like glass, the stillness was shattered by a single stone's blow, once more leaving their hearts numb, hardened, and bitterly cold.

* * *

Saul awoke with a start to see the sun chasing away the night's dark hue. He climbed stiffly out of bed with the nightmare still lingering in his mind. "Do the council remember it like I do?" he thought while stretching. Suddenly, the day's affairs rushed back to his mind, crowding out the pricks of conscience. With a smile he remembered the transaction about to take place and the responsibility that he had received from the Sanhedrin council. Damascus needed to be purged of those traitorous followers of Christ, and since Saul was going there soon, he had been commissioned to do the job. Dressed and ready, he rushed out the door, leaving behind the nightmare to live out his own dream.

Could it be that, like Saul, you ignore the promptings of God's Spirit to follow your own desires? Whose dream are you living?

~ Michael Hamel

January 11

Honored by God

Stephen was honored of God at the very period when he was dishonored of men. – Sketches from the Life of Paul, pg. 20

The year 1918 was significant in world history. On November 11 of that year, the peace treaty ending World War I was signed. During the next few years, monuments were built in the great cities of the world and the bodies of unknown soldiers were buried where people could see and remember the millions of soldiers who died to bring peace back to the world. In France, an unknown soldier was buried under the Arc de Triumphe, and above the grave a flame representing sacrifice is kept burning day and night. In England, an unknown soldier was buried in Westminster Abbey. In the United States, an unknown soldier was buried in Arlington National Cemetery on November 11, 1921. A marble tomb was erected ten years later with the simple inscription: "Here rests in honored glory an American soldier known but to God." Sentries, who are changed every hour during the day and every two hours during the night, keep guard over the tomb.

Stephen was a mighty warrior for God and a strong pillar in the early Christian church. He was cruelly martyred by the priests and rulers because of his love for Jesus, whom they hated. Although there is no large tombstone, no imposing monument marking the resting place of Stephen, he is honored in Heaven. Our supreme goal should be to be honored by God.

~ Rebecca Luchak

January 12

A Stirred Mind

The mind of Saul was greatly stirred by the triumphant death of Stephen. – Sketches from the Life of Paul, pg. 21

As he walked away from the council chamber, Saul pondered what had just transpired. He had sought for help from the council in answering some tough questions he had about Stephen's trial and stoning just two days before. Saul could not help but notice how peacefully Stephen had died, without any look of hatred or even of reproach. It was this that had made Saul wonder if the Pharisees had actually been right about Stephen. Had he really been just another rebel trying to upset the ancient laws? Or could he have been inspired by God, just as Moses was?

The other members of the council had assured Saul that they were right in their judgments, and to help ease his mind, they had "elected" him into the Sanhedrin council. Still the questions remained in Saul's mind: how was Stephen able to die so peacefully, even asking for the forgiveness of his murderers?

Our actions, whether great or small, always have an effect on those around us. Stephen's life and death had a great influence upon Saul. This influence began to lead Saul closer and closer to Christ, until he finally met and accepted Jesus on the way to Damascus.

"Let no man imagine that he has no influence. Whoever he maybe, and wherever he may be placed, that man who thinks becomes a light and a power." – Henry George

~ Brad Donesky

January 13

A Double Purpose

Saul was about to journey to Damascus upon his own business; but he was determined to accomplish a double purpose, by searching out, as he went, all the believers in Christ. – Sketches from the Life of Paul, pg. 21

    Saul was going to Damascus on his own business. He might have been visiting relatives, a doctor, or just shopping. But whatever the task was, he didn't travel anywhere without also looking for Christians to persecute. He felt that it was his personal duty to curb this "heretical" new teaching, and he did so even when he was about his own business.

    God saw in Saul some good character traits, which would be useful in His work. Saul was industrious, determined, and zealous. He was committed to his convictions and was always pursuing his purposes, even on personal trips to town. But Saul was obviously fighting for the wrong side. God miraculously turned Saul around and put his dedication to a superior cause. Suddenly, he was entirely devoted to sharing the gospel wherever he went. God sent him on several journeys through many countries as a missionary. Saul, whose name was changed to Paul, later wrote in a letter to his friend Timothy, "I have fought the good fight, I have finished the race, I have kept the faith" (2 Timothy 4:7 NIV). You see, wherever Paul's track went, he kept running towards one goal—the finish line.

    So wherever you may go today, and whatever you may do, keep in mind that you have a double purpose. There is no time for any vacations from witnessing. In every moment, look for an opportunity to share the One you love.

~ Melissa Butler

January 14

The Journey

While Saul, with his companions, was gazing and admiring, suddenly a light above the brightness of the sun shone round about him, "and he fell to the earth, and heard a voice saying unto him, Saul, Saul, why persecutest thou me? And he said, who art thou, Lord? And the Lord said, I am Jesus whom thou persecutest; it is hard for thee to kick against the pricks." – Sketches from the Life of Paul, pg. 22

Nearing Damascus, Saul admired the scenes of nature that surrounded the city. He found the fields of flowers, fruit-laden orchards, and gurgling roadside streams wonderfully refreshing after the taxing journey through the desert waste.

Suddenly, he and his companions found themselves trapped in an intensely bright light. Saul fell to the ground and waited for what he feared was his apparent doom. "And he…heard a voice saying unto him, Saul, Saul, why persecutest thou me? And he said, Who art thou, Lord? And the Lord said, I am Jesus whom thou persecutest: it is hard for thee to kick against the pricks" (Acts 9:4, 5 KJV).

Like a seed buried in the dirt, all the evidence in favor of Christ that Saul had hidden away began to sprout forth in the light of Christ's words. Stephen's trial and death had been the seed, and the death of other martyrs had watered the truth implanted in Saul's heart. Now the seed that had been planted began to grow into one of the strongest trees of faith that has been seen since Christ's.

Why don't you let God water the seeds in your heart, and then watch them grow into a tree of faith like Paul's?

~ Michael Hamel

January 15

Kicking a Cactus

It is hard for thee to kick against the pricks. – Acts 9:5 KJV

Have you ever kicked a cactus? Ouch! It hurts. Our consciences are very sensitive and will prick us until we listen. Most of us have experienced a situation where we strove against our consciences and used ridiculous logic to kick against something that, deep inside, we knew was wrong.

I remember sitting in front of the television fascinated with movies or shows that I insisted were okay. Hey, the family being portrayed was close knit, the moral of the story was great, and the setting even had God's scenery in it! (That's a lame one, I admit.) Then, all of a sudden, boom! It was too late. A graphic murder, horrid innuendos, or a torrent of profanity was suddenly added to the scars of past sights that were forever engraved on my mind. I hadn't listened to the prompting of the Holy Spirit. I kicked against a cactus. Ouch!

Saul experienced something similar. He was killing God's children—all in the name of Judaism. Inspiration tells us that Saul was horrified when he realized that he had closed his eyes and ears against the most striking evidence and continued to persecute the believers in Christ. Saul finally submitted his will and stopped kicking against the thorns of truth.

God has blessed all of us with the gift of the Holy Spirit. He is our conscience. We need to listen to Him and not kick back. If God is speaking to you, listen! You will never regret it.

~ Veronica Nudd

January 16

The Blessing of Solitude

He was taken to the house of the disciple Judas, and there he remained, in solitude…in lonely seclusion…in perfect blindness. – Sketches from the Life of Paul, pp. 26, 27

Darkness. Solitude. Spiritual awakening. For three days after his life-shaking vision on the Damascus Road, Paul was shut away from light and human companionship that he might repent of his sin and seek God's forgiveness. Yet during this bitter time, Paul was not left altogether alone; the loving Father was with him, speaking to his broken soul, guiding his search for truth, and preparing him to be a humble servant of the Gospel.

Throughout Scripture are examples of men and women who have had to endure times of lonely seclusion that they might deepen their communion with God and be fitted for a special work. Moses was sent to the wilderness of Midian; David to the shepherd's fields; Esther to the spiritual seclusion of a heathen palace; Christ to the desert of temptation.

God still uses times of quiet and solitude to turn our focus away from the things of this world and to draw out our souls in love to Him. When you find yourself on a lonely section of life's road, with few friends to share in your sunshine and storms, do not complain; rather use this opportunity to draw close to your heavenly Friend. To each one of us He will sometime call: "Come ye yourselves apart into a desert place, and rest a while" (Mark 6:31 KJV). When He calls you, do not be afraid to walk into the seeming shadows of solitude, for you will but find them to be a doorway into the brilliant light of friendship with God.

~ Cara Dewsberry

January 17

At a Crossroads

Overcome by a sense of his guilt, he cried out, "Lord, what wilt thou have me to do?" Jesus did not then and there inform him of the work he had assigned him, but sent him for instruction to the very disciples whom he had so bitterly persecuted. – Sketches from the Life of Paul, pg. 28

I think it's interesting how, when Saul asked Jesus what He wanted him to do, Jesus didn't tell him right away. Instead, He sent Saul to the very disciples whom he had so bitterly persecuted. In the same way, we sometimes ask God what He wants us to do, but we don't get a direct answer from Him. Sometimes the answer comes through someone else, and often the answer we get isn't what we wanted to hear. When that's the case, we start questioning God and saying, "No! I can't do that." For Saul, he had to go and face the people whom he had recently wanted to kill. I'm sure he was wishing for a better way out of that situation, but he trusted God, because he knew that that was what God wanted him to do.

If I surrender my life to God and trust in Him even when times are hard, He'll be with me every step of the way. God has a plan for my life and yours, and He knows what's best for us. Sometimes we find ourselves at a crossroads, and we don't know which way we should go. But God does, and if we leave everything in His hands, He'll be there for us and will guide us through even the most dark and difficult places.

~ Jennifer Atkins

January 18

Changed

But Jesus, whose name of all others he most hated and despised, had revealed himself to Saul, for the purpose of arresting him in his mad career, and of making, from this most unpromising subject, an instrument by which to bear the gospel... – Sketches from the Life of Paul, pg. 28

John Newton was an atheist and a slave merchant who did all he could to hurt the lives of others. On one particular voyage, his slave ship was caught in a violent storm. Realizing that his efforts to steer the ship were useless, Newton left his atheism and called upon God for mercy. He believed that his ship would have sunk had it not been for the grace of God. Through that experience, Newton came to know Jesus as his personal Savior and later wrote the song "Amazing Grace."

All of us have something to share about the love and grace of God. Even though we are unworthy of Christ's love and forgiveness, he freely extends it to all of us. If we will give our hearts unconditionally to God, He will do amazing things in and through us. He wants to change our hearts and make us instruments to spread the gospel to the world; but first we have to see our need of His help.

Today, Jesus is patiently waiting for you to make Him your very best friend. Just like Saul, we may have ventured into things that were not God's original plan for us, but if we will heed God's gentle voice calling us back, He will always forgive and give us a new beginning.

"I am not what I ought to be... I am not what I hope to be... But by the grace of God, I am certainly not what I was." – John Newton

~ Becky Brousson

January 19

Old Things are Passed Away

Therefore if any man be in Christ, he is a new creature: old things are passed away; behold, all things are become new. – 2 Corinthians 5:17 KJV

In this verse, Paul describes his own personal experience in saying that anyone who is converted is a new creature, and the old things are passed away. After his baptism, Paul began to preach the word of God in the synagogue. The brilliant and boastful Pharisee was now transformed into a humble fisher of men. Everyone who heard Paul was confounded by his drastic change; his new life was the exact opposite of the old one. Paul had become a new creature.

Paul's transformation was what Jesus described as true conversion. "Unless a kernel of wheat falls into the ground and dies, it remains by itself alone. But if it dies, it produces much grain" (John 12:24 NET). Jesus clearly teaches that the inevitable result of true conversion is a dying to the old ways. A person is not a true Christian unless he is willing to lay down riches, fame, and the pleasures of this world. Although God loves His children, it breaks His heart if they cling to their old sins. These cherished sins block the channel between God and man, making Him unable to reach the poor soul. God yearns for each one of His children to be saved. In fact, Jesus laid aside pleasure and life and gave everything just for you. He is calling you to give up your old self and live. Will you allow Him to grant you a new life?

~ David Chang

January 20

Two Sauls

I say then, Hath God cast away his people? God forbid. For I also am an Israelite, of the seed of Abraham, of the tribe of Benjamin. – Romans 11:1 KJV

Why did Saul's parents name him Saul? Did they want him to be a leader? Saul was from the tribe of Benjamin just like King Saul was. Maybe Saul of Tarsus was named after King Saul. Saul's parents sent him to the finest school to be taught by the distinguished Rabbi Gamaliel. Both Sauls had a choice to make, whether to follow God or to go their own ways.

King Saul was at first very dedicated to God; but after he became King, he trusted in himself instead of in God. "Trust in the Lord with all thine heart; and lean not unto thine own understanding. In all thy ways acknowledge him, and he shall direct thy paths. Be not wise in thine own eyes: fear the Lord, and depart from evil" (Proverbs 3:5-7 KJV).

Saul of Tarsus started out rebelling against God; but when he was converted, he became willing to die for his faith. When he was in trouble, he went to God with prayer and fasting, but when King Saul was in trouble, he went to the witch of Endor. These two men had so much in common: they had the same name and were from the same tribe; but they chose to follow totally different paths.

You too have a choice to make. Which path will you follow? "And thine ears shall hear a word behind thee, saying, This is the way, walk ye in it, when ye turn to the right hand, and when ye turn to the left" (Isaiah 30:21 KJV).

~ Jenny McCluskey

January 21

Lesson of Faith

Arise, and go into the street which is called Straight, and enquire in the house of Judas for one called Saul, of Tarsus. – Acts 9:11 KJV

One cold night, Ananias had a vision. In his vision, he saw Jesus in all His glory. While he was beholding the wonderful scene, Jesus came to his side and told him to go anoint Saul of Tarsus. However, Ananias recalled that this Saul was a murderer of Christians. In doubt and astonishment, Ananias asked for assurance of God's will. Immediately, Jesus gave him a promise that He would be with him. The following morning, Ananias went boldly to meet Saul.

In this story, Ananias displayed a strong faith in God, even though meeting with Saul must have been difficult for him. Saul could have rejected the conviction of the Holy Spirit, or he might have been playing a part in a new and sinister plan to kill all Christians. Despite the possibility of jeopardizing his own life and the lives of other believers, Ananias decided to follow God's command. He demonstrated what we call faith—obeying what is unseen without knowing what might happen.

Though Ananias couldn't see it at first, God had a plan for Saul of Tarsus, as He has for each one of us. The plan is to restore each one to His image. Unfortunately, we cannot do this for ourselves; we have to work with God. The only way God can restore us to His image is through allowing us to exercise faith, that we may learn how to trust and obey His Will.

~ David Chang

January 22

Immediate Action

He… immediately began to preach Jesus to the believers in the city…
– Sketches from the Life of Paul, pg. 32

Have you ever taken immediate action in a situation? It can be a good thing or a bad thing. Listening to the Holy Spirit is a good thing. Speaking quickly and harshly often has tragic consequences. Here are two situations where people acted immediately:

There was once a waitress who gave a man his bill, only to find that he was busily drawing a picture on his napkin. As the man got up to leave, he handed the waitress the napkin. She opened it, expecting to find a tip. Finding none, she flung it to the floor. Without even giving the man a chance to speak, she yelled, "You Cheap-skate!" Another customer, seeing her hasty reaction questioned her, "Do you know who that man is? He's Thomas Kinkade!" That very napkin was later sold for over twenty thousand dollars. Mr. Kinkade, the famous artist, knew exactly what he was doing when he drew that picture. I'm sure that the waitress was deeply sorry for her hasty judgment; but she couldn't take her words back.

After Paul was baptized by Ananias, he went immediately to tell the believers of Damascus about Jesus. He didn't wait until he was more knowledgeable, or until he thought the time was right. He knew he had a job to do, and he didn't hesitate to carry it out.

Throughout our lives, we are presented with opportunities and beset with temptations. Ponder carefully how you should react to these. Will your actions cause pain to someone else, or will they have amazing results? The choice is yours. Decide carefully, because you may never have another chance.

Veronica Nudd

January 23

Evidence of God's Love

Paul demonstrated to all who heard him that his change of faith was not from impulse nor fanaticism, but was brought about by overwhelming evidence. – Sketches form the Life of Paul, pg. 33

Have you ever wondered if someone "liked" you? You may have felt that they did, but you weren't sure. Yet as you saw continual evidence of their adoration in a heart-warming smile, an affectionate hug, or a carefully wrapped gift, then you would have become fully confident of their affection for you.

There are many in this world who question the Christian faith. They see God as someone who is full of anger and hatred, and they want nothing to do with Him. But how can that be true, when we have evidence that God loves us? Our belief is not based on impulse or fanaticism. God sent His one and only Son to die for us, and that should leave no doubt in our minds of His unselfish, unfailing love.

Saul did not act on his first impulse to follow Christ and believe in Him; rather it was by overwhelming evidence that he was compelled to follow the Savior. He was not easily convinced. However, it was by Christ's aggressive intervention and the Holy Spirit continually working on his heart that he was led to surrender all and accept this new truth.

~ Melody Hyde

January 24

Chosen

He was an apostle, not chosen of men, but chosen of God.
– Sketches from the Life of Paul, pg. 34

    Moses could not believe his ears. What was God thinking, choosing him, a lowly shepherd with a speech impediment, to visit Pharaoh and demand the freedom of the Israelites? Anyone in his right mind would have chosen someone strong and imposing for such a job—someone Pharaoh would listen to. But anyone didn't choose Moses—God did.

    In fact, many of the people God uses to accomplish great works are the last people we would think of. Take the disciples, for example. They were just a bunch of young, uneducated, quarrelsome fishermen; but Jesus chose them to be His personal companions while on earth. Or look at Paul the persecutor-turned-disciple of Christ; if anyone was an unpromising candidate for apostleship, it was Paul.

    Often we think that God has no work for us to do, that our talents can't possibly be good enough for Him to use. But God gave us our talents, and He has a purpose for each one of us to fulfill. He may send you to the other side of the world or to the other side of the street; but wherever it may be, He has a work only you can do. Don't hesitate or make excuses. Just listen…God is calling.

~ Cara Dewsberry

January 25

Preaching to Pagans

He was an apostle…chosen of God, and his work was plainly stated to be among the Gentiles. – Sketches from the Life of Paul, pg. 34

Paul, a zealot for the Jewish race, sent to the Gentiles he was trained to abhor? These were the very ones who had trampled upon the Jews, kept them in bondage and whose armies occupied their cities! But it was to these Gentiles that Paul, a "Hebrew of Hebrews" (Philippians 3:5 NET), was to proclaim the Good News of Jesus Christ. Who could have foreseen that Paul would later proclaim this as a blessing? In his letter to the Ephesians Paul exclaims, "To me—less than the least of all the saints—this grace was given, to proclaim to the Gentiles the unfathomable riches of Christ" (Ephesians 3:8 NET).

This is an amazing example for us! Just as Paul, we too can be happy as we witness. Regardless of whether we preach to friends or enemies, Christ is for us. While we might not be as Jonah sent to Nineveh, we have our own sphere of influence. We have our own "Gentiles" around us. Christ sends us to witness to these. The people that seem to be the farthest away from Christ are the very ones that need Him the most. No sinner is too sinful for the forgiveness of Christ. As He extended His love to us when we were still in our sins, so we must extend His love to the "Gentiles" in our lives. Christ desires you to be a worker in the saving of souls. This self-denying path is the only one that leads to the abundant life.

~ Luke Gonzalez

January 26

Chosen People

It was necessary that the word of God should first have been spoken to you; but seeing ye put it from you, and judge yourselves unworthy of everlasting life, lo, we turn to the Gentiles. – Acts 13:46 KJV

God had chosen the people of Israel to spread His light over the whole world, but they continually turned from Him and worshipped idols. The Son of God was born among them, and they crucified Him. When the apostles gave the last appeal to the Jews, they contradicted and blasphemed. How different their history could have been if they had only known that this was the last invitation to be extended to them as a nation. They were God's chosen people, but they still missed the great truth of the gospel.

Once, a young man went to Chicago as a tourist and rented a room in a hotel. After getting settled, he wandered around the shopping section and got lost. He tried to find his way back, but in his excitement, he had forgotten the name and address of the hotel. He was too embarrassed to appeal to the police for help, and at last had to take another room. For five days, he vainly sought to find the first hotel where his luggage was, but finally he was compelled to ask the police for help. They phoned several hotels and found his name in the register of the hotel next door to the one where he was staying! He was so near, but was lost.

God has called us to be His messengers, bringing a message of light and peace to a world in darkness. He has given you the invitation—will you accept it? Don't miss this chance to impact the world for good.

~ Rebecca Luchak

January 27

Arabia

While in Arabia…Paul came in close connection with Heaven, and Jesus communed with him, and established him in his faith… – Sketches from the Life of Paul, pg. 34

In the quiet of the wilderness, God was near. Perched atop the rocky hillside, I admired the beautiful valley that lay before me. In this solitary place, I was privileged to connect with Heaven. For hours I lingered, simply talking with Jesus and reading His word. As I spent time with God, my faith in Him grew. Invigorated, our friendship was strengthened. This refuge proved to be a huge blessing!

Soon after his miraculous conversion, Paul lived in a similar "wilderness." Guided by the Holy Spirit, he traveled to the land of Arabia. There, separated from the commotion of everyday life, he "…came in close connection with Heaven…" He spent time with God—alone. It was here that God prepared Paul for his mission; faith was established. Through intimate conversation, Paul came to know and love the Jesus that he had once hated.

Many years earlier, Jacob also experienced this special closeness with God. While sleeping on the rough ground, he dreamed of a stairway that connected him with Heaven. He heard God speak to him and promise him many things. Through this direct encounter with God, Jacob learned to trust Him more. In the midst of a secluded wasteland, his confidence in God began to flourish.

Just as these great men of faith discovered the place of quiet seclusion, you also may find that intimate communion with God. If you will separate yourself to be with Jesus, you will attain a "…close connection with Heaven…" Faith will be established as you travel through the "wilderness." Daily devotions are essential, but the "wilderness" includes much more. When was the last time you went to Arabia? Maybe it's time to plan a trip.

~ Jonathan Sharley

January 28

Don't Give up

He would not give up the conflict until he had the assurance… that his repentance was accepted, and his great sin pardoned. – Sketches from the Life of Paul, pg. 34

This winter I went snowboarding for the second time. I was learning how to carve, and the experience was very painful because I kept falling. I just could not get it, but I refused to give up. The clouds of failure seemed intent on making me downcast. I knew that if I kept on trying, I would accomplish the goal that I had in mind. Each time I fell, I immediately got back up. It took time, but finally at the end of the day, I mastered it.

I think it should be the same in our Christian walk. No matter how many times we fall, we should keep our eyes focused on Jesus and keep getting back up. We should not rest till we know that we are right with God and that our sins our forgiven.

Satan will try to discourage us and tell us that we are not good enough, that our sins are too great for God to forgive. But we must not listen to that voice. In 1 John 1:9 it says, "If we confess our sins, he is faithful and just to forgive us our sins, and to cleanse us from all unrighteousness" (KJV). Jesus has given us that promise. No matter what Satan tries to tell us, we can know that what he says is not true.

We are all sinners in need of a Savior. Don't be discouraged. When the road gets rough, just know that Jesus will be with you every step of the way. He is holding on to you with a cord of love that can never be broken.

~ Becky Brousson

January 29

A Ride in a Basket

Finally they conceived a plan by which he was let down from a window, and lowered over the wall in a basket at night. In this humiliating manner Paul made his escape from Damascus. – Sketches from the Life of Paul, pg. 34

Paul was trapped in Damascus with the city's Jews just waiting for an opportunity to catch and slay him. The city gates were being watched night and day to cut off any attempt at escape. How was he to get out of the city? The believers in Damascus knew that only God could save Paul, and they prayed unceasingly for wisdom and guidance. God answered their prayers and gave them the idea to hide Paul in a large basket and lower him over the wall during the night. In this unusual way, God rescued Paul from the hateful Jews, and he escaped to the safety of Jerusalem.

During our lifetime, we will all face problems, either physical or spiritual, that are beyond our ability to solve. God Himself tells us that "in the world ye shall have tribulation," but He also promises to "make a way to escape," that we might not be overwhelmed (John 16:33; 1 Corinthians 10:13 KJV). If you find yourself in a difficult circumstance today, remember that God is only a prayer away. He will always hear and answer you. No matter how hopeless the situation seems, know that God can and will deliver you, even if it means giving you a ride in a basket.

~ Cara Dewsberry

January 30

Rejection and Acceptance

They remembered his former persecutions, and suspected him of acting a part to deceive and destroy them. – Sketches from the Life of Paul, pg. 35

After his conversion and baptism, Paul was eager to begin laboring in God's work. Unfortunately, he wasn't received with open arms. Resentful of all that he had done to them, the disciples of Christ were frightened that his murderous nature would resurface to annihilate them. Though most of the disciples didn't want to receive this black sheep into their company, one of them made a difference that still stands today.

Barnabas knew of Paul as a persecutor of Christians. However, he bravely stepped out to receive the converted Pharisee, and thus their relationship began. Barnabas believed Paul's testimony and was assured of his change of heart. He accepted Paul for who he was now.

At the school that I attended as a toddler, many of my friends played sports during recess. There's always the same dilemma whether it be in soccer, in basketball or in volleyball: choosing the best players, and forsaking everybody else. I was one of those kids who longed to play but was never offered the opportunity.

Paul went through the same experience. He had passion, and he felt God's calling, but nobody trusted in his potential. Everybody anticipated a fiasco to be the outcome. But in the end, Paul became one of the foremost Gospel workers in history.

So, if you notice somebody who wants to serve the Lord with all his heart, and you witness that God is requesting him to do His work, never doubt his aptitude, because God can use even the rejected and weak. Sometimes those people make the biggest difference.

~ David Ortiz

January 31

Left Out

And, lo, I am with you alway, even unto the end of the world.
– Matthew 28:20 KJV

 Feelings of loneliness, solitude, and misery crept in as Jake watched the other kids play basketball. The unmistakable feeling that he was not wanted kept clawing at him. Other kids were allowed to play, yet he was not. When he had almost reached his lowest, Joseph came up to him and asked him to play on his team. The other members of the team where very hesitant to add him to their team, after all he didn't look like a basketball player, but they soon realized that Jake was an exceptional player. Soon everybody wanted Jake on their team. Jake's potential was hidden until he was given the opportunity to show it.

 Paul had similar feelings. His excitement and joy in following Christ was dampened by the disciples untrusting spirit. The disciples where letting fear and suspicion choke them. This hurt Paul deeply, but Barnabas stretched out his hand in friendship to Paul. He proved that Paul was worthy of their trust and that the disciples' expectations were false. Once this was proven to them, they accepted Paul without hesitation.

 Being left out is not a good feeling, and many times it seems that nobody cares; but God is always there to give you the courage and help you need. And when you are at your lowest point, He sends Barnabases to extend the hand of friendship.

~ Jourdain Smith

February 1

Earnestly Dedicated

...Paul was eager to get about his Master's business...
– Sketches from the Life of Paul, pg. 37

Eagerness filled the heart of Paul as he went to Jerusalem to meet with Peter and James. There the two key players of the new faith met: Peter, who had been with Jesus on earth, and Paul who had spoken with and seen Jesus on the road to Damascus. This first discussion was vital to both apostles; but Paul was so *eager* to start preaching and teaching about Christ, that the conference was soon adjourned.

It was my 15th birthday. I had been waiting for this day for years because I was going to get my drivers permit. I was so excited that I would do almost anything to get my parents to move just a little faster, so that we could get to the DMV as soon as possible.

If only we would be as eager in the work of bringing souls to Christ, as I was to get my driver's permit. I want to challenge you to reach out to the lonely, rejected outcasts of this world, with joyful eagerness. It doesn't matter how old you are, or whether you have a disability or some other excuse; there is work to be done, and there is something you can do to help.

~ Joey Heagy

February 2

Never Too Far

Soon the voice which had so earnestly disputed with Stephen, was heard in the same synagogue fearlessly proclaiming that Jesus was the Son of God—advocating the same cause that Stephen had died to vindicate. – Sketches from the Life of Paul, pg. 37

There are times when we doubt that certain people we know will be in heaven because of how far they have wandered from God. Our doubts may be reasonable if they have grieved away the Holy Spirit; but many times a person will turn around completely. An example of this is Saul, who was later known as Paul.

Saul, before his name was changed, fiercely persecuted the early church. He was instrumental in many arrests and deaths including the stoning of Stephen. Then God struck him blind and gave him a vision on the way to Damascus. At this point, he finally listened to his conscience and realized how far he had gone from God. He, with the help of God and the disciples in Damascus, turned his life around and became one of the strongest leaders of the early church.

Can you imagine the surprise Stephen is going to have in heaven? The very man who was instrumental in his death will be there to greet him. That just totally blows me away.

I think we need to remember to pray for those we don't think will be saved. They may seem headed in the wrong direction, but God has a plan, and He may just be waiting for your help. We need to let God use us to reach out to others and show them His mercy and grace.

~ Amy Windels

February 3

Whisked Away from Danger

While Paul…was praying earnestly to God in the temple, the Savior appeared to him in vision, saying, "Make haste, and get thee quickly out of Jerusalem; for they will not receive thy testimony concerning me. – Sketches from the Life of Paul, pg. 37

God has promised to guide the feet of His servants. Isaiah 30:21 says, "And thine ears shall hear a word behind thee, saying, This is the way, walk ye in it, when ye turn to the right hand, and when ye turn to the left" (KJV). This is what God did for Paul to keep him alive to work for Him.

In Andra Pradesh, India, some missionaries were just finishing their meetings. They planned to leave by train on the following Friday, but God had another plan. In a dream, God told them to leave that night on a bus. The missionaries obeyed and left as soon as the meeting was finished. Later, the missionaries learned that a man had been waiting for them at the train station to do them harm. God had whisked His workers away from danger.

God has promised that if His people spread the gospel, He will be with them to the end. Mathew 28:20 says, "And, lo, I am with you alway, even unto the end of the world" (KJV). When God asks us to do something, we should obey immediately. He only wants to do what's best for us and to protect us from danger.

~ Jenny McCluskey

February 4

The Joy of Doing God's Will

"Make haste, and get thee quickly out of Jerusalem; for they will not receive thy testimony concerning me." Paul even then hesitated to leave Jerusalem… – Sketches from the Life of Paul, pg. 37

Joy, peace, and renewed faith are the result of doing God's will. I realized this one Monday when I was doing a worship talk. I had doubts about my talk because I wasn't ready and was stuttering and making mistakes. But as everyone prayed together afterwards, I was confirmed that they were blessed. I was used as God's tool; for on my own, I can't do anything. Being used of God was such a blessing! I said, "Lord, if this is what doing your will is all about, then take me and use me!"

Paul had an experience similar to mine when God told him to leave Jerusalem. Paul first hesitated, but when God told him again, he knew he must go. It must have been hard for him to leave the hopes of converting his old friends; yet he still followed God's will, and as a result, more people were added to the church.

Put your imagination cap on and think of a person just about to enter a door labeled "God's Will". He goes through the door with uncertainty, but he comes out with confidence in every step. Doing God's will might be fearful at first, but the result is always the same—content, joy, and renewed faith. Today, God offers these blessings like a basket of sweet flowers, if we will but enter the door of His will.

~ Sharon Jeon

February 5

Animosity

The animosity existing between the Jews and Samaritans decreased, and it could no longer be said that they had no dealing with each other. – Sketches from the Life of Paul, pg. 39

The early church had many racial disputes among themselves. The Jews were taught that Gentiles were lowly, and God was not trying to save them. A Jewish person would not even do business with a Gentile customer. On the other hand, Gentiles harbored similar animosity towards the Jews. Christians had to rethink their stand when it came to races, and with time, it was widely accepted that "there is neither Greek nor Jew… but Christ is all and in all" (Colossians 3:11 KJV).

Is there animosity between you and someone else? Malice, anger, and hatred come in quietly, and your preconceived ideas may be veiling your sense of right and wrong. Counterintuitive though it may be, we cannot let these feelings fester inside us. We must uproot them if we count ourselves as one with Christ, for "if any man will come after me, let him deny himself…" (Matthew 16:24 KJV).

The devil will do all in his power to keep you from noticing and dealing with this flaw. He appeals to our selfish nature, which wants only what benefits itself. If we are to follow Jesus, we must put away our selfishness, and embrace the unselfish love of Jesus. Remember, it is through Him that we will gain the victory.

~ Robby Folkenberg

February 6

Life Theme

It was here [at Antioch] that the disciples were first called Christians. This name was given them because Christ was the main theme of their preaching, teaching and conversation. – Sketches from the Life of Paul, pp. 40, 41

To the disciples at Antioch, life was about Christ. He who had set them free, now sat upon the throne of their heart. From this throne Christ's will and love became evident in everyday life. Their words, thoughts and actions reflected those of their Savior. They talked endlessly of their Master's life on earth, ranging from His Healing, to His death, to His raising of the dead.

Due to this way of life, the Gentiles called the disciples Christians. Yet this was not the only result that was evident from their lifestyle. Through the Christians' hearts, Christ was able to bring the Gentiles into contact with His saving love. And as the seeds that were planted in hearts of these Gentiles' grew, more people were able to come into contact with the Savior.

There are millions of "Christians" today, but what do their lives tell you about them? Is their speech about the One that died for them? Are their actions prompted by His love? Is their greatest joy thinking about God and his amazing grace and love? To the true Christian, who is really a disciple of Christ, this is what life is about.

~ Michael Hamel

February 7

Good News!

This name [Christians] was given them because Christ was the main theme of their preaching, teaching, and conversation. They were continually recounting the incidents of his life, during the time in which his disciples were blessed with his personal company. – Sketches from the Life of Paul, pp. 40, 41

Have you ever been excited to the point of bursting? Have you ever had such good news that you felt you must either share it or explode? I have an amusing habit of tripping over my tongue when I have something especially exciting to say; it seems I just can't get it out fast enough. But sadly, I don't always talk that way about Christ. Has my walk with Him become too dull to talk about?

The believers in Antioch were called Christians because they couldn't stop talking about Christ, whom they loved so much. The word "gospel" means "good news." Christ's followers had the wonderful news of what Jesus had done for them, and they couldn't wait to share it. How do you think the people in Antioch found out about Jesus? It was by one person experiencing Jesus' love and sharing it with someone else. The news spread like wildfire and eventually reached even you.

Do you call yourself a Christian? I do, and I've seen Jesus work in marvelous ways. It's a miracle that I even woke up this morning! But when I look at my words and thoughts, I'm ashamed that Christ doesn't come up more often. Jesus is coming very soon, and we are to spread the good news to as many people as we can. Make it your goal to share Him with someone today.

~ Melissa Butler

February 8

Where is Your Focus?

...Christ was the main theme of their... conversation. They were continually recounting the incidents of His life...They dwelt untiringly upon His teachings, his miracles of healing the sick, casting out devils, and raising the dead to life. – Sketches from the Life of Paul, pp. 40, 41

It was A.D. 33 in the ancient city of Antioch. Paul the Apostle had just arrived to encourage and strengthen the believers there, and he found them ready to soak up all the truth. His vast knowledge of the scriptures, along with his passion and love for Christ seemed to hold the people spellbound. It was here at Antioch that the believers were first called Christians.

This name was given to them because they continually kept Christ at the center of their attention. They spoke of his miracles, teachings, death and resurrection with unending enthusiasm. Although it was not considered "cool" to be a Christian at this time, their joy could not be repressed; they let their Savior shine through them to the inhabitants of Antioch.

We as Christians should also make Christ the main theme of our lives. Sometimes we seem to think that being Christians is something to hide, and we feel ashamed to talk about Christ because we're afraid that we may look "un-cool." So we "hide" Christ by replacing Him with worldly actions and conversations. By doing this we are insulting Him and are not worthy to be called Christians. But if we place our focus on Christ, the things of this world will fade away and leave Him as the only theme of our lives.

~ Dave White

February 9

Joy in Jesus

And straightway he preached Christ in the synagogues, that he is the Son of God. – Acts 9:20

After Paul had been converted, Ananias baptized him in the river of Damascus. Like a child with a new friend, Paul went on his way with the purpose of testifying about the joy he had found in Jesus Christ. Do you, like Paul, possess joy when you know Christ is in your heart?

The conversion of Paul did not come without opposition. When Paul began to spread the news of his conversion, the rage of the Pharisees escalated against him. The man who had once been a fervent worker for the destruction of the believers was now a powerful witness for their faith, and the Pharisees planned to silence his voice. But Paul stood above the crowd and followed through with the plan that God had for him, even under the pain of death. As with Paul, God has a purpose for you, are you willing to give your life to that purpose?

Fill your life with Christ, so that in that final day you may be able to stand unyieldingly, regardless of the cost. No sacrifice is too great in order to be a child of God.

~ Leighton Sjoren

February 10

A Purposeful Life

The apostles next visited Iconium. This place was a great resort for pleasure-seekers, and persons who had no particular object in life. – Sketches from the Life of Paul, pg. 52

The people of Iconium, many of whom had no object in life, needed to find their true purpose. They needed to experience a relationship with God. If you know God, you will have that true purpose which will move you to tell the world to prepare for God's soon return.

There is a parable in Luke 12:42-47 that talks about doing our work and being prepared. There once was a master who went away for a long time and left a servant in charge of his household. When the master delayed his coming, the servant started to slack off, party, and abuse the other servants. Then the master came back unexpectedly, and found that the servant had not done his work, and the servant was severely chastised for his laziness.

The master in this story represents Christ, and we are the servant. We need to remember that Christ will come at an hour when no one expects Him to come. We need to be found at the work God has given us; and if we do our work for God, we will have a true sense of purpose in our lives. Do you have a purpose in life? Are you doing your Master's work?

~ Amy Windels

February 11

Lovers of Pleasure

Iconium… was a great resort for pleasure-seekers, and persons who had no particular object in life. – Sketches from the Life of Paul, pg. 52

So many things can cloud our focus—our warm houses, food, entertainment. We get so wrapped up in the empty folly that we forget about what will last for eternity— communing with God and leading others to Him. Think about it; how long can you go without breathing? Not very long, I'm sure. We shouldn't be able to go without thinking of Jesus for longer than we can go without breathing.

Iconium was a wealthy place. It had everything necessary to entice visitors to its streets. We are told that the people there had no particular object in life. They were "content". Can you imagine how hard it must have been for Paul to show these people that there was something better than what their money could buy? The Jews made matters worse by stirring the city officers against Paul. Yet Paul knew that he had been called of God and that he had a special work to do. He didn't just sit back and let someone else worry about it, he actively took part in God's service to lost humanity.

This is the age of the Laodicean church. Just like the Iconians, we have so much to take our focus off God. We're lovers of pleasure and are repulsed at the thought of stepping outside our comfort zones to stand up for Jesus. But we each have a choice to make: either to sit back, enjoy the world or to become like Paul. We must deny ourselves of earthly pleasure and step out to do God's work. Will you accept His high calling?

~ Veronica Nudd

February 12

Heaven's Resort

The apostles next visited Iconium. This place was the resort for pleasure-seekers, and persons who had no particular object in life. – Sketches from the Life of Paul, pg. 52

Paul, in going to Iconium, found a resort for all manner of people. They all sought pleasure, and many possessed no true purpose in life. In this city, Paul chose to share the truth. He knew that among these pleasure-seeking, aimless people were many who could be saved.

In 1905, a little railroad town was founded in Nevada. Through the years, little Las Vegas has grown into a thriving "Sin City" that boasts almost every pleasure and vice imaginable. People go to its many resorts and casinos seeking pleasure and wealth to fulfil their lives. As is often said, history repeats itself, and Las Vegas is simply a modern Iconium in great need of a modern Paul.

You and I live in a world full of pleasure-seekers and people without purpose. It is our duty to lead these lost souls to reach the higher standard of heaven, our eternal resort. There will live those who have sought and found the real object of life—the pleasure of serving the Lord. As we seek to lead others to God, the evil one will attempt to hinder us, but God will always guide the earnest seeker to Himself. Decide today to reach out to others, so that you can bring many with you to the "heavenly resort."

~ Douglas Schappert

February 13

You're There!

The apostles here, as at Antioch, first commenced their labors in the synagogues for their own people, the Jews. – Sketches form the life of Paul, pg. 52

Have you ever felt God calling you to the mission field? Even as a small child, I wished I could become a missionary. My siblings and I grew up hearing our mother read mission stories of far away countries. In my heart, a burning desire grew to go to those places and share God's love. However, I knew that I would have to wait until I was older. I never fully realized that, as essential as it is for natives in distant lands to hear the gospel, there are many people close by that just as desperately need to know how they can be saved.

As a child, Jesus' mission field was right at home. There His life was an example of all that was pure and just. He was a constant reminder to His playmates of what they should be: true, honest, kind, obedient, and understanding. There was never a careless or unkind word that left His lips, and Jesus would never have been seen doing anything wrong.

The apostles had a message to share, and there were many places that had never heard the gospel. But many chose to stay in their own hometowns, where they worked with the people they knew best. I believe that this is what we need to do. We can't just wait until later to accomplish what Jesus desires us to do. It is when we begin right where we are that God can use and prepare us best for His purpose.

~ Melody Hyde

February 14

Pink

...Many were daily embracing the doctrine of Christ. – Sketches from the Life of Paul, pg. 52

Did you know that God loves Valentine's Day? Hugs and kisses express His very nature. Love is the essence of His character. This love was revealed in the greatest Valentine's gift *ever*! As Jesus hung on the cross, He opened for you the way of salvation.

On this special day, I want you to imagine a happy couple. For his Valentine, Mr. Right buys a gorgeous bouquet of pink flowers. Upon receiving this gift of love, his wife throws herself into her lover's arms. And there, as the two embrace, she whispers, "I love you too!"

When you hear the word "embrace," what do you think of? Perhaps words such as "love", "adoration", and "commitment" come to mind.

As Paul and Barnabas preached the gospel of love, many responded by "embracing the doctrine of Christ." They accepted God's gift by loving, adoring, and committing themselves to the Good News. In His life, Jesus showed that this doctrine is all about salvation.

Jesus loves you; in fact, He is just plain crazy about you! And right now, He is giving you the opportunity to have eternal joy. What is your response? Will you run into His open arms, embracing His promise of salvation (Heb. 11:13), or will you refuse "to love the truth" (2 Thessalonians 2:10 NIV)? When we truly cherish God's love-gift, we say "Thank you" to our Savior. Today, as you see the pinks, reds, and other symbols of love, remember to respond to your True Lover and embrace the doctrine of Christ.

~ Jonathan Sharley

February 15

Doing Right

The apostles, however, were not easily turned from their work, for many were daily embracing the doctrine of Christ. – Sketches from the Life of Paul, pg. 52

Guilt clogged Adrian's mind. Why did he join his friends in their sabotaging endeavors? He didn't mean to go that far, but they went overboard. Mr. Jenkins's garden, orchard, and even some equipment had been damaged. Adrian decided that the problem must be fixed. He went to Mr. Jenkins and apologized for all he did, and promised to make up for everything. He began the process of restoration by replanting the garden, cleaning up the orchard, and fixing the equipment. His friends mocked and jeered him, saying he was a goody-to-shoes. They also made his labor harder by undoing some of the work he had done. But Adrian was not deterred. He continued until the job was finished, and his friends came to the realization that what he had done was right even though they wouldn't help him.

Paul was doing what was right in sharing Jesus with other people; yet the unbelieving Jews sought to discredit his work. They tried to influence the Gentiles against Paul by presenting unreasonable opposition and even turning new converts away from Christ. But through all this, Paul continued to work against the prejudice and malice of the Jews, and his efforts proved God's power. Those who witnessed Paul's work were convicted by his message.

When we are doing what is right and others make fun of us, we should never give up or get discouraged because, eventually, they will see our motives. Then they too could be changed by our efforts.

~ Jourdain Smith

February 16

Unmovable Faith

They were filled with envy and hatred, and determined to stop the apostles at once. – Sketches from the Life of Paul, pg. 53

Shortly after becoming a Bible worker in un-entered part of western Zambia, Charles Simopolkwe began a series of evangelistic meetings. For the first three nights, no one came; but he preached anyway. On the fourth night, one woman and her husband began coming to the meetings; they were the only ones that attended the series. When the meetings concluded, the couple continued studying the Bible and were eventually baptized. It turned out that the husband was the headman of the area and had a strong influence. As a result of his conversion, about thirty-five people came to Christ, and now they worship every Sabbath in a little grass-covered church. Despite the obstacles that Satan threw in their way, Charles and his co-workers overcame through their faith in God, and many souls were reached.

At Iconium, the apostles became popular by preaching the doctrine of Christ, making the Jews very jealous. By bombarding the apostles with false accusations, the Jews tried to end their work. However, the apostles, anchored in their faith in God, firmly withstood the false accusations. Their convincing arguments caused many people to believe in Christ.

Satan is constantly attempting to discourage you from doing God's will. He plants obstacles in your pathway to dampen your spirits and turn you away from your task. Trusting God is the only way to withstand the hardships Satan will place in your path. Daily, you must yield yourself to God, inviting Him to fulfill His plan for your life.

~ Jeremy Grabiner

February 17

Reformation, not Revolution

They could but acknowledge that the teachings of the apostles were calculated to make men virtuous, law-abiding citizens. – Sketches from the Life of Paul, pg. 53

Revolution! Revolution! This was the rallying cry of the French during one of the darkest times in their history. This cry led to one of the bloodiest massacres of both men and freedom. Death sentences flowed from the government like wine from a broken bottle. Men became lower than the basest of animals. All revolutions demand death and the destruction of order. This was the charge brought against the apostles in Iconium.

The magistrates of the city ordered for the apostles to defend themselves. The apostles had so successfully shown how the Gospel uplifts man, that they wanted them to continue preaching! The Gospel uplifts the morals of man and teaches us to live peacefully with others. Peter showed this in his first letter when he wrote, "Honor all people, love the family of believers, fear God, honor the king" (1 Peter 2:17 NET). Paul also tells us, in his second letter to the Corinthians, "Finally, brothers and sisters, rejoice, set things right, be encouraged, agree with one another, live in peace…" (2 Corinthians 13:11 NET). Men who are empowered by the Prince of Peace will always resort to reform, not revolt. The Jews, on the other hand, illustrated the spirit of Satan—rebellion. Reform wishes to build up, revolt will tear down. We, as the beacons of truth, must ever keep this before us; we are reformers, not revolutionaries. The Prince of Peace ever sought to correct error. Whenever you see a brother in sin or an error in the church, think reformation, not revolt.

~ Luke Gonzalez

February 18

Life through Death

For we who live are always delivered to death for Jesus' sake, that the life of Jesus also may be manifested in our mortal flesh.
– 2 Corinthians 4:11 NKJV

When Christ was here on earth, many people didn't believe that He was the Son of God. Many people wanted nothing to do with Him. Even after all the miracles Christ had performed, many chose not to believe in Him. They wished for Him to be crucified.

Christ came to this earth for the purpose of being an example of true love. It wasn't easy for God to send His Son to this sinful planet to pay the price so that we may have eternal life with Him.

Paul was called to preach the gospel to the entire world, and he had surrendered his whole life to God. No matter what he was faced with, he trusted in God. Death didn't matter to him. He was doing the work of God, and he knew that when his life ended here, he would have a better life in the hereafter.

At the crucifixion, many could see that Jesus really was the Son of God; and through his death and resurrection, many chose to sacrifice all and follow Him. If we stand strong in our faith, and focus on the crown of life, it doesn't matter if we live or die, for we have a much higher reward waiting for us in Heaven.

~ Jennifer Atkins

February 19

Blessed Are the Persecuted

While persecution and opposition met them on every hand, victory still crowned their efforts, and converts were daily added to the faith.
– Sketches from the Life of Paul, pg. 55

Some days I feel like I'm stuck in a hole of quicksand. I'm assailed by homework and lack of sleep, and to top it off, find out that I've been talked about behind my back. It's days like these that make me feel like crawling under my covers and until the sun emerges again. There has to be a cure for feeling this way.

Paul and Barnabas went to Lystra to preach to the heathen. At first, the people welcomed them, but when the Jewish rulers interfered and told the people lies about Christians, the crowd suddenly turned on Paul and Barnabas, stoning them nearly to death. This was not the only time the apostles had suffered for Jesus. Though beaten, imprisoned, and ridiculed, the work never faltered. In fact, more converts were brought to the faith. As the people saw that nothing could sway Paul and Barnabas, they decided that they wanted to be Christians too.

Matthew 5:10 says, "Blessed are those who are persecuted" (NKJV). Maybe you are not being persecuted for your faith, but Satan is trying to discourage you with trials. When it seems you cannot bear them, turn to Jesus. He is waiting to carry your burdens and lighten your load. If you grasp His hand, your crisis will shrink in importance, and Jesus will grow to be everything to you. As others witness your remedy for trials, they will want to take hold of Christ too.

~ Melissa Butler

February 20

Thoughts from Nature

He directed their attention to the firmament…the lofty trees, and the varied wonders of nature…Through these visible works of the Almighty, the apostle led the minds of the heathen to the contemplation of the great Mind of the universe. – Sketches from the Life of Paul, pg. 56

The beauty of nature encircles you if you look beyond our manmade structures. God created and bestowed this gift as a beacon of His love. Back in Eden, God would often take strolls in the garden to commune with Adam and Eve, and even now, there is still a holy blessing to be gained by meditating in nature's awe-inspiring atmosphere.

When I was younger, I would stroll through the woods on cool mornings to a log that spanned a ravine. There in the ravine I could see the remains of long, fallen trees. Here, away from the hustle of the morning, I would sit in stillness talking to God. From these moments I left refreshed and filled with love. The years went by though, and new elements began to take the place of my time in the forest. The things that God created no longer interested me. Time in nature became a drag for me because I always wanted to be indoors checking out the latest gadgets.

We need to take a break from the technological tornado that is always sucking us in. For so many of us, technological advances are taking the place of nature in our contemplations. Even so, nature still stands as a witness of God's love, beckoning us to become better acquainted with Him.

~ Buddy Taylor

February 21

Stand Up!

Paul commanded the cripple to stand upright upon his feet. Hitherto he had only been able to take a sitting posture; but he now grasped with faith the words of Paul, and instantly obeyed his command. – Sketches from the Life of Paul, pp. 56, 57

Imagine you are a cripple who has never walked on his own two legs. You spend your days crawling through the city streets begging for handouts from sympathetic passersby. Then one day, you see a crowd gathered around a stranger who is preaching about a loving God in heaven, Who sent His Son to die for the sins of the world. As you sit, longing to know this amazing God, the preacher fixes his gaze upon you, and pausing in his sermon, he commands, "Stand up upon your feet!"

How would you respond? Would you instantly jump up and stand on those lame, useless feet? Or would you laugh and say, "I've been a cripple all my life. Stand up? You're out of your mind"? Sadly, I think most of us would respond with faithless scorn. It seems that the majority of Christians today have less faith than a heathen cripple. We so easily forget about our all-powerful Father, that at the slightest trial our faith fails us. God could do so much through us if we would simply depend on His word to do what it promises to do. When God tests your trust, do not be faithless; rather allow such trials to deepen your reliance upon Him. Remember the cripple of Lystra, and stand up and leap into complete faith in God.

~ Cara Dewsberry

February 22

Stepping Out

In the presence of that idolatrous assembly, Paul commanded the cripple to stand upright upon his feet...Strength came with this effort of faith; and he who had been a cripple walked and leaped as though he had never experienced an infirmity. – Sketches from the Life of Paul, pg. 57

Fountainview Academy was going to Panama on a music/ mission trip, and I wanted to go too. But it cost three thousand dollars that I didn't have. After much thought, I concluded that, if God wanted me to go, He would have to open the way. I left everything in His hands, and stepping out in faith, started to practice the music. My faith in God's ability to provide grew as I practiced. I knew that He would work things out. A few days later, my parents told me that an anonymous donor had given me all the money.

Jesus is waiting for us to grasp with faith the wonderful things He wants to do for us. But because we don't believe, He can't work for us. Just as practice helps us improve at something, the exercise of faith will make it easier to trust Jesus even more. "Strength came with his effort of faith." The cripple not only trusted Jesus; he stepped out in faith. When we realize that in our own strength we are weak, we become strong because Jesus gives us His strength. In 2 Corinthians 12:9 Jesus says, "My grace is sufficient for thee: for my strength is made perfect in weakness" (KJV).

If you desire to see God work in your life, then believe even when you cannot see the evidence. That's when miracles happen.

~ Becky Brousson

February 23

Standing Before God

Sirs, why do ye these things? We also are men of like passions with you… – Sketches from the Life of Paul, pg. 58

Pride, egotism, self-glorification: these are tendencies that we all have. If we do not see someone who is better than we are, then we tend to be proud of ourselves.

When I was eleven years old, I played my violin in a children's recital. None of the other kids played as well as I did, and as I compared myself to them, my heart puffed up with pride. But at my next violin lesson, criticism came out like a bullet from my teacher's mouth, and I realized that I wasn't really so good.

"Sirs, why do ye these things? We also are men of like passions with you," Paul cried out to the multitude that was praising him after he had healed a cripple. Paul was so upset that the people were worshiping him, that he tore his clothes. Why was he upset?

I believe that Paul felt the same humility before God that I felt before my violin teacher. If my teacher had been at the recital, I would not have been so proud of myself. Paul was always standing before God, and because he realized how imperfect he was compared to God, he felt upset and embarrassed when he was praised instead of God. Just like Paul, we also need to realize how perfect God is; and if we are constantly in His presence, our selfish pride will shrink away. We will be embarrassed to say, "I am the best" in the presence of God.

~ Ryo Fusamae

February 24

Lessons from an Ordeal

The Lystrians rushed upon the apostles with great rage and fury. They hurled stones violently; and Paul, bruised, battered, and fainting, felt that his end had come. – Sketches from the Life of Paul, pg. 61

Charging frantically, the Lystrians rushed upon Paul to stone him. He thought that his time to die for Jesus' sake had come. However, God had more work for his servant to do; and Paul rose up praising God. Even through this hard experience, Paul demonstrated a Christ-like character that was an example to the other believers.

God uses hard trials to teach us how to be like Him. If it had not been for Paul's excruciating experience at Lystra, the new Christians might never have learned what it takes to be a Christian. A trying experience conveys a deep lesson that no words can describe. When a person is having a hard time, he is open for the Spirit of God to work within him. This enables God to heal him not only physically, but spiritually. I believe God reveals the most profound things through trials because this is when we are most open to the Holy Spirit.

Furthermore, it is by trials that we desperately feel our need of Christ. Unfortunately, in our daily life, we think we can do everything by ourselves, while in reality we can't do anything without God. God is still pleading for men to soften their hearts and listen to His calling. If you have a hard experience today, think, what is God trying to tell me?

~ David Chang

February 25

Stones

Then Jews from Antioch and Iconium came there; and having persuaded the multitudes, they stoned Paul and dragged him out of the city, supposing him to be dead. – Acts 14:19 NKJV

The disciples surrounded Paul's body as it lay on the hard, rocky ground. Sorrow drowned their souls as they lamented their fallen comrade. The disciples shed tears as the thought of their friend's death clouded their minds. In a surprising twist, Paul jumped to his feet, and his lips proclaimed praises to God! This baffled Paul's comrades; he acted as if nothing had happened!

Moments before, the frenzied Lystrians had hurled stones at them. The helpless disciples had desperately tried to protect themselves. As his body wilted, and rocks rained on his head, Paul's mind had pictured the scenes of Stephen's martyrdom. He was so weak that his body collapsed to the ground; he was "dead".

This barrage of stones foreshadowed Paul's later ordeals. Many of Christ's disciples faced a similar fate. Peter's crucifixion, the beheading of John the Baptist, the stoning of Stephen, and other examples have shown us that Satan heavily targets those working in God's mission.

Rejection, persecution, judgment, imprisonment, and torture are the stones hurled by Satan's hand. His oppressive attacks overwhelm us; but with God's aid and guiding hand, those satanic strikes are futile.

"Blessed is the man that endureth temptation; for when he is tried, he shall receive the crown of life which the Lord hath promised to those who love Him" (James 1:12 NKJV).

~ David Ortiz

February 26

Rejoice

… He suddenly lifted his head, and arose to his feet with the praise of God upon his lips. – Sketches from the Life of Paul, pg. 61
Rejoice evermore…In every thing give thanks.
– 1 Thessalonians 5:16, 18 KJV

Job listened helplessly as his terrified servants reported the destruction that had come upon him. First, the Sabeans had stolen all his oxen and donkeys; next, fire from heaven had burned up his sheep; then, the Chaldeans had taken his camels; and as a last blow, a violent wind had blown down the house where his children were gathered, killing them all. In one day, Job's entire world was swept away. After such a day, I'd probably begin to seriously doubt God's love for me and even His very existence. But listen to Job's reaction: "Then Job arose, and rent his mantle, and shaved his head, and fell down upon the ground, and worshipped, and said, Naked came I out of my mother's womb, and naked shall I return thither: the Lord gave, and the Lord hath taken away: blessed be the name of the Lord" (Job 1:20, 21 KJV). Wow! Can you imagine blessing the Lord just after He has apparently ruined your life?

Paul had a similar experience when he was brutally stoned by the Lystrians and afterward rose up praising and glorifying God. In a later epistle, he commands the believers to "Rejoice in the Lord always" (Philippians 4:4 NKJV). Paul and Job were able to respond so positively to adverse circumstances because they trusted God's love for them implicitly. You can do the same. If you put your faith completely in God, He will give you the grace to rejoice in every situation.

~ Cara Dewsberry

February 27

Contrasting Characters

In fact, the unreasoning opposition of those wicked men had only confirmed these devoted brethren in the faith of Christ: and the restoration of Paul to life seemed to set the signet of God upon their belief. – Sketches from the Life of Paul, pg. 61

Jesus descended to this world to reveal the opposite of sin. When Jesus and Barabbas were put face to face, the distinction between sinner and Savior was clear. Barabbas was a perfect example of what sin does to man, and when Jesus was put next to him, the difference was too obvious to ignore. When two opposites are put side by side, it is easier to distinguish between them.

This was the case in the story of Paul's near-death incident. Paul was stoned and thrown out of the city; but while some new converts were weeping over him, he suddenly rose to his feet, praising God! You would think that they would lose faith during persecution, but actually, their faith in God grew. They saw the contrast between the unreasonable mob that stoned Paul out of anger, and Paul, who got back up with praises on his lips.

If there is any advantage of living in a sinful world, it is because the more we see sin, the more we realize God's mercy and love. When we hear of end-time events and the sins in this world, instead of being depressed, we rejoice. Why? Because Jesus is coming soon. Sometimes God needs to show us the contrast between the character of sin and His character in order to establish our faith in Him. He wants us to identify true religion with a true God.

~ Sharon Jeon

February 28

The Greatest Honor

He stood by his apparently dead body, and saw him arise, bruised and covered with blood, not with groans or murmurings upon his lips, but with praises to Jesus Christ, that he was permitted to suffer for his name. – Sketches from the Life of Paul, pg. 62

Paul was greatly honored by God at the very time he was dishonored by men. He was chosen and found worthy to suffer for Jesus' sake. Paul followed the example of his Lord and did not complain when he was beaten. Paul even sang praises to God because he was able to suffer for His name.

"Blessed are ye, when men shall revile you, and persecute you and shall say all manner of evil against you falsely, for my sake. Rejoice and be exceeding glad for great is your reward in heaven; for so persecuted they the prophets which were before you" (Matthew 5:11, 12 KJV).

"Fear none of those things which thou shalt suffer: behold, the devil shall cast some of you into prison, that ye maybe tried…be thou faithful unto death, and I will give you a crown of life" (Revelation 2:10 KJV).

Next time you are under persecution, grasp the reality that you are receiving heaven's highest honor, and know there is a crown of life awaiting you.

~ Jenny McCluskey

March 1

Willingness

But both Paul and Barnabas returned again to visit Antioch, Iconium, and Lystra, the fields of labor where they had met such opposition and persecution. – Sketches from the Life of Paul, pg. 62

Dedication and eagerness for their work drove Paul and Barnabas to return to where persecution had previously hindered them. Even though persecution was highly probable, the two men felt it was their duty to strengthen and encourage their persecuted brethren.

A few years ago my family went on a mission trip to Grenada. We had been trying for several years to go on a mission trip, but nothing ever worked out before. Even though I knew we were going on this trip to help people, all I could think about was how much fun I was going to have flying, snorkeling, and just experiencing a different country. The whole time we were there, I complained or argued about everything I was supposed to do. I don't think I even really understood why we were there, every time we saw or did anything that was slightly boring, I was negative about it. Now, as I look back, I wish I would have had a better attitude towards the whole trip. If I had, the trip might have been such a great blessing; but I had been unwilling to give up myself and be used by Christ.

True service is rarely easy. We must be willing to help wherever we are needed, even if it means going to a place where you might be persecuted like Paul and Barnabas. No matter where you are, or what circumstances you are under, still remember that it is our duty to show others the unselfish life of Christ in everything we do.

~ Joey Heagy

March 2

Move

The Jews were not generally prepared to move as fast as the providence of God opened the way. – Sketches from the Life of Paul, pg. 64

Moving is hard. Not long ago, my father received a job offer in Washington State. Accepting the offer would mean moving across the country away from my home and friends. Even though my family sensed that God was leading us to this "unexplored territory," I felt somewhat reluctant.

As Paul ministered to the Gentiles, he came in contact with Jews that had this same problem. They were not "prepared to move as fast as the providence of God opened the way." For ages, they had been accustomed to following the ceremonial laws that pointed forward to the Messiah. But after Jesus came as a fulfillment of these regulations, many converted Jews still thought them to be necessary. Moreover, they tried to force these rules on the Gentile converts. Although God had opened the way to a new covenant, the Jews were hesitant to move into "new territory".

Many years earlier, God opened the door for the Jews to return to their own land. But after living in Babylon for so long, some were slow to take advantage of God's providence. After asking for those who wanted to return, Ezra "found that not one Levite had volunteered to come along" (Ezra 8:15 NLT).

Think of how much more God could accomplish if we were always ready to move. Although the new might not seem as comfortable as the old, it is where God wants you to be. My family *did* decide to move, and as a result, we have experienced many blessings. As God leads you into "unexplored territories," ask Him to give you strength to keep moving.

~ Jonathan Sharley

March 3

The Greatest Scientist

God had given these injunctions to the Jews for the purpose of preserving their health and strength. – Sketches from the Life of Paul, pg. 66

In the 1800's, germs had not yet been discovered. People didn't realize the need to wash their hands and the necessity of cleanliness. A man named Ignaz Semmelweis introduced hand washing to some interns at the clinic where he worked. The number of deaths from contamination was immediately reduced. In spite of such an amazing discovery, many thought Semmelweis was insane, and he was admitted to an asylum. Many years later, Louis Pasteur discovered germs, and today most people are aware of the need to wash their hands.

Semmelweis, however, was not really the first to discover the need to wash your hands, nor was Pasteur the first to discover germs. Over 3,000 years ago, God gave the Jews some special instructions about cleanliness. Simple things like washing hands, properly disposing of waste, not touching dead animals, and proper eating habits are all covered in the Bible. The Jews have been spared many diseases and plagues because of their understanding of cleanliness.

Jesus said, "I am come that they might have life, and that they might have it more abundantly" (John 10:10 KJV). Not only does He want you to be spiritually healthy, but also physically healthy. He has given us many guidelines in the Bible, and in order to be entirely healthy, we must follow them. After all, God has always been and always will be the greatest scientist.

~ Melissa Butler

March 4

Self-control

God had given these injunctions to the Jews for the purpose of preserving their health and strength. – Sketches from the Life of Paul, pg. 66

Satan knew that if he could tempt Eve to eat the forbidden fruit, it would open the door for sin. If we pollute our bodies with refined foods, our mental and moral powers will be weakened, making it harder to resist temptations. If we eat more wholesome foods, we will be able to think more clearly and discern between right and wrong. The tempter of souls uses many things to entice and lure us. In our own strength, we cannot resist these temptations, but Philippians 4:13 tells us that we can do anything in the strength of Jesus.

God wants us to be in the best state mentally, physically and spiritually; and He has given us the principles for having a healthy, happy, and long life. "Indulgence in any unhealthful practice makes it more difficult for one to discriminate between right and wrong, and hence more difficult to resist evil" (*Ministry of Healing*, pg.128). If we could control our appetite, we could control almost every part of our lives. "The body is the only medium through which the mind and the soul are developed for the up building of character. Hence it is that the adversary of souls directs his temptations to the enfeebling and degrading of the physical powers" (*Ministry of Healing*, pg. 130).

God has given us our health, but we must do our part to preserve it. Our bodies are the temple of the Holy Spirit, so why not keep them in the best state possible? Since I have been choosing to eat healthier foods, I feel so much stronger, physically and mentally. Do you want Jesus to be living in a trashed and tarnished body or in one that is pure and holy? I challenge you to make changes today.

~ Becky Brousson

March 5

No Matter Who You Are

This message showed that God was no respecter of persons, but accepted and acknowledged those who feared Him, and worked righteousness. – Sketches from the Life of Paul, pg. 67

Have you ever questioned your worth? You may have found yourself looking around at your friends and comparing yourself with them. Perhaps some of these thoughts entered your mind: "I'm not good enough," "Nobody loves me," or "There's no point in trying." This is the very mindset that Satan wants us to cultivate. He wants us to be dissatisfied with who we are, so that we will begin to doubt our value. But how do we measure our worth? Do we look to God or to what we can achieve?

Mary Magdalene's life was one of abuse, shame, and rejection. She knew she was despised and saw herself as unvalued. But when she met the Savior, she found Someone who loved and valued her, not because she was perfect, but because she was a child of God. Christ looked beyond her sinful past to what she could become through Him.

As the early church began, the gospel message was being shared with the Gentiles. Some of the Jews felt that they were better than these new followers because they knew and followed every truth. However, God saw these same people sincerely seeking to follow His will, and He endowed them with the Holy Spirit, regardless of their nationality. No matter who you are, God sees your potential and what you can become through Him.

~ Melody Hyde

March 6

Reaching Out

The Jews had prided themselves upon their divinely appointed services… – Sketches from the Life of Paul, pg. 64

Marty Marion was a shortstop for the St. Louis Cardinals. When Marty began his career, he was called the "ugly duckling" of baseball because he was not good at hitting or fielding. Marty had a friend who encouraged him and helped him get his major breakthrough in the world of baseball. After his breakthrough, Marty showed that he had exceptional talent. Sports writers nicknamed him "The Octopus" because of his ability to get grounders. He helped his team win the World Series in 1942 and won the MVP award in 1944. Although at first he seemed awkward and clumsy, he ended with great statistics as both a player and manager. This was because someone boosted his confidence and encouraged him to be something greater.

Paul felt convicted that God had specifically chosen him to bring the gospel to the Gentiles. However, the prejudice of the Jews hindered him from preaching to the Gentiles. The Jews, planted in their traditions, refused to share the gospel with the Gentiles. Paul reasoned with church leaders to follow Christ's example and not withhold the truth from any man. Paul ignored their hatred and reached out to a people regarded for generations as untouchables.

Like Marty, there are people who are awkward, clumsy, and weird. They do not have friends because they are not athletic enough or do not wear the right clothes. Like Paul, God summons you to cross over that dividing line and reach out to those people. Let Christ's love shine from you as you give them words of encouragement and become their friend.

~ Jeremy Grabiner

March 7

What's In Your Eye?

They indulged in murmuring and fault-finding… and seeking to pull down the work of the experienced men whom God had ordained to teach the doctrine of Christ. – Sketches from the Life of Paul, pg. 70

Have you ever noticed other people's faults? Your roommate might be messy, maybe your best friend never brings her Bible to church, or your little brother might be unbearably annoying. It is so easy to see these faults and think that you are better than they are. For myself, I tend to notice the problems in others and not even notice my own bad habits. In Matthew 7:3 it says, "And why beholdest thou the mote that is in thy brother's eye, but considerest not the beam that is in thine own eye?" (KJV).

God chose Moses to deliver His people from their bondage in Egypt. It was hard for the people to trust Moses because he was human and had not always followed what was right. There never seemed to be a moment when the Israelites were not complaining or finding fault with what Moses did. Even other leaders of Israel, such as Aaron and Miriam, Moses' own family, doubted some of Moses' actions making it even more difficult for the people to be content. But, by their constant complaining no one was benefited, and it only made matters worse.

Nobody is perfect. It is when you look for the good and uplift others that they will want to change. Sometimes it may be necessary to give guidance to your friends, but only advise them with a spirit of love. Then, when you allow God to use you to encourage others, you will find that you have become truly happy and content.

~ Melody Hyde

March 8

Weight of Potatoes

Peter saw the error into which he had fallen and immediately set about repairing it as far as possible. – Sketches from the Life of Paul, pg. 72

A teacher once told her students to put potatoes into a plastic bag—one potato for each person they hadn't forgiven. She told them to take the bag of potatoes wherever they went for one week: in the car, to their desks, and even to bed at night. After some time, the potatoes began to get moldy and rotten. This lesson was to show them how much spiritual weight they carried around when they didn't ask God's forgiveness for sin right away. God wants us to ask for His forgiveness immediately because, the longer we carry our sins around, the more they "stink up" our lives with mold and rot.

Peter showed prejudice towards the Gentiles, and because of Peter's strong influence in the church, Paul openly rebuked him for his sin. When Peter realized what he had done, he tried right away to repair the broken relationships. King David also asked forgiveness for his sins to "repair the damage" when God opened his eyes to the extent of his sins (Psalm 51:10).

Someone once said, "Don't be afraid that your life will end, be afraid that it will never begin!" In the same way, when we ask for forgiveness right away, a new life of opportunity opens to us. God can show us so much more when we have everything right with Him. The "bags of potatoes" we keep in our lives will only worsen the longer we hold on to them.

~ Sharon Jeon

March 9

Move Up a Little

God…permitted Peter to exhibit this weakness of character, in order that he might see that there was nothing in himself whereof he might boast. – Sketches from the Life of Paul pg. 72

The Jews and Gentiles had been at odds for years, and Peter was not exempted from this struggle. While visiting Antioch, Peter at first tried to treat the Gentile as equals; but when other Jews influenced him against them, his attitude changed. The Gentile believers saw this and received a bad impression of Peter and his message. However, soon Peter realized that he had been wrong in treating them differently and tried to repair the damage as much as possible.

A little girl was visiting Switzerland with her mother, and while she was there, she faithfully practiced her five-finger piano exercises every day. Soon the other guests tired of her playing but were too kind to say anything. One day a guest came up to the little girl and said, "Move up a little and make room for me". The guest then sat down with the little girl and began to play along with her, turning her simple tunes into beautiful melodies. The other guests soon asked, "Who is that man playing with the little girl?" The hotel manager whispered, "The great pianist, Josef Hoffmann; he is here on a vacation to get a little rest." The little girl playing by herself nearly drove the guests crazy, but together the little girl and the great pianist produced beautiful music.

God gave Peter his humbling experience to show him his great need of being wholly in tune with Christ. This is how it is with us. We often play wrong notes and fail to get the timing right. At best our efforts are not at all melodious or sufficient, but if we will "move up a little" and make a place for the Master in our lives, then his life and ours, side by side, will produce sweet harmonies.

~ Rebecca Luchak

March 10

The Artist's Touch

God, who knoweth the end from the beginning, permitted Peter to exhibit this weakness of character, in order that he might see that there was nothing in himself whereof he might boast.
– Sketches from the Life of Paul, pg. 72

Everyone wants to be the most important. We boast about what we can do in order to impress those around us. Then we rely on our own strength to support our boastful claims.

There once was a jar full of many young, untrained paintbrushes. One said, "I can paint the most perfect circles." Another quickly retorted, "Well, I'm the squiggle master!" Among the group was an older, more experienced paintbrush. This paintbrush reminded the others that it was not by their own efforts that they could achieve great works; it was only under the guidance of the Master's hand that they could create something wonderful.

In this illustration, we find that it is when we are humble and submissive that we can be used by the Master. A brush is only a brush; it can never paint a picture on its own. It is only when the artist uses the brush that it does anything. It was when Peter was weak that God could do something through him, because then Peter knew that it was not by his own strength that he could do good works, but by God's power. It is very important for us to realize that we can do nothing on our own. Only when we are guided by God, can we have a great impact on this world.

~ Melody Hyde

March 11

Timothy: God's Man

Paul found that Timothy was closely bound to him by the ties of Christian union. This man had been instructed in the Holy Scriptures from his childhood, and educated for a strictly religious life. – Sketches from the Life of Paul, pg. 73

Among those who witnessed the stoning and miraculous recovery of Paul at Lystra was a young man named Timothy. Timothy had been brought up in a Christian environment by his mother Eunice and grandmother Lois. They had trained him to be a man of integrity and to live his life in service to others.

God's plan for this youth was to join Paul in doing service for Him. Timothy felt the call of the Holy Spirit and joined Paul in his labours, becoming one of his closest companions. Timothy proved to be a faithful minister of the Gospel, eventually taking control of the Ephesian church. Paul grew to love Timothy as a son and requested his presence in Rome after the trial before Caesar. Because Timothy learned godliness and discipline as a child, He was able to be used and blessed of God in the work of rescuing the lost.

Today, God is calling you and me. He has a plan for each of our lives. Like Timothy, we must prepare while we are young to serve God. Won't you join me in seeking God's purpose for your life? I know He has a wonderful plan for you.

~ Douglas Schappert

March 12

No Price too High

Timothy... was not appalled at the prospect of suffering and persecution. – Sketches from the Life of Paul, pg. 73

Suffering. Persecution. These words strike fear in even the bravest of hearts. Being a Christian is serious business. It's not the well-trodden path. Yet when we get to Heaven, we will find that the price we had to pay was cheap enough.

There was once a group of believers who were told by their captors to renounce God or die a humiliating death. They chose to die. They were led out to a frozen lake, told to take off their clothes, and to lie on the ice. As they lay there, they sang hymns. One believer who was unable to take the suffering any longer got up off the ice and renounced his Lord. One of the captors who was especially touched by the devotion of these followers took off his clothes and gave them to the one who had just renounced Jesus. He joined the dying soldiers of Christ and sang until he died. He did not find the price too high. He looked beyond this terrible trial and saw the ultimate reward in store.

In this world, a true Christian WILL suffer for Christ. Do you find the price to be too high? Are you willing to give your dreams, goals, and ambitions—maybe even your life—for the cause of Jesus? I challenge you to go for it! You will find the price to be cheap enough.

~ Veronica Nudd

March 13

Back Off!

...Paul, under inspiration of the Spirit of God, commanded the evil spirit to leave the woman. Satan was thus met and rebuked.
– Sketches from the Life of Paul, pg. 74

When I was six or seven years old, I was playing with friends on our property when a strange dog came through a hole in the fence and started barking and charging at us. Afraid it would attack, we picked up sticks and raced across the field hollering and waving our "weapons." The dog immediately stopped, stared at us, then turned and ran back through the fence. We had scared off the intruder by our childish display of boldness.

The same tactic works in our fight with Satan. James 4:7 says, "Submit yourselves therefore to God. Resist the devil, and he will flee from you" (KJV). But how often do we really follow this counsel? When Satan comes storming in for the attack, we usually cower in fear and confusion; but if we would have a little boldness, we could easily drive him away. All the power of heaven is on our side, and God has made sure that we have no reason to lose.

When Satan tries to back you into a corner and intimidate you, tell him to back off! You are the one with the REAL power—you are a child of the mightiest Warrior in the universe, and He will always be at your side. Don't be afraid to resist the devil—he WILL flee from you.

~ Cara Dewsberry

March 14

Worthy

They suffered extreme torture; yet they did not groan nor complain, but conversed with and encouraged each other, and praised God with grateful hearts that they were found worthy to suffer the shame for his dear name. – Sketches from the Life of Paul, pg. 75

Paul's stoning at Lystra was not his last ordeal. He trekked to Philippi with another companion named Silas, and the chances of suffering persecutions and torture were high, but this did not upset Paul's faith. Unfortunately, Satan stirred up a frenzy among the people, and the next thing Paul and Silas knew, they were in jail. The jailer scourged the poor disciples and left them flogged and bleeding.

Though they were not enjoying a comfortable stay in prison, their hearts did not get discouraged. They encouraged each other by singing hymns and praising God! Both were grateful to find themselves worthy to suffer shame for God's name. In the end, both knew that it was worth it. Paul, especially felt privileged to suffer for the doctrine he had once despised.

When facing any challenge in life, remember that you are not the only one struggling in this fight. The pains of life can bring you closer to God. He is standing by you to pick you up when you stumble. Our Heavenly Father uses these times of testing so that you can develop trust in His power. Paul and Silas overcame through their optimism, and God's power freed them from their chains.

Whether fire or lightning burst into your life, stay close to God and believe in His power to save you. Every single trial that you experience can edify you, making such trials worth going through.

~ David Ortiz

March 15

Always Cheerful

There in the pitchy darkness and desolation of the dungeon, Paul and Silas prayed, and sung songs of praise to God. – Sketches from the Life of Paul, pg. 76

"Melody, it's your turn to wash the dishes," my mother informed me.

"Not again!" I sighed. It seemed that I was always the one doing the dishes. In my opinion, it was the worst job in the whole world. It was like cleaning up after an army, because there are eleven people in our family, and we don't have a dishwasher!

My dad would always tell me, "You can choose to be happy, even when you don't feel like it." I would then force a smile on my face and start humming a little tune. After a few minutes, I would be singing and thoroughly enjoying myself. Now, what was once the worst job of my childhood has been transformed into one of my favorites.

It's amazing to me how my outlook could change everything. It made me want to choose to always be happy, even when I assumed that nothing could ever help. I always found that singing was the best way to lift my spirits, even when I was at my deepest point of despair.

Paul and Silas had chosen to be cheerful in every situation they faced. When in prison, they went straight to God and praised Him for His goodness. If they had not cultivated the habit of praising the Savior, they would have easily been drawn into discouragement. So whether you are doing the dishes or some other distasteful job, choose to be cheerful and see the great difference it will make.

~ Melody Hyde

March 16

When Right Seems Wrong

There in the pitchy darkness and desolation of the dungeon, Paul and Silas prayed, and sung songs of praise to God. – Sketches from the Life of Paul, pg. 76

Pain and suffering were the exact thoughts of Daniel, as he looked at the big "F" across the front of his college science final. "I can't in clear conscience agree with what they are trying to teach me," he mumbled to himself. "All I did was express my beliefs, and this is what I get for it. Why me?"

Suddenly two verses flashed into his mind: "In every thing give thanks…" (1 Thessalonians 5:18 KJV); "And we know that all things work together for good to them that love God, to them who are the called according to his purpose" (Romans 8:28 KJV). "No, God must have a bigger plan," Daniel decided. So, he resolved to give thanks.

When his friends asked him what he received on his test, he told them that he had failed. "Well aren't you depressed?" they inquired. To this, he replied, "In all things we should give thanks."

Later, a teacher who had been impressed by the stand that Daniel had taken approached him and asked if he would share more about what he believed. "Sure, I would love to," he replied thinking with a smile, "In every thing give thanks."

Paul and Silas were beaten and thrown into prison for sharing Jesus. Feelings of despondency and bitterness could have filled their minds, yet they chose to sing and be cheerful. This attitude helped convert not only some prisoners but also the jailer. This, in the end, made their pain worth it.

When we do right and things don't turn out as expected, we can thank God for those trials. He sees the big picture and can cause unexpected good to come from them.

~ Jourdain Smith

March 17

Influence

He had expected to hear bitter wailing, groans, and imprecations; but lo! his ears were greeted with joyful praise. – Sketches from the Life of Paul, pg. 77

Joyful singing and words of praise rang through the prison hall that night. All the inmates turned with rapt attention towards Paul and Silas' cell. Instead of hearing the usual swearing and ranting, the bewildered inmates were soothed by glorious hymns.

During that eventful night, an earthquake ensued, shaking the prison walls like dry leaves and opening the gates. Awakening in the midst of this chaos, the jailer instantly thought that all the prisoners had escaped. Fearing the consequences of his carelessness, he decided to end his own life. Just before his sword touched his belly, a loud voice cried out, "Do thyself no harm; for we are all here" (Acts 16:28 KJV).

The jailer was shocked that Paul, whom he had so cruelly tortured, was not resentful but compassionate and forgiving. Falling to his knees, the jailer begged for forgiveness and inquired, "Sirs, what must I do to be saved?" (verse 30). They responded by telling him, "Believe on the Lord Jesus Christ, and thou shall be saved…" (verse 31). This prison keeper did believe and was baptized with his household. The inmates, impressed by the experience, also opened their hearts to God.

Paul and Silas' cheerfulness under distress astonished the inmates. Though terribly treated, they exhibited compassion and Christ-like love towards their antagonists.

When you have a close connection with God, people will notice it; and those impressions will point them towards our Savior.

~ David Ortiz

March 18

Watch my Mouth, Lord!

Set a guard, O Lord, over my mouth; keep watch over the door of my lips. – Psalm 141:3 NKJV

The other morning, I was reading the above verse in my morning devotions, and a few days later I read about Paul and Silas' imprisonment at Philippi. Paul and Silas were thought to be evil criminals and the judge told the jailer to keep them in jail, or else he would have to pay with his life. The jailer put them in the innermost cell, bound them in stocks, and had them watched by guards.

Now, if the worst criminal had guards and watchmen set before the door of his cell, and David prayed that God would set a guard over his mouth, then that must mean that our mouths and what comes out of them can be extremely dangerous. Indeed, James 3:8 says, "But no man can tame the tongue. It is an unruly evil, full of deadly poison" (KJV). Verse 9 also mentions how we bless God with our tongues one minute, but the next are saying something mean to someone who annoys us. This means that I need to be asking God to set a watch over my lips, my mouth, or my tongue because they are the worst of criminals we have. Are you willing to let God put a sentry over your mouth? Do you want to only bless God and others and not to curse? Try setting a goal to see if you could make it through one day only saying kind words to those around you. That is something I really want. How about you?

~ Amy Windels

March 19

Killed with Kindness
Part 1

Therefore if thine enemy hunger, feed him; if he thirst, give him drink: for in so doing thou shalt heap coals of fire on his head. Be not overcome of evil, but overcome evil with good. – Romans 12:20, 21 KJV

Jim and Cora had just moved into a new house. Nobody seemed to want to live there, and they were going to figure out why. They discovered it was because of an old man, Mr. Grimes. He was the most evil old man anybody had ever known or seen. Jim decided to make old Mr. Grimes his new challenge. He wanted to see if he could still love him no matter what he did. "I will kill that old devil!" Jim exclaimed. After a few months of not being seen, the grouch finally started to live up to his name.

First, old "Grouch" Grimes chopped Jim and Cora's fence to smithereens and let the cows escape. So Jim went and fixed the fence, putting in a gate with a latch, which he left unlocked. Then, old Grimes cut a unit of pipe out of their water system, leaving them waterless. Jim went out to the pasture and fixed it, but instead of putting all the soil around it again, he left it loose, so that, if Mr. Grimes wanted to do something to their water again, it would be easier for him. That afternoon, Cora made some pies and insisted that Jim go and take them to Mr. Grimes along with a basket of fruit. When Jim got there, he was quite surprised to see the old guy's place. It had a little run down house, a weedy garden and there was only one tree—a crab-apple tree. "No wonder he is such a crab," Jim told Cora jokingly.

When we have difficult people in our lives, how do we deal with them? When someone does something mean to you, try doing something kind in return and see what happens.

~ Becky Brousson

March 20

Killed with Kindness
Part 2

The severity with which the jailer had treated the apostles had not roused their resentment ...But their hearts were filled with the love of Christ, and they held no malice against their persecutors. – Sketches from the Life of Paul, pgs. 77, 78

Yesterday, we saw that Jim and Cora had just moved into their new house. They encountered many trials, but determined to love old Mr. Grimes anyway.

One night, Cora left the laundry hanging out on the line. In the morning, they found their clothesline cut in half and the laundry strewn on the ground with muddy boot marks all over it. Then a few days later, when Jim went out to work, he called for his dog, Roger; but no Roger came. Jim went to the barn to see if the dog was there and found him on a heap of hay, dead. Old Mr. Grimes had poisoned him! That evening, Jim read for worship, "Ye have heard that it hath been said, An eye for an eye, and a tooth for a tooth: But I say unto you, That ye resist not evil: but whosoever shall smite thee on thy right cheek, turn to him the other also" (Matthew 5:38, 39 KJV); "For if ye forgive men their trespasses, your heavenly Father will also forgive you" (Matthew 6:14 KJV).

The next morning, Cora baked old Grimes some fresh bread and took it to him. That afternoon, as Mr. Grimes was going to town, he got stuck right in front of their house. Jim took his tractor, and without a word, pulled Grimes out. Just as Jim was about to leave, old Mr. Grimes threw open his truck door and exclaimed, "This is just too much for me. You are killing me! Every time I do something mean to you, you do something nice back to me!" Jim smiled and thought to himself, *I killed that old devil.* Yes, he was killed—killed with kindness.

If we truly love Jesus with all of our hearts, no matter what people do to us, we will be able to love them back. If you are having a hard time with someone, try turning the other cheek, and see if you can "kill" them with kindness.

~ Becky Brousson

March 21

Open Hand

But their hearts were filled with the love of Christ, and they held no malice against their persecutors. – Sketches from the Life of Paul, pg. 78

Envy and greed led the fiendish mob to imprison Paul and Silas at Philippi. Though they were in a discouraging situation, they chose to focus on holy things. Their holy influence illuminated the blinded souls of the other prisoners, pleading with them to turn away from their wicked ways. For an entire day, the apostles' sweet melodious words touched the hearts of everyone in the prison. However, that same night, an earthquake shook the whole dungeon, flinging the doors open. The jailer, who woke up in terror, knew the terrible consequence of sleeping on duty. In his despair, he decided to commit suicide. As he was about to thrust the cold steel blade into his throat, Paul cried out to him. Paul told him that they were all there, and no one had escaped. This action not only saved the jailer's physical life, but also led to his becoming a born-again Christian.

I believe Paul manifested opening one's hand to others. Though that same jailer had lacerated Paul's back, Paul didn't hesistate to relieve the poor soul from trouble. It is written that Christ gave his whole meal to people that needed it more than He did. You are called to live like Christ. If Christ gave His meal to those around Him, aren't you supposed to do the same? You may have passed by a homeless person shivering out in the cold of winter while you did nothing to help him. What would Jesus have done if He were there? I'm sure He would have given His own coat for that person. Jesus bids us do the same, not just for the benefit of others, but to express our devotion to Him. So if you see anyone in need of your help today, open your hand and do what Jesus would do.

~ David Chang

March 22

Brilliant Light

He saw the light of Heaven mirrored in their countenances.
– Sketches from the Life of Paul, pg. 78

As the speaker completed the meeting, she invited all who desired to give their hearts to Jesus to come up into the courtyard of the model sanctuary. As the Spanish strains of the song "I'd Rather have Jesus" progressed to the second and third verses, the outer court of the sanctuary was filled; people overflowed into the holy and most holy rooms, and some even stood on the steps descending from the huge stage. As she sang, the speaker shook hands with the guests in God's tent. Her heart was bursting with joy because more than ninety percent of the audience had moved forward to walk with Christ. She knew heaven was having a celebration.

In the crowd, a woman named Eva, who had been experiencing much depression and pain, was watching the speaker's face as she sang, "I'd rather have Jesus than anything." Suddenly, Eva saw a bright light in front of the speaker, and a large bright being passed in front of her. Eva could not describe the joy that thrilled her at seeing such a sight. As she gazed at this bright being, a flood of peace and joy came over her and wiped out all the depression. Her pain was relieved, and she had no more suffering. The experience was so amazing that Eva feared to tell anyone because they might think she was crazy. But after three days, she could not wait any longer and went to the speaker's motel door to tell her about it. Eva's gratitude for what Jesus did for her was evident all over her face. Her heart was full of love for Jesus, and she wanted to work for Him.

When people look at us, they can tell if we are Christians by the way we look and act. If you and I have the love Christ, it will be mirrored in our faces.

~ Jenny McCluskey

March 23

A Prism of Light

You are the light of the world. - Matthew 5:14 NET

Jesus is the Light of the world. He is the "radiance of his [Father's] glory" (Hebrews 1:3 NET). His life was the "light of mankind" (John 1:4 NET). This is what the jailor witnessed in Paul and Silas. He saw Christ's character in their lives. When tormented and unjustly imprisoned, they did not murmur. When mocked and tortured, they uttered the words of Christ. The apostles shone with a brightness that no man can ever produce.

Light has always puzzled scientists. Sir Isaac Newton was one of them. He found out that light, when shown through a prism (glass pyramid), would split into several different colors! The human race is like a prism for light. As the gospel shines through us, we each bring out what speaks to us the most. It is all light, just different perspectives, different pieces of the same puzzle. There are those who will only see the light through a different shade. There are those who only we can convert. Every man has his plot of land to nurture, to cultivate in his own way. Christ wishes for you to work among your friends, your family, and your community. You are Christ's doorway to shine light on this Earth. "For, look, darkness covers the earth and deep darkness covers the nations, but the LORD shines on you" (Isaiah 60:2 NET). Today there is somebody who needs this light; today there is a jailor who gropes in darkness. Let God shine through you.

~ Luke Gonzalez

March 24

Sinners

He saw his own deplorable condition in contrast with that of the disciples, and with deep humility and reverence asked them to show him the way of life. – Sketches from the Life of Paul, pg. 78

We are all familiar with the story of the proud Pharisee who prayed, "God, I thank thee, that I am not as other men are…I fast twice in the week, I give tithes of all that I possess" (Luke 18:11, 12 KJV). When we read that story, we roll our eyes and think what a proud, self-centered prayer! Imagine behaving in such a self-righteous way! But really, how often do we display the same mindset? We look at ourselves and think, "Hey, I'm doing pretty well. I lead an upright life and am surely much better than a lot of people in the world." For us humans, it is so easy to forget that we are helpless sinners in need of Christ.

Now do you remember the other character in the story? He was a despised tax collector, who realized his hopeless condition and in anguish cried out, "God be merciful to me a sinner" (verse 13). Jesus said that "this man went down to his house justified rather than the other" (verse 14). God can't do much for us when we think we're already good enough. He needs a humble, contrite heart to work with. When you find yourself feeling proud of your "good" life, remember the Pharisee and the tax collector. Which one went home justified? The one who saw his great need. We all have need of our Savior, Jesus Christ. Don't blind yourself to your faults; go to Jesus, for "if we confess our sins, he is faithful and just to forgive us our sins, and to cleanse us from all unrighteousness" (1 John 1:9 KJV).

~ Cara Dewsberry

March 25

Don't be a Hog

They went rejoicing from the prison…and related all the wonderful dealings of God… – Sketches from the Life of Paul, pg. 80

"Get away from my train set!" shouted Tommy as he smacked his little brother. Tommy did not know how to share. After wanting this toy for so long, his father had finally allowed him to play with it. But it was not Tommy's to keep; Daddy had merely loaned it to him. When Father found out how selfish Tommy had been, he thought it best to take back the train set.

The lives of the apostles, however, were quite different from Tommy's. Instead of keeping it to themselves, they were always sharing with others "the wonderful dealings of God." After being thrown into a Philippian dungeon, Paul and Silas spent the night singing praises to God. But before morning, God sent an angel to deliver them. The ground shook, and the prison doors were opened. But instead of escaping, Paul and Silas were able to share the Good News with the jailor as well as the other prisoners. When the apostles finally left the dungeon, they did not hoard their miraculous experiences, but instead told the believers all that God had done for them.

What about you? Are you hogging "all the wonderful dealings of God"? Are you keeping them to yourself? If you do not share them, you might lose them. It does not have to be complicated. Simply share with someone an experience that you have had with God. May you say like the psalmist: "O God…I constantly tell others about the wonderful things you do" (Psalm 71:17 NLT).

~ Jonathan Sharley

March 26

Pressing Forward

They there met much opposition and persecution; but the intervention of Providence in their behalf ... atoned for the disgrace and suffering they had endured. – Sketches from the Life of Paul, pg. 80

John Weidner was a Dutchman who lived in Paris during WW II. During the war, he decided to help Jews escape from German territories. He did this through organizing an "underground railroad" that helped over one thousand Jews and Allied servicemen escape. Weidner was captured many times, tortured frequently, and yet found ways to escape. Though arrested more than four times by the Gestapo, he kept at his work of saving people, risking his own life in the process.

Late in the war, one of his associates was arrested and tortured. She confessed to being a part of the underground and gave many names. The Gestapo arrested several leaders and posted a reward for Weidner. However, he persisted and rebuilt his network of helpers. Shortly after this incident, the Gestapo arrested him. Again, he was placed in the trying situation of being tortured if he would not reveal his contacts. The Gestapo set a date for his execution, but the night before, a French guard helped him escape. Although, John was captured and tortured several times and even faced death, yet each time he was able to escape. He did not cower in a corner or stop what he was doing; instead he knew God had given him another opportunity that he must use to help others.

Jesus calls you to be his messenger of truth. You must guide those who are spiritually blind, showing them that Jesus is the only solution to sin. When you are met with opposition, do not get discouraged; press forward with determination, boldness, and with the faith to get up and continue your work.

~ Jeremy Grabiner

March 27

Stand for Your Faith

The apostles might have fled when the earthquake opened their prison doors and loosened their fetters; but that would have been an acknowledgment that they were criminals, which would have been a disgrace to the gospel of Christ; the jailer would have been exposed to the penalty of death, and the general influence would have been bad. – Sketches from the Life of Paul, pg. 80

Jesus had a hard decision to make. He had to be willing to come down to this sinful earth and go through trials and temptations so that we may have eternal life. Just before His crucifixion, He prayed, "O my Father, if it be possible, let this cup pass from me: nevertheless not as I will, but as Thou wilt" (Matthew 26:39 KJV).

What He was about to go through was so difficult for Him that He sweated blood. Jesus longed to be back in Heaven with His Father, but He knew that if He didn't give His life for us, we wouldn't be able to have eternal life with Him.

When He prayed the second time, He said, "O my Father, if this cup may not pass away from me, except I drink it, Thy will be done" (verse 42).

It was possible for Jesus to go back to Heaven and not have to be crucified. He could have turned His back on His mission to save us. But He chose not to. Jesus chose to go through death no matter how hard it was. Just think of all the people who were making fun of Him on the cross and telling Him to prove to them that He really was the Son of God by coming down from the cross.

Paul, too, saw the door of opportunity open for him, but he chose not to take it. Instead, he chose to stand for what he believed in and not to run because he had a chance to save himself.

What would you do? Would you stand for your faith, or would you turn your back and run to save your own life?

~ Jennifer Atkins

March 28

Treasure It

They highly prized the precious truths for which the apostle had sacrificed so much... – Sketches from the Life of Paul, pg. 81

Savoring each bite, I thought of my mom who had made these coconut sticks for me. They were a real treat! When living in a dormitory far from home, homemade food is scarce. But its scarcity was not the only thing that made it special. As I bit into the yummy crunchiness, I thought about how my mom had taken time out of her busy schedule to make them for me. With this thought in mind, I treasured my coconut sticks even more.

The Christians who lived in Philippi were amazed to see how willing Paul was to go through trials. They saw how he was tortured because of his love for Jesus. When they realized how much he had given up in order to share with them the plan of salvation, these truths became even more precious to them.

Throughout the ages, many have sacrificed much in order to preserve and spread the "precious truths" of the Gospel. Many advocates for the truth "died by stoning, some were sawed in half, and others were killed with the sword. Some went about wearing skins of sheep and goats, destitute and oppressed and mistreated" (Hebrews 11:37 NLT). Starting with the patriarchs, many have suffered for Jesus since the beginning of this world. The prophets were continually being persecuted for proclaiming their God-given messages. Our wonderful Savior, Jesus, certainly knew what sacrificing was all about. His life was full of trials. The apostles were always being thrown into prison for preaching Christ. During the Dark Ages and the Reformation, countless seekers of truth were martyred.

"Therefore, since we are surrounded by such a huge crowd of witnesses" (Hebrews 12:1 NLT), let us join with them and prize these "precious truths" for which so many have sacrificed.

~ Jonathan Sharley

March 29

Rejoicing

Their appearance bore evidence of their recent shameful treatment, and necessitated an explanation of what they had endured. This they made without exalting themselves, but magnified the grace of God, which had wrought their deliverance. The apostles, however, felt that they had no time to dwell upon their own afflictions. They were burdened with the message of Christ, and deeply in earnest in his work. – Sketches from the Life of Paul, pp. 81, 82

The apostles had gone to Thessalonica after their imprisonment and release in Philippi. Their wounds were still evident, and the people asked what had happened. The apostles told their story, but in a way that would not exalt themselves. Instead, they gave glory to God that the jailer had been converted as well as his family. They wanted to tell the people more about what Christ had done for them through their suffering and what He could do in their lives.

We should remember this story today. We have the same message to give as the apostles did back in Thessalonica. More than likely we haven't been put in jail or whipped for our faith, but we do face trials everyday. Much of the time we make a big thing out of something really small that happened to upset our day. Then we go tell our friends what happened and how bad our day was when we really should be telling them about what God has done in our lives. There are times when it is good to talk to your friends about some of your trials, but I believe there should be more rejoicing over how God helps us instead of complaining. Let's start practicing this together.

~ Amy Windels

March 30

No Time

The apostles, however, felt that they had no time to dwell upon their own afflictions. They were burdened with the message of Christ, and deeply in earnest in his work. – Sketches from the Life of Paul, pg. 82

If anyone ever had the right to complain about difficulties, the apostles did. Paul had been rejected by his Jewish friends; mistrusted by the believers; stoned unconscious at Lystra, and finally he and Silas had been unjustly beaten and imprisoned at Philippi. No one would have blamed the apostles if they had bellyached a bit about their trials. But they felt they had no time to dwell on their own sufferings while souls hungered for the gospel. When they did tell of their afflictions, it was to glorify God, not have a pity party.

Now I want you to take a moment and think of all the things you grumbled about in the last day or two. How much time did you spend complaining? Was it more time than you thought?

We all probably complain a bit too much, but is it that big of a deal? Well, the apostles felt they had no time to complain because God's message needed to be preached. Could it be that, while we wallow in self-pity, opportunities to witness and save lives slip quietly by? It's a sobering thought. Now more than ever our world needs the Good News. We don't have time to waste complaining. Like the apostles, we need to turn our focus from ourselves to saving the lost souls around us before it's too late.

~ Cara Dewsberry

March 31

Burdened With the Message

They were burdened with the message of Christ, and deeply in earnest in his work. – Sketches from the Life of Paul, pg. 82

Paul and Silas had just gone through a very traumatizing time. They had been beaten, thrown into prison, and then, by the grace of God, redeemed and set free with the apologies of their offenders. Through this experience they had grown closer to Christ and now were even more dedicated to the work that He had called them to.

John Baker is part of an elite rock-climbing group known as the "hard men." Climbing mountains and scaling sheer rock faces is a way of life for them. In his lifetime, John has free-soloed some of the most difficult rock faces in the U.S. with no safety ropes or climbing equipment. How has he accomplished this feat of human strength and endurance? According to his wife, he has accomplished his goals only through commitment, dedication, and many hours of training.

While John might not have any safety ropes to rely upon, you have Jesus Christ, and He is willing to help you if you dedicate your life to the work that He has called you to do. It may not be easy to commit all that you are to Him, and at times you may be discouraged and think it too difficult. But as long as you take the much-needed time to "train" and strengthen yourself in Christ, He will give you the power that you need to accomplish your goals and to live the life that He has called you to live.

~ Leighton Sjoren

April 1

Tradition

He taught them that all their religious services and ceremonies would have been valueless if they should now reject the Savior, who was revealed to them, and who was represented in those ceremonies. – Sketches from the Life of Paul, pg. 83

Hard, arduous, and exacting was the perfect description of Judaism. The over-emphasis on ceremonial and traditional laws taxed the people so much that it led them away from seeing the symbolic meaning that each law carried. Into this darkness, God graciously sent Paul to illuminate the people and show them that it was Christ who was important, and not their traditions.

Though Paul died a long time ago, the principle of his teachings is still applicable. Paul addressed the Jews as formalists who taxed people to the point that following God was hard labor instead of joyous service. However, don't we do the same thing in our churches today? Whenever a new convert steps into the church, don't we expect him to accept all church "traditions"? Furthermore, we often emphasize health, dress, and other messages to the point that they become a salvation issue. By over-emphasizing tradition, we are doing what the Jews were condemned for. Imagine how many people we could uplift if we were to focus on Jesus more than our traditions. Tradition was the stumbling block for the Jews that led them away from Christ. Could it become a stumbling block in our Christian walk today? Let me suggest that we re-adopt Paul's focus and fix our eyes upon Jesus.

~ David Chang

April 2

Learn from Your Disappointments

...There was danger of his words being misinterpreted, and that some would claim that he, by special revelation, warned the people of the immediate coming of Christ. This he knew would cause confusion of faith; for disappointment usually brings unbelief. – Sketches from the Life of Paul, pp. 83, 84

It was October 21, 1844, and the time had almost arrived. A group of people, called Millerites, was excitedly awaiting the conclusion of the 2,300-day prophecy and the second coming of Jesus on October 22. As the day approached, the excitement of the Millerites soared. They had been so sure of this event that they hadn't even harvested their crops to store for the winter. They spent so much of their time spreading the news and preparing themselves that they had time for little else.

Now it was, Oct 22, 1844: the day they believed Jesus would come! All day long they anticipated his return, watching and waiting faithfully. But alas, He did not come! They had unknowingly discovered the day He would enter the Most Holy Place in the heavenly sanctuary, not the day he would return to take them home. When He did not return, they were intensely disappointed and several thousand of the believers left the faith because of it.

Sometimes God can use a situation of disappointment to help bring us closer and teach us to rely more fully on Him. We need to learn that even though disappointments may come, we can learn from them and choose to rely on God to help us through these disappointments.

~ Dave White

April 3

Rejected Truth

Those who preach unpopular truth... need expect no more favorable reception from a large majority of professed Christians then did Paul from his Jewish brethren – Sketches from the Life of Paul, pg. 86

While in Thessalonica, Paul preached three consecutive Sabbaths, reasoning with the Thessalonians from the Scriptures about the life of Christ. He showed them that the expectations of the Jews about the Messiah were not the same as prophecy had foretold. Paul, during this talk, also spoke about the second coming of Christ and of certain events, which must take place, before He comes.

However the truth was rejected. The Jews saw how successful the apostles were in acquiring large congregations, even converting some leading woman of the city, and they were filled with hatred and jealousy. By cunningly devised falsehoods, the Jews stirred up a tumult, and a large mob assaulted the house of Jason, where the apostles were staying. In all their fury, the people broke into the house; but friends of the apostles had already sent them out of the city.

Here is one more of the many examples of Paul being persecuted for preaching unpopular truths. Although Paul was faced with all these trials, he chose to go through them with Jesus. When we preach, there will always be people who don't appreciate what we are saying and who will resist it. But we can go through it with Jesus by our side, as Paul did. Someone once put it this way, "In the game of life, resistance will always follow us; but it doesn't matter for Christians because Christ is on our side, and He's the best player."

~ Joey Heagy

April 4

Present Truth

Those who preach unpopular truth in our day meet with determined resistance, as did the apostles. – Sketches from the Life of Paul, pg. 86

Nominal Christians don't usually want to discuss character building, subduing of base passions, or the Judgment because it makes them uncomfortable. These messages rebuke their naturally selfish desires. However, we are called to present the Gospel the way Jesus reveals it to us. He never compromised the word of God to please people. He always presented the plain truth, regardless of its popularity. However, whenever Jesus gave a message, he uttered every word with deep compassion. We are suppose to follow His example and fearlessly preach the truth, but with love for the blinded soul.

On the other hand, I must admit that I don't feel like standing up and preaching the truth all the time. I might be scorned or criticized; but, is it about my feelings, or is it about God? God sees in His infinite wisdom that His people are forgetful of His grace. He sends servant after servant to remind and encourage His church to follow after Him. However, following Jesus is building character, loving God with all your soul. It is not always comfortable, but it is the only way to become like Him. Think of how many people may be walking in darkness because you refuse to give the message that God is placing on your heart. Though it can be scary to go against the mainstream, God encourages us by saying, "Do not be afraid for I am with you" (Genesis 26:24 KJV). If God is on your side, you are invincible because you have the Almighty protecting you. So why don't you go preach the truth that God wants you to preach?

~ David Chang

April 5

Right Course, Right Reason

Those who preach unpopular truth in our day meet with determined resistance, as did the apostles. – Sketches from the Life of Paul, pg. 86

Do you like being popular? Do you want to be the top dog at work, at school, in music, in fashion, or with friends? Deep within us we all desire to be the best, but isn't that rather selfish? Generally, if we're on top, someone else is on the bottom. If we're lifted up, someone else is pushed down. It's more Christ-like to lift someone else up, to put someone else on the top; but far too often, we let self conquer conscience in these matters.

It gets even worse, though. Could it be that we are seeking popularity and the highest place in regards to religion? Do we go to church to be in God's presence or to be in man's presence? Do we dress up Sabbath mornings for God or for man? Are we Christ-like in order to be like Christ or to impress our friends?

Really living the truth will often be unpopular and challenging. More often than not, it will be necessary to go against the flow as we follow Christ, but how can we do this if we are always allowing ourselves to be swept along by those around us? The only way to head the right direction is to disconnect from this world's motives, to go the right way for the right reasons. Proceeding in that way, we'll surely reach our destination.

~ Robby Folkenberg

April 6

Animal Behavior

Those who will not themselves accept the truth are most zealous that others shall not receive it; and those are not wanting who perseveringly manufacture falsehoods, and stir up the base passions of the people to make the truth of God of none effect.
– Sketches from the Life of Paul, pg. 86

My family lives deep in the wilderness of Montana and has succeeded in befriending some of the wild forest creatures, even getting deer and birds to eat from our hands. Because we have been able to get so close to the animals, we have been able to observe their behavior. I've noticed, that when we put food out for them, it's "every man for himself." The deer especially manifest a pervasive "me first" attitude. Some are so busy chasing others away from the piles of food that they themselves don't get a single bite. By the time one chases its neighbor away, another is at the opposite end, stuffing its face. The frenzied animal tries harder and harder to hoard all the grain for itself, but fails to reach its goal of getting its own food. It seems totally incapable of realizing that this doesn't ensure itself any more food.

Deer are just animals. How many times do we as humans, and even worse, as Christians, decide that, if others won't see things our way, we're going to make their lives miserable? All too often, we manifest a spirit more like the animals than the God we claim to represent. When our hearts feel the calling of the Holy Spirit, we are confronted with two choices: either heed the voice, or try to convince ourselves and others of its fallacy.

The only way you can escape this ensnaring attitude is to be on your knees constantly. Prayer will keep you close to the Savior and will guide your actions. "The messengers of Christ must arm themselves with watchfulness and prayer, move forward with faith, firmness, and courage, and, in the name of Jesus, keep at their work, as did the apostles" (*Sketches from the Life of Paul*, pg. 86).

~ Jonathan Fink

April 7

Shooting with a Book

The messengers of Christ must arm themselves with watchfulness and prayer, and move forward with faith, firmness, and courage, and, in the name of Jesus, keep at their work, as did the apostles. – Sketches from the Life of Paul, pg. 86

There is a story told of a young man named Paul, who was selling Adventist literature. On the last day of a hard week he noticed a tall stranger following him. At the end of the day, Paul boarded a train and was about to lie down in his private compartment when the door opened and in came that same tall stranger!

"Do you carry much money with you?" the stranger asked.

"No," Paul said. "But why do you ask?"

"Are you armed?"

Paul hesitated then said, "Yes. Are you?"

"Yes," said the man, pulling out a pistol. "Now show me yours." Paul reached into his briefcase and took out his Bible. "Here's mine," he said.

"You're crazy," said the man. "That's not a gun; that's a book!"

"It shoots better than yours," said Paul. "Your gun can only shoot the man it's pointing at, but this book is certain death to every wicked man who will listen to its words."

"How do you shoot with a book?" questioned the stranger.

"Put your gun away and I'll show you," Paul replied.

The man put away his gun, and Paul opened his Bible and read verses that told the story of how sin entered the world and how Jesus, the Son of God, came to save mankind.

"Tell me more, quickly. My station is the next stop," said the man.

Then Paul told of the new earth where there would be no more sin, sorrow, or death for those who believe in Christ. The stranger grasped Paul warmly by the hand and said, "No one will know what your gun saved me from tonight."

The word of God is the ultimate source of wisdom and help. Only through watchfulness and prayer may we be victorious in our spiritual battles over evil.

~ Rebecca Luchak

April 8

Open the Book

These [the Bereans] were more noble than those in Thessalonica, in that they received the word with all readiness of mind, and searched the scriptures daily, whether those things were so. – Acts 17:11 KJV

The Bible is the voice of God speaking to us on Earth. Before sin, we used to be able to converse directly with God. Now, in this sinful world, most of us don't hear God's voice audibly. The Bible is one of the ways that He communicates with us. It is His love letter to us. In it, we can find directions on how to live, how to treat others, and how to serve Him better. It is our life guide.

The people in the church at Berea were considered to be nobler than those in the Thessalonian church. Why? They didn't just accept the word of anyone as truth. They pored over the holy writings, to see if the new doctrine was true. I think they set a very good example for us.

When you hear something at church that you have never heard before, go home and look it up! God will honor your diligent search for truth with increased knowledge and love for Him. Hear Him say, "You will seek me and find me when you seek me with all your heart" (Jeremiah 29:13 NIV). When you look for the things of God, He will become so real to you that it will seem like you are sitting on your front porch chatting with Him. Think about what that really means! You have the privilege of conversing face-to-face with the Supreme Creator of the universe! To make things even better, He wants to talk with you. He says, "Here I am! I stand at the door and knock. If anyone hears my voice and opens the door, I will come in and eat with him, and he with me" (Revelation 3:20 NIV). Open the Book. All He is waiting for is your acceptance of His "dinner" invitation.

~ Jonathan Fink

April 9

Honestly Seeking

In the presentation of the truth, those who honestly desire to be right will be awakened to a diligent searching of the Scriptures. – Sketches from the Life of Paul, pg. 87

The labors of the apostles in Berea met with great results; and their teachings provoked the people to think about the Word of God for themselves. The people honestly desired to know the truth, and they studied the Bible with diligence.

Those who teach the truth in our age rarely meet with the same results as the apostles met with in Berea. Those who hear the truth often approach it with the greatest reluctance. They cannot change the truth that they hear, so they refuse to approach the light given and diligently investigate it for themselves. They think it is of little consequence whether they believe the message is truth or not. They think that their current faith and customs are sufficient for them.

"God will judge all according to the light which has been presented to them, whether it be plain or not" (*Sketches from the Life of Paul*, pg. 87). It is your duty, like the Bereans, to study the Word for yourself, to learn the Bible's teachings, and to apply them in your life. Do not be ignorant of the truth like many people in the world are. Seek the truth with all your heart, and be burdened to live that truth in your everyday life.

~ Leighton Sjoren

April 10

Transformation

They think that their old faith and customs are good enough for them.
– Sketches from the Life of Paul, pg. 87

    Traditions are customs that you have become familiar with; they ways of thinking and acting. When you are in the habit of doing things a certain way, it is very hard to change and do things differently. It becomes easy to believe that your way is the only way to do things.

    One dark, drizzly night, two girls who were colporteuring were making their way through a shady part of town. Feeling a bit nervous, they stopped to pray. Just as they opened their eyes, they saw a group of rough, dirty men gathering around them. As crude insults were hurled at them, the girls tried to stay calm and told the men that God loved them and could change their lives. One girl handed her Bible to one of the men, hoping it would impact his life. Impressed, the man ordered the others to leave the girls alone, enabling them to quietly slip away.

    A while later, the girls attended a meeting and saw a familiar-looking man standing by the door of the church. The man stepped up to the girls and asked, "Do you remember me? You gave me this." He held out a familiar Bible, and immediately the girls recognized him as their protector from that frightening night. Inside the church, the girls found all the men who had accosted them sitting in the front row, completely changed and glowing with the light of Christ's love.

    These men did not think that they needed to change because they had become so accustomed to being on the streets. This lifestyle had become their "tradition" and had shaped their way of thinking and acting. However, the Christ-like example of the girls had touched their hearts, and they desired something better. We need to make sure that in our lives we don't become so accustomed to the way we do things that we are not willing to allow God to transform our lives.

~ Melody Hyde

April 11

Respect

But the Lord, who sent out his ambassadors with a message to the world, will hold the people responsible for the manner in which they treat the words of his servants. God will judge all according to the light which has been presented to them, whether it is plain to them or not. It was their duty to investigate as did the Bereans. It is the Lord who says though the prophet Hosea: "My people are destroyed for lack of knowledge, I will also reject thee." – Sketches from the Life of Paul, pg. 87

In one African village where my mom and I were doing mission work, the people were very disrespectful to us and accused us of disturbing the peace. After much prayer and fasting, a letter came from the General Conference, recommending us and instructing the people to respect our work. The letter cleared the way for us to continue with the meetings. But the government leaders were stilled concerned about us because of the history of genocide in that area where even pastors killed those who came to church. The leaders provided lodging, water, and a generator for us. They demanded full support of the doctor and nurse who came to help them. They even appointed special soldiers to guard us and to keep the peace at our meetings. These guards gave their hearts to Jesus and were baptized along with more than one hundred others. Even the wrath and disrespect of men ended up bringing praise to God.

It is our duty to give respect to our teachers and pastors. We need to make sure that we are not rejecting something that is important. You and I need to study to show ourselves "approved unto God, a workman that needeth not to be ashamed, rightly dividing the word of truth" (2 Timothy 2:15 KJV).

~ Jenny McCluskey

April 12

School of Life

God will judge all according to the light which has been presented to them, whether it is plain to them or not. – Sketches from the Life of Paul, pg. 87

When I was in Social Studies class last semester, I had a teacher who only taught Social Studies and English. Being a Canadian, I am required to learn about Canadian history, but it is up to me to actually listen in class and take notes. There were times when I didn't study as diligently as I needed to, and I had a test the next day. So I would either stay up late or get up early, so that I would have a better chance of passing the test and getting a good grade. This method of cramming would sometimes work, but not always.

Our characters are much the same way. God is the principal of our school of life and he has workers, like pastors and teachers, who teach us the way to go. But it is up to us to listen to them and to apply what we learn to our lives. Unlike school, we won't have the ability to do last minute studying before the final exam, which is the judgment. When it comes to our characters, we need to prepare today. Are you getting ready right now for that final exam?

~ Amy Windels

April 13

Dig Deeper

These were more noble than those in Thessalonica, in that they received the word with all readiness of mind, and searched the scriptures daily, whether those things were so.
– Acts 17:11 KJV

There is a story told of a young man in South Africa named John who had just graduated from high school and needed money for college. He decided to find a piece of unclaimed ground and begin digging for diamonds. Each week he and his partner found enough diamonds to pay expenses and to save for school; but the fortune that they dreamed of never turned up. Now diamonds are generally found in a layer of gravel near the surface. So John and his partner worked the gravel thoroughly right down to what they thought was basic dirt. They noticed that their neighbors were digging deeper, but decided that the surface gravel on their neighbors' land just went deeper than their own. They did not think of digging a hole to see if there was more gravel under what appeared to be basic dirt, and when they had thoroughly worked the surface gravel, they moved on.

Later, someone else came along and dug a hole on their old plot. They found more gravel deeper down and in that gravel was the fortune! Many thousands of dollars worth of diamonds were dug from that plot of ground. If John and his partner had only dug a little deeper, they could have found the fortune! But they had been satisfied to skim over the surface, so they missed it.

There is a "fortune" in the Word of God, but you have to search for it. Skimming over the surface and just reading the stories will give you some blessing, but the richest blessings come when you study, think, and compare your life with the ideas found in the Word of God. So "dig" a little deeper in the Bible, and you'll find a "fortune."

~ Rebecca Luchak

April 14

Craving God's Word

If the people of our time would follow the example of the noble Bereans, in searching the Scriptures daily... there would be thousands loyal to God's law where there is one today.
– Sketches from the Life of Paul, pg. 88

Have you ever searched for a lost item? There is a big difference between going on a search and taking a leisurely walk, enjoying the scenery. Searching may involve some digging, dirty knees, and putting on of glasses.

Many people of our time are not searching the scriptures enough. We do not realize the power of God's word. In Hebrews 4:12 it says, "For the word of God is quick, and powerful, and sharper than any twoedged sword..." (KJV). God desires us to search the Scriptures, and that doesn't mean merely reading over them.

The Bereans were willing to search and to get their hands dirty because they desired truth. Why does searching God's word come so hard for us? Why do we find reading God's word so boring? It is because we don't have the desire to know the truth. Friends, we have fallen so low that truth is not appetizing to us anymore. When God makes truth appealing, than we are able to search God's word with renewed energy. We must crave for more truth so that more people can be loyal to God's law.

~ Sharon Jeon

April 15

Usable

I tell you the truth, unless a kernel of wheat is planted in the soil and dies, it remains alone. But its death will produce many new kernels - a plentiful harvest of new lives. – John 12:24 NLT

In a Chinese farmer's garden, there grew a beautiful bamboo plant. Each day the farmer would stroll through his garden at the cool of dusk, lovingly admiring his plants. One day, he paused by the beautiful bamboo plant.

"Bamboo, I need to use you," he intoned. As the farmer listened, he heard the melodious voice of the plant respond:

"Here I am, Master, use me as you see best."

"I need to cut off your leaves and branches, and lay you in the dust," said the farmer gently.

" What? No!" shrieked the bamboo. "Use me—but in some other way!"

"If I don't do this," the farmer warned, "I cannot use you. Also, I will need to split you open and take your heart from you."

At this revelation, the bamboo almost wilted. "Please! Am I not the most beautiful of your plants?"

"If you want me to use you, this is what I must do. Believe me, as your Master; I know your purpose best."

So the master cut, trimmed, split, and took the heart from the bamboo. When rice- planting time came, the farmer took the coarse, dry bamboo shell out to one of his fields, using it as a trough to transport water from one of his springs. As the pure, clear liquid flowed through the dead plant, it imparted life to others. By giving up its beauty in death, the bamboo became even more beautiful in fulfilling its Master's plan.

All too often we, like the bamboo plant, have our own plans and desires for our lives; but are we sure that they are God's will? Are we fulfilling our true calling? The apostle Paul recognized this need when he said, "I die daily" (1 Corinthians 15:31 KJV). It is when you decide to let go of everything you are, that the "Master Farmer" can step in and use you to nourish His "crop."

~ Jonathan Fink

April 16

Do You Dream?

Yet the faithful apostle steadily pressed on…to carry out the purpose of God as revealed to him in the vision at Jerusalem… – Sketches from the Life of Paul, pp. 88, 89

I dream of living in the Swiss Alps! From my little mountain chalet, I will gaze across the meadow at the jagged mountains, covered with snow. All around me, a sea of wild flowers will brighten the view. On the adjacent knoll, bleating goats will graze on the lush grass. A yodeler's echo will be heard reverberating through the valley. It is in this paradise that I plan to retire. Without a dream, the reality of this is impossible.

The apostle Paul was a dreamer. While in the temple at Jerusalem, God gave him a vision—a plan for his future. His desire to share the love of Jesus was strengthened. God instructed him, "Depart, for I will send you far from here to the Gentiles" (Acts 22:21 NKJV). Dreaming about spreading the Good News and equipped with a vision, Paul was now able to fulfill the "purpose of God" in his life.

Has God given you a vision? Have you received a glimpse of His purpose for you? The vision is an essential component of progress. Without a vision—without a goal—we wander through life carrying out our *own* purposes. Without ambition, God's purpose will never become a reality in your life. "Where there is no vision, the people perish…" (Proverbs 29:18 KJV). Ask God to give you a dream. It may not be a prophetic vision as was Paul's, but God will reveal His plan for you just the same.

~ Jonathan Sharley

April 17

Idols

The senses of the people were entranced by the beauty and glory of art. – Sketches from the Life of Paul, pg. 89

When Paul arrived at Athens, he encountered a people famous for their intelligence and education. They built magnificent statues of their gods and took pride in their architecture and art. The Athenians, entranced by their architecture, art, and idols, could not accept the truth presented by Paul. They were so fixed on their idols that they could not see the truth plainly presented to them.

What do you think about when you hear the word "idols"? People usually think of idols as small wooden figures worshiped by natives on a remote island. However, common things such as your favorite movie star or sport can also be an idol in your life.

I love soccer. Soccer is definitely my favorite sport. I am constantly reading soccer news, checking which team won a game and who got hurt. I stay up late watching games, I collect soccer shirts, and I play soccer every chance I get. I am so fascinated with soccer that I do not leave enough time to spend with God. Soccer is my idol. I spend so much time with soccer that I do not put my focus on the more important things in life.

What is your idol? What keeps you from focusing on Christ? Is it TV, video games, movies, Internet, or sports? Christ beckons us to put less attention on our idols and more attention on our walk with God.

~ Jeremy Grabiner

April 18

No In-Between

He [Paul] perceived that human art had done its best to make falsehood attractive. – Sketches from the Life of Paul, pg. 90

Satan has developed so many lies to entice us. What is it with sin that attracts us? Why did Eve eat that apple when God had told her what would happen? She ate it because it was attractive.

During my life, whenever I was struggling to understand the difference between something right and wrong, my mom would ask me, "If I baked you a batch of brownies, but I put just a pinch of poison in them, would you eat them?" I would reply with an emphatic no. My mom explained to me that a little bit of bad spoils the whole thing.

Something cannot be both bad and good. There are no "gray areas" in God's eyes. Satan is working hard to make us stumble. If he can get us to fall in just one area, then he's got us. Men cannot serve two masters. A house divided against itself cannot stand. Will you choose to give not 99.9%, but 100% to Jesus? Don't try to get the approval of both God and the world. It doesn't work. Satan's pleasures always turn out to be what they are—lies.

When you give your heart to Jesus, you will discover just as Paul found, that Jesus is the only thing worth giving your life to. He is the only one that can fill that space in your heart. He is the right side. There is no in-between.

~ Veronica Nudd

April 19

Values

And when the chief Shepherd shall appear, ye shall receive a crown of glory that fadeth not away. – 1 Peter 5:4 KJV

A little girl went to the store with her mom. There she saw a cheap plastic pearl necklace that she wanted. She begged her mom to get her the necklace, and after much coaxing, her mom gave in to her pleas. The little girl loved that necklace and wouldn't give it up for anything. She wore it everywhere so that she could show it off.

One night, when her dad was tucking her into bed, he asked her if she would give him her necklace. Not wanting to give it up, she offered to give up her teddy bear instead. Her dad calmly said that it was all right and that she didn't have to give it to him. This same situation happened several more times, but she didn't want to give up her necklace. A few days later, her dad found her crying. When he asked her what was wrong, she replied that she had finally decided to give up her necklace. When she handed it to him, her dad smilingly reached into his pocket, took out a real pearl necklace, and placed it around her neck. He had wanted to give it to her for several days, but she had to be willing to give up her plastic necklace first.

Sometimes, I have earthly things that I hold on to. Yet, God wants to give me so much more, if I will let go of my earthly things. As I let Him change me, they will fade from view. Just as for the apostle Paul, those things will appear valueless in comparison to what God holds in store for me.

~ Jourdain Smith

April 20

Priorities

The moral nature of the apostle was so alive to the attraction of heavenly things, that the joy and splendor of those riches that will never fade occupied his mind, and made valueless the earthly pomp and glory with which he was surrounded. – Sketches from the Life of Paul, pg. 90

Enoch, though surrounded by sinful, pleasure-loving people, lived in the very atmosphere of heaven. He was so close to God that earthy things had no control over him. His mind, heart, and conversation were on heavenly things. He knew where his treasure lay, and his heart was there. "The greater the existing iniquity, the more earnest was his longing for the home of God" (*Patriarchs and Prophets*, pg. 87). The closer he grew to Jesus, the deeper he sensed his own weaknesses and imperfections.

Earthly fame, wealth, or power did not distract Enoch because heavenly things were constantly on his mind; they were of more importance to him. No matter what the cost, if Jesus is important to us, other things will be able to wait. We will want to give our time to Him. The things of this world will fade away when compared to the joys and splendor of heaven. That doesn't mean that we will be unaware to the times that we are living in; it means that the things of this world will hold no value compared to what Jesus is to us.

This world will try to make riches and honor look appealing to us. If something is valuable to us, we will be able to make time for it. Jesus gave His life for you. Can't you just give Him some of your time? Make Him your priority, there is nothing to lose, rather eternal life to gain.

~ Becky Brousson

April 21

Focus

The moral nature of the apostle was so alive to the attraction of heavenly things, that the joy...of those riches...occupied his mind, and made valueless the earthly pomp and glory with which he was surrounded. – Sketches from the Life of Paul, pg. 90

Spotting motion in a ditch, a naturalist went to investigate. Upon closer examination, he discovered a turtle striving to push a telephone pole out of its way. The naturalist picked up the small creature and moved it around the pole, and it continued walking. When the animal reached the next pole, it repeated the process! A biological study showed that some species of turtles will travel only in a straight line. If something is in the way, they will push against it forever. In the same study, it was found that buzzards won't fly out of a cage that is smaller than eight feet wide, even if there's no roof. A bumblebee, when placed in a glass cup, will expend the rest of its energy and life trying to get through the bottom.

These animals are so obsessed with their own problems and phobias that they can't see the bigger picture, the easy solution. When focusing on the things of Christ, your impossibilities will vanish. The light of heaven will illuminate your steps. Everything here on earth fades away in the glory of the Eternal. When you willingly give all your plans, aspirations, dreams, and desires to the One who had your life planned out from the very beginning, you'll be able to see past all of your obstacles, and walk in His straight path. It all boils down to one thing: Where's your focus?

~ Jonathan Fink

April 22

Art Worship

The religion of the Athenians...consisted in a great part, of art worship, and a round of dissipating amusement and festivities.
– Sketches from the Life of Paul, pg. 91

As the latest electronic gadget nears its release date the world is flooded with advertisements. The day it is released, millions flock to the stores hoping to get their hands on this wonder. The glitz and glamour of the newest fashion enthralls the crowd and occupies their dreams for days. The Internet is flooded with reviews of a video game that has just been released to the public and boasts the most stunning graphics of its genre. It is as if the object's beauty is revered and worshipped above its practicality or usefulness. We find ourselves worshipping the extravagance and enjoying the ease and comfort of a "world" that we have invented.

Numerous incidents come to mind of times when I got caught up in the latest craze. I remember when the Nintendo Wii ©, a game platform, came out. I looked in awe at its shiny white case. It seemed to be calling for me to be its owner. The Wii © occupied all my thoughts and energies, and as a result my life was unproductive. As long as I worshipped it, my spiritual life lay in ruins.

It was the same with the Athenians. They had become worshippers of art and seekers of pleasure. The problem didn't lie in the art necessarily. It was the high place given it in their minds that gave them their false religion of idolatry. Art in itself is not a religion; the object may be perfectly good, but you run into problems when that object is elevated to a central position in your thoughts. This is when a good thing can become bad, because your focus is no longer on Christ but instead on the object. Experience a paradigm shift so that the Holy Spirit can point out the idols in your life, even if they are beautiful pieces of art, so that you may cast them away.

~ Buddy Taylor

April 23

Fill in the Blank

On the very stones of the altar in Athens this great want was expressed by the inscription, "To the Unknown God."
– Sketches from the Life of Paul, pg. 91

Athens was a heathen place full of idols and sculptures. As Paul looked around, his eyes caught the words "To the Unknown God" inscribed on an altar. He could see that the people of Athens wanted something more. Even with all the gods they made, they still had a hole in their lives, a desire which nothing seemed to fill. They recognized this longing and called it "unknown." They realized the emptiness of their hearts, and Paul used this God-given chance to tell them about the "Unknown God."

When you desire something, you may not always be able to find it on your own. It is like after eating, you know you need some other food to make the meal complete, but you just can't put your finger on it. Suddenly, someone suggests a _____, and you say to yourself, that's it! Your desire is fulfilled and the search is over.

There are people in darkness who are looking and searching for the light. They spend their lives chasing after different gods. They try different things to satisfy their want, things such as buying, drinking, eating—fill in the blank. Despite their searching, they still have something missing in their hearts. The Holy Spirit has already convicted them of the blank space in their hearts. God wants us to show them the substance for that emptiness. To fill in the blank of somebody's life should be the focus and purpose of every Christian.

~ Sharon Jeon

April 24

Unknown

Though boasting of their wisdom, wealth, and skill in art and science, the learned Athenians could but acknowledge that the great Ruler of the universe was unknown to them. – Sketches from the Life of Paul, pg. 91

In A.D. 768, Charlemagne became king of France, and in his heart, he decided to conquer his smaller neighboring nations and rule the whole world. Thus, he conquered the Lombards in Italy, the Saxons in Germany, and after fifty campaigns he was made emperor of Rome in A.D. 800. He then ruled nearly all the western part of the Roman Empire. But he died in A.D. 814, without his dream of a world empire coming true, and was buried in a large marble tomb.

Nine hundred years went by, and then one day his tomb was opened. There was his skeleton, still clothed in kingly robes, sitting on a marble slab. His golden scepter was still in his hand. On his knee was an open scroll and a bony finger was pointing at the words, "What doth it profit a man, if he shall gain the whole world, and lose his own soul?" (Mark 8:36 KJV). At the end of his life, Charlemagne finally realized that even though he was emperor of the largest nation on earth, the One who gave him his wealth and power was unknown to him.

The Athenians were satisfied with their accomplishments and felt no need for the salvation Paul talked about; they didn't see its overwhelming importance. Never let worldly wisdom, wealth, or ambition block the way between you and God. The salvation of your soul is more important than anything else.

~ Rebecca Luchak

April 25

Image of God

Man was created in the image of this infinite God, blessed with intellectual power and a perfect and symmetrical body.
– Sketches from the Life of Paul, pg. 94

"Just once man, I guarantee you, it tastes awesome!" Two cigarettes lay in my hand given to me by my buddies who both smoke and drank. We were on top of the house, where no one could see, and I sat there sweating, with a couple guys around me who were anxious to see me smoke. They thought that I would love it, but I did not want to do it because I knew smoking was bad. I knew it would harm my health.

Finally I said, "Hey, I don't think I'm ready now; I'll save it for later... maybe." On the way home, I threw the cigarettes away in a public trashcan.

"Just once man, I guarantee you, it tastes awesome!" I was hearing the same thing again. I was with my cousins, who were non-Christians, and they wanted me to drink.

"Yeah dude, don't chicken out!" my other cousin put in. When I declined, they made fun of me but never brought the alcohol can again. Two weeks later, I was informed that one of my cousins, who had been tempting me to drink, had died in a motorbike accident. He only nineteen years old, and he was drunk.

Man was created in God's image, and our body has laws that must be followed. If we don't obey God's will, we will lose our minds. God requires all of us human beings to follow his laws and take care of our bodies because if we don't, we will put ourselves in danger.

~ Ryo Fusamae

April 26

Now That's Big!

The heavens are not large enough to contain God; how much less could those temples made with hands contain him. – Sketches from the Life of Paul, pg. 95

God is huge. Trying to fit God into a human category is like trying to squeeze the Empire State Building into a golf ball... an infinite number of times! It's impossible, right? God is so huge, that we can't even fathom His greatness. Now that's big! Paul used this concept to show the Athenians how impossible it was for an idol to be God. How could an image made with hands hold Him who created hands in the first place? Furthermore, how could man's imperfection hold God's perfection?

In this Being of immense proportions we see immense love. "For God so loved the world that He gave His only begotten Son, that whoever believes in Him should not perish but have everlasting life" (John 3:16 NKJV). To see God stretching out his arms of love to those who rebelled against Him is amazing. And to see that God's arms are still outstretched towards us today gives me hope and a sense of belonging.

God wants to be a part of your life today. Immensity longs to interact with the infinitesimal. When you allow God to run your life, He fills you right up with His love. You'll be overflowing! Seriously, you'll want to talk about God's love, return love and adoration to God, and give others the chance to experience God's love for themselves. Infinity can fill up an infinite number of lives. Now that's big!

~ Robby Folkenberg

April 27

Unknown God

The heavens are not large enough to contain God; how much less could those temples made with hands contain him. Paul, under the inspiration of his subject, soared above the comprehension of the idolatrous assembly, and sought to draw their minds beyond the limits of their false religion to correct views of the true Deity.
– Sketches from the Life of Paul, pg. 95

Athens was one of the world's most prestigious and sophisticated cities during the time of the Roman Empire. There, many scholars formulated philosophies and created extraordinary pieces of art. Athens was a home of art and philosophy, and the Greeks were proud of it. However, the Athenians cherished the sin of idolatry. The Greeks served many different gods, and they even had an altar for the "Unknown God."

Man has an inborn desire to worship something; it is a wonderful gift that God endowed us with. However, Satan perverted this desire so much that man began to worship his creations, and the Greeks were no exception. Though these Gentiles ignorantly committed this great sin, Paul could tell that the erected altar to the "Unknown God" showed their inborn desire to know the true God. In infinite love, Jesus sent Paul to tell the Athenians about the God they did not know and to teach them that He does not dwell in graven images.

As the Athenians had to learn that God does not dwell in idols, we too need to learn that we should not worship idols. But what is an idol? An idol can be anything that you love more than God. It can be your car, money, education, work, entertainment, or anything; it could even be theology. Man in his perverted mind tends to worship what is man-made. This is so senseless because God created man in perfection, but we degrade ourselves by worshiping work, money, or other worldly things, and doing so greatly insults the God of Heaven. Many times we are so unfamiliar with this "Unknown God"; yet He yearns for us to know and experience Him. He says that to know Him is "life eternal" (John 17:3 KJV). So why don't we start getting to know this "Unknown God"?

~ David Chang

April 28

Rescue the Lost

This divine Ruler had, in the dark ages of the world, passed lightly over heathen idolatry; but now he had sent them the light of truth, through his Son; and he exacted from all men repentance unto salvation. – Sketches from the Life of Paul, pg. 95

As we split into different groups to descend Mount Askom at the close of a weekend camping excursion, we expected to see everyone at the bottom in a matter of hours. All the groups had radios so that no one could easily get lost, and communication would be possible. Everything was expected to go just as planned. How wrong we were! One of the radios didn't work, and as one of the groups lost their way in the dense fog on the mountaintop, they found that their connection with help was severed.

Within hours everyone else was off the mountain, wondering what had happened to the missing group. Soon search and rescue was underway, with helicopters, search personnel, and even a military plane capable of sensing heat and taking high quality aerial photographs for later examination. Everything possible was being done to find the lost hikers.

Many people today don't follow Christ, and they have no way of locating Him or even knowing that they are off course. They wander around in a wilderness of hopelessness and inner desperation. The difference between them and those who were lost on Mount Askom is that those on Askom were truly isolated. Those in darkness today are often right next to those with the truth; we underestimate the magnitude of the situation, but they are still lost!

When a helicopter pilot located the lost hikers, immediate action was taken, and they were rescued. Had they been out there much longer, frostbite and hypothermia could have taken a serious toll on their lives. Salvation was just in time. There are those around you who are lost, and they need to be saved! Jesus is coming soon, and the time has come for them to get on the right track. Will you rescue them?

~ Robby Folkenberg

April 29

Reluctance

Many who listened to the words of Paul were convinced of the truths presented, but they would not humble themselves to acknowledge God, and to accept the plan of salvation. – Sketches from the Life of Paul, pg. 96

After fleeing from Berea, Paul arrived at Athens accompanied by a group of converted Bereans. The Athenian architecture and artistry would have been a feast for our eyes, but Paul immediately saw its pagan roots. The Athenians' intellect and fascinating philosophies were rooted in idolatry. Their minds encompassed every shred of knowledge, but their intelligence was oblivious to the one true God. Paul noticed the Athenians' longing for this "unknown" light through the inscription in the stones of the altar in Athens: "To the Unknown God."

After the Athenians were acquainted with Paul, they invited him to speak on Mars' Hill. This sacred hill became the stage where Paul would step into action. There the apostle drew the Athenians' minds away from heathen deities and revealed to them the true God. He declared to them that art, temples, and man's devices could not represent God. Paul's overwhelming evidence and ardent eloquence satisfied the Athenians' hunger, but did not lower their proud defenses. They could not humble themselves to accept the heavenly truth.

Don't we behave like that? There are moments in our lives when we long for solutions to certain mysteries, but when somebody provides the answer, we do not accept it! Possibly the answer is not enough, or could it be our arrogance?

Speeches, arguments—any method of rhetoric cannot convert the sinner. Only the power of God and the blessing of His Holy Spirit can change the heart. Are you willing to let Him transform you?

~ David Ortiz

April 30

Bought Back

Of the Athenians it may be said, "The preaching of the cross is to them that perish foolishness, but to them that are saved it is the power of God." – Sketches from the Life of Paul, pg. 96

There is a lovely story told about a little boy who built a toy boat. With his father's help, he shaped and painted it. He put a mast and sails on it; then proudly took it to the park to sail it on the lake. A long string was tied to the little boat, and the boy joyfully watched it sail farther and farther out on the water. Suddenly, the string slipped out of his hand, and he could not bring his boat back to shore. He called for help, but no one came, and he ran home to bring his father. But by the time they got back to the lake, the little boat was gone. Someone had found and taken it. The little boy was heartbroken.

Then one day, while he was downtown, the boy saw a beautiful little boat in a toyshop window. Of course, it was his boat. He could tell by the size, the paint, the mast, and sails. But rather than start an argument with the shop owner, he went in and bought it, paying the full price for it. Then he went home, hugging his little boat to his heart while he whispered, "Dear little boat, how I love you! You are mine—twice mine; for I made you, and now I've bought you back!"

That's what Jesus says about you and me. "Oh, how I love you, My child. You are mine—twice mine; for I made you, and I've bought you back!" The cross is where Christ bought us back with his blood. Some may think of it as "foolishness," like the Athenians did. But if we are Christ's, we know the cross is the love and power of God!

~ Rebecca Luchak

May 1

Are You Bored?

The Hebrews had been instructed of God, by his servant Moses, to train up their children to industrious habits. That people were thus led to look upon indolence as a great sin, and their children were all required to learn some trade by which, if necessary, they could gain a livelihood. Those who neglected to do this were regarded as departing from the instruction of the Lord. – Sketches from the Life of Paul, pg. 100

"What should I do?" is the question of many people today. We live in a state of "idleness" because we are always "bored". There is a saying that states, "The devil gives work to idle hands."

I was sitting on my bed wondering what to do when my mom told me to put the car in the garage. As I sluggishly made my way to the car, my mind was looking for something to do like a computer searching its hard drive for a file; but nothing seemed worthwhile. As I slid behind the steering wheel, a "genius" thought popped into my head. I would quickly drive around the block then put the car in the garage without anyone knowing. As I pulled off, I looked all around to make sure nobody was looking. Driving a little faster then normal, I sped around the corner—I had to make it before Mom noticed. But as I turned the last corner, I nearly collided with another car. Thankfully, God protected me from crashing.

My idleness could have caused serious damage, injury, or even a death. If I had been occupied with something useful, this experience probably would not have happened. Paul, by having experience in tent making remained productive, even when he was not actively preaching. Hebrew families emphasized the importance of learning a trade so that their children wouldn't be idle. If we spend "down time" gaining useful knowledge, we might escape the monster boredom, and thus escape the devil because, "Idle hands are the devil's workshop."

~ Jourdain Smith

May 2

The Blessing of Work

He rejoiced that he was able to support himself by manual labor, and frequently declared that his own hands had ministered to his necessities. – Sketches from the Life of Paul, 100

To Paul, manual labor was a blessing. He rejoiced in the fact that he could support himself and his ministry with his own two hands. He was a skilled workman in the art of tent making, and through this trade supported his ministry when income was scarce.

Manual labor is a blessing. It strengthens the body, enlivens the mind, and enriches the soul. Fresh air and sunlight are probably the most essential elements of the human body, and when working outside you'll most likely take in both of these. Pure air is the strength of your system, and sunlight gives you the essential vitamin D that is now known to strengthen your immune system.

God gave us the blessing of work, but often Satan distorts this blessing to make it look unappealing to the carnal mind. Doing a hard job gives a sense of accomplishment to the worker, makes the body healthy, and provides for one's needs. When performing a daily task, do not begrudge your efforts; work with all diligence and sincerity knowing that, once accomplished, the work done will benefit you and further the work of Christ.

~ Leighton Sjoren

May 3

Let God Lead

He crossed the seas, and traveled far and near, until a large portion of the world had learned from his lips the story of the cross of Christ. He possessed a burning desire to bring perishing men to a knowledge of the truth through a Savior's love. – Sketches from the Life of Paul, pg. 101

Have you ever tried to make your own plans for your future? I know that I have. It is so easy to fill your mind with what is yet to happen. What will I do after I graduate? Where should I go to college? When will I get married? It is so easy to try to figure everything out, yet I need to scoot over and let God sit in the pilot's seat.

David Livingstone was a man of dreams. His desire was to serve God with all his heart. He dreamed of going to China to share God's love and the plan of salvation. However, when he met Robert Moffat and heard of the great need in Africa, Livingstone became convicted that the people there were just as needy. He chose to go to Africa rather then waiting to go to China; by doing this he won many souls for God's kingdom.

Paul was also given a mission field: the city of Corinth. In this region there were many unbelievers. But because Paul followed God's will and shared his knowledge of truth and the Savior's love, many were led to Christ.

Livingstone had thought that his mission field would be China, but God had another plan. The truth is that we all have a special mission field, and we will be a blessing to many if we will allow God to lead us every step of the way.

~ Melody Hyde

May 4

Let the Savior Shine Through

He possessed a burning desire to bring perishing men to a knowledge of the truth through the Savior's love. – Sketches from the Life of Paul, pg. 101

Time period: the Dark Ages. Place: Oxford, England. A young boy and his family had just been driven out of their town by a stone-throwing crowd and were now residing in a larger city, where they were more likely to remain inconspicuous. The reason for their banishment was their religion, because they were not Catholic, but Lutheran. After they had been in the city for awhile, there was a "cleansing" of heretics during which the city gates were locked and the "heretics" were tortured, killed, or exiled. The Lutheran family decided that their best chance of escaping torture or death was to try to escape from the city and take refuge in a different country.

The family split up, and the boy hid in a farmer's wagon with hopes of gaining his freedom as the wagon passed through the gates. Unfortunately, the gatekeepers found the boy and brought him to trial. During his trial, he was asked if he had been baptized into the Lutheran church. To this he truthfully answered no. Then, after they offered him freedom, he boldly proclaimed his love for his Savior and began to tell the judges about the truth that they had shunned.
Because of his desire to bring these worldly men to the Savior, he gave up his own comfort and endured many hardships including torture and exile.

I think that sometimes, when we see an opportunity to share, either by our words or actions, we think of the inconveniences of witnessing and justify that we are to busy or that we don't know how. But in the story, we saw a little boy, who had, it seemed, every reason to leave without preaching. But he had such a burning desire to show God's love, that he didn't let even the most trying circumstances become a barrier to sharing the truth. Think about this today when you come into a trying situation, and remember to let God shine through.

~ Dave White

May 5

Be the Moon

While thus preaching and working, he presented the highest type of Christianity. – Sketches from the Life of Paul, pg. 101

Aviation is an activity I really enjoy. The thrill of soaring through the air is unparalleled. However, guiding a virtual missile through the heavens and bringing it safely back to earth is quite a responsibility. It's not something you can just do without prior instruction. You can't simply climb behind the yoke, taxi out, and take to the air. It takes many hours of bookwork and actual flight time with an instructor to learn how to skillfully command your aircraft. When some of the basics are learned by actual experience, flying is exhilarating, but also safe. Hitting the books is a necessary part of learning to fly, but if that's all you ever did, and then thought you could control a plane, you'd be sadly mistaken.

Such is the case with almost everything in life. You can't just read about something on the weekends and then expect to be perfect at it on the first try. Paul knew he could preach all he wanted, but if he didn't have love and the desire to live his faith out in the open, it did him absolutely no good (1 Corinthians 13:1-3). He knew that the "highest type of Christianity" is one that is lived out in a day-to-day life that portrays the Savior we claim to serve. I heard a saying that goes, "Be the moon. Reflect the Son." This should be our entire goal in life. Are you a billboard of your Creator's goodness and mercy? Is Jesus shining from you? In how you live, in what you do and say, are you being the moon?

~ Jonathan Fink

May 6

In Everything a Purpose

He combined teaching with his labor...In pursuing this course, he had access to many whom he could not otherwise have reached.
– Sketches from the Life of Paul, pg. 101

Have you ever thought why am I going to school if I can be doing mission work right now, saving souls? Or have you felt like what you're doing is wasting time? Paul, in his earlier years, wasn't just a Pharisee, but he was also a tent maker. He might not have known why he was becoming one, but God had a plan for him.

When Paul was at Corinth, he put his tent making skills into practice. He wanted to support himself, so that he didn't have to depend on other believers for food and shelter. He didn't want to give the idea that he was preaching for profit. God expected more of Paul because He knew that he was capable. By making tents, Paul was able to reach people he could not have otherwise.

I've also felt like school was a waste of time, but I know that God will use my education for a purpose. In Romans 8:28 it says, "And we know that all things work together for good to them that love God, to them who are the called according to his purpose" (KJV). God has a purpose for us in everything we do. He wants to use us, and we must do all in our power to do our best. As we do our part faithfully, as Paul did, God can use us to reach others who couldn't be reached otherwise.

~ Sharon Jeon

May 7

Living by Faith

That your faith should stand not in the wisdom of men, but in the power of God. – 1 Corinthians 2:5 KJV

There was once a small boy who lived for biking. One balmy, summer day this small boy and his dad were enjoying a relaxing ride when the small boy decided to ride ahead and see what was over the next hill. The scenery in this area was breathtaking with a neat row of hedges on the left and open fields of wildflowers on the right. As the father was taking in the beautiful view, he failed to notice the intersection, unusually quiet for this time of day, looming up ahead.

When the small boy saw the intersection, he thought it looked harmless and decided to pass right through without stopping. As he neared it, the father realized what was going on. He immediately looked over the hedges and spied a large truck speeding toward the intersection. Quickly assessing the situation, he yelled for his son to wait. Time seemed to go into slow motion, making the father feel helpless. Then, right before the small boy crossed the intersection, he decided to trust his father and wait, stopping just in time for the truck to pass harmlessly by.

In this story, the small boy had to put his trust in his father and believe what he said. He could not, because of his small size, look over the hedges and see the truck. The intersection looked harmless because of the lack of traffic, and from his viewpoint, it looked perfectly safe to cross. But his father could see the danger ahead and warned his son.

Many times in our Christian walk, we can't see the danger looming ahead because of our limited viewpoint; but God, who knows all things, can see ahead and warn us of the danger. At that point, we need to place our faith in Him, trusting that He knows what's best and will help us avoid those situations that may seem harmless to us, but in reality are very dangerous. Why not let God guide you? He knows the way much better.

~ Dave White

May 8

Change

The Apostle did not labor to charm the ear with oratory, nor engage the mind with philosophic discussions… he preached the cross of Christ… and his words moved the people. – Sketches from the Life of Paul, pg. 105

A disappointed Paul left Athens and traveled to Corinth, the metropolis of commerce. Corinth was radically different from Athens; instead of the arts and philosophy of Athens, the hustling busy schedule of a market center was displayed in the city of the Corinthians. Paul decided to change his approach in preaching the gospel. His preaching method at Athens was using logic to discuss religion. This time, he avoided elaborate discussions and decided to use simple but deep messages, urging the sinners to accept Christ. Adapting his approach yielded more fruit.

Once there was a man walking down a street who fell into a deep hole in the sidewalk. It took him forever to get out. The next day, he walked on the same street and fell into the same hole. It still took him a long time to get out. The following day, he fell into the same hole, but since it had become a habit, he got out immediately. The next day, he walked down the sidewalk and saw the same hole but decided to walk around it. The man knew he was getting nowhere, and the next day, in order to improve his situation, he decided to take a different road. And that was the change he needed.

Just like Paul, when we reach out to others, let us make sure to think outside the box. Showing God's light does not only mean delivering sermons or intelligent arguments: it can be shown through a smile, a flower given to someone who is discouraged—even a "be happy" card counts! Get out of your comfort zone! You will be surprised to see yourself reaching somebody through unexpected and previously untried ways.

~ David Ortiz

May 9

Mother

Honor your father and mother, which is the first commandment with promise: that it may be well with you and you may live long on the earth. – Ephesians 6:2, 3 NKJV

When James A. Garfield was elected president in 1880, he wrote to his dear old mother and said, "I want you to go to Washington, D.C., with me for the inauguration."

"Oh, no," she said, "I could not go. I would feel out of place with all those great people. I'll stay home and pray for you."

But James Garfield wrote back: "Mother, I will not go without you." So they traveled to Washington together, stayed in the same hotel, and when he went to the capitol, his mother was leaning on his arm. When he got on the platform, he put his mother in the chair that had been provided for him, and he sat in a seat beside her. Then, after he had delivered his address and taken the oath to be true to his high office, he turned around, put his arms around his mother, and kissed her; and more then one hundred thousand people cheered and applauded. They all thought it was one of the most beautiful acts they had ever seen.

Ellen White says, in *Messages to Young People*, pg. 330: "When the judgment shall sit, and the books shell be opened; when the 'well done' of the great judge is pronounced, and the crown of immortal glory is placed upon the brow of the victor, many will raise their crowns in the sight of the assembled universe and, pointing to their mother, say, 'She made me all I am through the grace of God. Her instruction, her prayers, have been blessed to my eternal salvation.'"

Mothers are some of the most special people on earth. They're the ones that do the most for their children. Today, don't miss the chance to thank your mother for all her prayers and instruction that have made you a better person.

~ Rebecca Luchak

May 10

Keep it Simple

The apostle did not labor to charm the ear with oratory, nor to engage the mind with philosophic discussions…He preached the cross of Christ, not with labored eloquence of speech, but with the grace and power of God… – Sketches from the Life of Paul, pg. 105

Once when I was little, our church's new pastor gave a sermon on David and Mephibosheth. Little kids don't usually pay much attention in church, since the sermons are often over their heads; but this pastor spoke so simply and interestingly that I was captivated. He made the story descriptive, fascinating, and easy to understand. It made such an impression that I still remember it today.

So often, we think that important things must be complicated. Legal documents are written in bewildering jargon; assembly instructions for kids' toys need a military code-breaker to decipher; even the Gospel has been so entangled with human rituals and dogma that the simple truth is often obscured. But Jesus says, "Except ye…become as little children, ye shall not enter into the kingdom of heaven" (Matthew 18:3 KJV). It takes the simplicity of a child to grasp the unfathomable things of God.

When Paul went to Corinth, he chose not to use oratory and argument in his preaching, as he had done in Athens, for it yielded few souls. He "determined not to know any thing…save Jesus Christ, and him crucified" (1 Corinthians 2:2 KJV). Paul chose to keep the Gospel simple, as did that pastor who made such an impression on me as a child. God's love isn't complicated; His salvation plan can be comprehended by the feeblest mind. Let's not complicate His love, but keep it simple.

~ Cara Dewsberry

May 11

The Voice of my Shepherd
Part 1

The apostle did not labor to charm the ear with oratory, nor to engage the mind with philosophic discussions, which would leave the heart untouched. He preached the cross of Christ, not with labored eloquence of speech, but with the grace and power of God; and his words moved the people. – Sketches from the Life of Paul, pg. 105

There was once a Shakespearean actor who was known everywhere for his one-man show of readings and recitations from the classics. He would always end his performances with a dramatic reading of Psalm 23. Each night, without exception, as the actor began his recitation, "The Lord is my Shepherd. I shall not want..." the crowd would listen attentively and at the conclusion of the psalm, they would rise in thunderous applause and appreciation of the actor's incredible ability to bring the verses to life.

But one night, just before the actor was to offer his customary recital of Psalm 23, a young man from the audience spoke up. "Sir, do you mind if, tonight, I recite Psalm 23?" The actor was quite taken aback by this unusual request, but he allowed the young man to come forward and to stand front and center on the stage to recite the psalm, knowing that the ability of this unskilled youth would be no match for his own talent.

The Pharisees prided themselves on their strict obedience to the laws and traditions of Moses and felt that they were above the rest of the world. Yet they had forgotten the God of grace and mercy Who had given the laws to Moses and Whom Paul preached. They thought that keeping the law was enough, but the truth has ever been that Christ's love alone will save us.

~ Michael Hamel

May 12

The Voice of my Shepherd
Part 2

My sheep hear my voice, and I know them, and they follow me.
– John 10: 27

Yesterday we saw how a seasoned Shakespearean actor was shocked by the request of a young man from the audience to take his place on the stage and recite the 23rd Psalm. Although reluctant, the actor allowed the young man to come forward.

With a soft voice, the young man began to recite the words of the psalm. When he was finished, there was no applause. There was no standing ovation as on other nights. All that could be heard was the sound of weeping. The audience had been so moved by the young man's recitation that every eye was full of tears.

Amazed by what he had heard, the actor said to the youth, "I don't understand. I have been performing Psalm 23 for years. I have a lifetime of experience and training, but I have never been able to move an audience as you have tonight. Tell me, what is your secret?"

The young man humbly replied, "Well, sir, you know the psalm... but I know the Shepherd."

The secret to Paul's success was not the fact that he could say amazing things, but that he knew an amazing Savior. This is the very thing that should set us apart from the world, the voice of our Shepherd. We, as His sheep, have a very special ability that is given to us, to be able to hear the voice of the Master, and this is how we are able to tell the world that He loves them. So listen to the voice of the Master today and ask Him to tell you who needs to be loved.

~ Michael Hamel

May 13

Glass Heartbeat

The Thessalonians…had carefully guarded the lives of their friends…But, one after another, death had laid their loved ones low…The friends of the righteous dead should not sorrow as those who lose their loved ones and have no hope in Jesus Christ…
– Sketches from the Life of Paul, pp. 111, 112

Life is fragile. Just a couple of years ago, my own grandpa died suddenly of a heart attack. His death was completely unexpected, and it broke our hearts. Every day hundreds of lives are snuffed out by old age, car accidents, murders, wars, and genocide. Right now, while you sit comfortably reading this, someone on this planet is taking his last breath.

The Thessalonians were very concerned about the death of their loved ones. They didn't understand the state of the dead or the resurrection, and mistakenly believed that if their loved ones died, they would lose their salvation and be gone forever. In a letter to alleviate their fears and correct their errors, Paul wrote: "But I would not have you to be ignorant, brethren, concerning them which are asleep, that ye sorrow not even as others which have no hope…For the Lord himself shall descend from heaven with a shout…and the dead in Christ shall rise first: Then we which are alive and remain shall be caught up together with them in the clouds…and so shall we ever be with the Lord" (1Thessalonians 4:13, 16, 17 KJV).

Life is fragile. But if we believe in Jesus, we have no need to fear death for ourselves or for those we love. Though our hearts may cease to beat on this earth, we have the blessed hope, that someday soon we will behold our Redeemer coming in the clouds to gather us all home. Do you have this hope?

~ Cara Dewsberry

May 14

Consolation

What consolation was afforded them by those words which revealed the true state of the dead. – Sketches from the Life of Paul, pg. 112

Jairus could not believe what he was hearing. His beloved daughter was dead! He had anxiously struggled to reach Jesus, so that He could heal her; but every drop of sweat had trickled in vain. His sight became hazy, his legs were trembling, and as his mind cried out in desperation, Jesus' hand touched his shoulder.

The multitude quieted as Jesus spoke these gentle words, "Do not be afraid; only believe, and she will be made well" (Luke 8:50 NKJV). After making His way to Jairus' house, Jesus entered upon a scene of mourning for the deceased girl. The Master spoke again, "Do not weep; she is not dead, but sleeping" (verse 52). The unbelieving hearts of the people met Jesus' declaration with ridicule and even bewilderment. Our dear Savior entered the girl's room, took her by the hand, and called, "Little girl, arise" (verse 54). Instantly, her eyes opened, and her parents were overjoyed. While the people did not believe Jesus' striking words, Jairus did! Deep inside, he knew that his daughter would live again.

Paul wrote of his faith in the resurrection in his epistles to the Thessalonians. He assured them that their deceased relatives were sleeping, and would arise on the day of the Second Coming. His hopeful words were heeded with joy, not mockery.

God tells us the same; He offers consolation and aid through each struggle. Are you going to doubt and laugh at Him, or believe His words?

~ David Ortiz

May 15

Always Faithful

But of the times and seasons, brethren, ye have no need that I write to you; for yourselves know perfectly that the day of the Lord so cometh as a thief in the night. – 1 Thessalonians 5:1 KJV

A traveler visiting Switzerland came across a beautiful home in the midst of an immaculate garden on the shore of a crystalline lake. It looked so inviting that he thought he would like to visit a while with the owner. So he knocked on the garden gate, and soon an aged gardener appeared. He opened the gate and invited the stranger in. The aged man seemed glad to have a visitor and showed him all around the wonderful garden.

"How long have you worked here?" asked the visitor.
"Twenty-four years," said the old gardener.
"How often has your employer been here during that time?"
"Four times."
"When was he here last?"
"Twelve years ago."
"Does he write you often?"
"Never once!"
"Then from whom do you receive your wages?"
"From his agent in Mailand."
"Does his agent come here often?"
"He has never been here. The agent posts me my wages."
"Then who does come here?"
"I am almost always alone, except for an occasional visitor like yourself."
"Yet you keep the garden in such perfect order, just as if you were expecting your employer tomorrow."
"Not tomorrow, sir, as if he were coming today," smiled the old man.

Doesn't the gardener's loyal service to his employer motivate you to be ready to meet our Savior? I was inspired by this story to be more faithful, and it made me want to start getting ready right now for Jesus' soon return—as if He were coming today!

~ Rebecca Luchak

May 16

Jesus is Coming Again?

But ye, brethren, are not in darkness, that that day should overtake you as a thief. Ye are all the children of light, and the children of the day; we are not of the night, nor of darkness. Therefore let us not sleep, as do others; but let us watch and be sober. – 1 Thessalonians 5:4-6 KJV

"Did you hear that?" my friend asked.

"I think I heard that." My friend and I were in the cafeteria when we heard loud music outside of the building. Wondering what was going on, we decided to go check it out. So, we jumped out of our seats and opened the door. Lo and behold, we saw a cloud unfolding like a scroll and angels of God singing praises to Jesus. This was the most awesome sight that I had ever seen in my life; it filled me with amazement to think that I was seeing my living Savior calling me to live with Him eternally! While pondering this excitement, I saw the dead in Christ rising with immortal bodies and ascending to meet their Lord. I saw my friends around me ascending too. However, while my friends ascended, I never did. At that instant, the awesome excitement became a dreadful fear. I thought I was going to die and just as I was about to be consumed, I woke up in terror. Though it was a terrifying dream, I knew it was God's warning to me.

In today's world, everything around us is so busy that we have little time to rest, think, or spend time with God. Even Christians ask, "Is Jesus really coming again?" as if they knew nothing. Although this is a very sad reality, it is the state of our church today. We have no time to waste. The prophecies are being fulfilled around us. The clock is ticking; what are we doing to prepare ourselves? Though I had a frightening dream, I got the message. The message God was trying to convey was that I was spiritually sleeping and that it is time to wake up because Jesus might come immediately. Think about it, if Jesus comes at this moment, would you be ready to meet Him? Jesus calls us to wake up. Listen to Him.

~ David Chang

May 17

Wake Up!

Let us not sleep, as do others; but let us watch and be sober.
– 1 Thessalonians 5:6 KJV

    On Christmas Day, 1776, Colonel Johann Gottlieb Rall was the commanding officer of the Hessian troops at Trenton, New Jersey. Up to this time, the American rebels had shown themselves to be undisciplined fighters and had not won a single battle. The Americans were deserting and lacked ammunition, food, and other provisions. Colonel Rall decided to allow his troops to enjoy Christmas and most of them drank too much during the festivities. The weather was very cold, and there was sleet, hail, and ice. Rall thought the Continental Army was too weak to mount an attack from Pennsylvania. However, Rall was wrong. That very night, General Washington took five hundred American soldiers in three boats across the Delaware River. At 4 a.m., they marched on the garrison at Trenton. The sleeping and dazed Hessian Army never knew what overpowered them. Within thirty-five minutes the Battle of Trenton was over. The Continental Army used surprise as their greatest weapon to capture Trenton.

    The Hessians at Trenton could have easily defeated the Continental Army, if only they had kept watch. In our Christian walk, we become relaxed and feel that everything will be "okay." However, Satan is a clever enemy who is always looking for an opportunity to attack. When everything seems to be going well and you let your guard down, he will attack, and you will not be able to prevail against him. Today, keep up your guard and pray that you will be able to resist Satan's surprises.

~ Jeremy Grabiner

May 18

Watchfulness

The watchful Christian is a working Christian, seeking zealously to purify his life, and to do all in his power for the cause of God.
– Sketches from the Life of Paul, pg. 115

The twenty-eight crewmembers of the sunken ship, *The Endurance*, miraculously found themselves on uninhabited Elephant Island after being at sea for 497 days. After resting, their captain, Sir Ernest Shackleton, took five men, and left for South Georgia Island, some eight hundred miles away. But there was a big problem: they had only an open seventeen-foot boat with which to cross the most dangerous sea passage in the world. Incredibly they made it, with God's help. Shackleton then had to go back to rescue the rest of his crew that were left on Elephant Island. This he attempted three times; but each time something happened that stopped him. Finally, on the fourth try, he succeeded.

As he approached Elephant Island, I am sure he was wondering what he would discover. How many men were still alive and what kind of condition were they in? Had any of them gone insane from all the solitude and silence? The answer he got when he arrived was that everyone was alive and in good spirits. Why was this, you might ask? Because the man Shackleton had left in charge told the men every day: "Get ready boys, the boss might come back today." Everyday they got ready, watched, and waited. At last, the day came when Shackleton did return.

We need to be just as watchful and prepared as those men. And we need to be preparing each and every day because Christ is coming back very soon. Are you ready and watching today?

~ Amy Windels

May 19

Warning!

The watchful Christian is a working Christian, seeking zealously to purify his life, and to do all in his power for the cause of God...
– Sketches from the Life of Paul, pg. 115

It was May 18, 1980, and the eyes of America were focused on two things: the imminent eruption of the 9,677-foot Mount St. Helens, and a man who defied the signs and refused to evacuate his lodge at the mountain's base.

Volcanologists studying the mountain noticed major changes in the months leading up to the eruption. It didn't take much experience to notice the huge bulge growing on the mountain's north face. Warnings and calls for evacuation were given over a month before the eruption, and the days before the eruption were filled with tiny earthquakes under the mountain! Surely enough warning was given. This thing was going to blow! And yet, Harry R. Truman refused to leave his mountain-side home. He thought that the mountain could never erupt, saying that the situation was "over-exaggerated." No one could get him to leave.

The end is near for this old world. End time events are erupting onto the scene; we can already see the signs. But do people hear the warnings? In Revelation, Christ calls His people to spread the warning about the times we live in. "Fear God, and give glory to Him; for the hour of His judgment is come: and worship Him that made heaven, and earth, and the sea, and the fountains of waters" (Revelation 14:7 NKJV). Urgency drove the government to evacuate the area around Mount St. Helens and to beg Harry Truman to flee for his life. Likewise let us with urgency tell the world that the time of the end is at hand, begging them to flee into the saving arms of Jesus Christ.

~ Robby Folkenberg

May 20

Watchful

Therefore let us not sleep, as do others; but let us watch and be sober.
– 1 Thessalonians 5:6 KJV

Steve Green knew some men who worked as "riggers" for large auditoriums. These men had to walk the four-inch rafter beams, which were often a hundred feet above the concrete floor, to hang sound speakers and spotlights.

One of the guys he knew said that looking down a hundred feet didn't bother him. What he didn't like was those jobs in buildings that had false ceilings of acoustical tile slung just a couple of feet below the rafters. He was still high in the air, and if he slipped his weight would smash right through the flimsy tile. But even though he knew the ceiling wasn't sturdy, his mind seemed to play tricks on him, lulling him into carelessness.

Satan doesn't want so much to scare us to death, as he does to persuade us that the danger of a spiritual fall is minimal. Paul advises us in 1 Thessalonians 5:6 to be watchful and sober, because the devil is always ready to pull us into his trap. If we let up one bit, he will seize the opportunity. Like a spider, which weaves its web and waits for its unsuspecting prey, so the devil waits for us. If we don't watch for the web, he will catch us. "Watch and pray, that ye enter not into temptation" (Matthew 26:41 KJV).

~ Jourdain Smith

May 21

Making a Difference

Their work had been appointed them of God; by their faithful adherence to the truth they were to communicate to others the light which they had received. He bade them not to become weary in well-doing... – Sketches from the Life of Paul, pg. 118

Todd was walking along a beach when he came across a man who kept bending over, picking objects up, and throwing them into the ocean. Todd asked him, "What are you doing?"

The man answered, "It's low tide, so I'm saving these starfish who are stranded on the beach and throwing them back into the ocean before they die." Todd didn't quite understand. There were thousands of starfish stranded on the sandy beach.

"Sir," he replied doubtfully, "you can't possibly make a difference. Why are you doing this? Can't you see how useless it is?"

The man smiled as he threw another starfish into the waves, "I made a difference to that one!"

Have you ever felt that it was useless to try to save lost souls? You watch the news or simply walk down the street, and you see hopeless people everywhere you look. I used to think that there were just too many to even *try* to tell them about Jesus. What difference could it make anyway? Let me assure you that since Jesus came into my heart, He has changed me. He would have come down from heaven and died even if it was just for one person! Satan wants you to get discouraged and think that you can never make a difference. But God has appointed you to do a special work. Just think of what joy there will be when you make a difference to even one.

~ Melissa Butler

May 22

Thoughts

The spiritual senses must be matured by continual advancement in the knowledge of heavenly things. – Sketches from the Life of Paul, pg. 124

What you think about now is what you are going to become in the future. You may not even realize what you are thinking. This is why taking note of the things that you think about every day is important.

The murder, that happened on October 31, 2006, shocked many people who saw the news. The newspaper headline read, "17-Year-Old Boy Kills Brother, Shows No Emotion." No emotions? Many thought, how can someone kill his brother without feeling any emotions? Usually, killings are preceded by intense emotions of hate or rage. The news article explained what had happen to this 17-year-old boy. The boy was into computer/video games, especially games that involved violence and murder. From his early years, going to a net-café to play games was a very common daily activity. Eventually, he started to feel the desire to kill somebody. He didn't care whom. He wasn't feeling angry. He just wanted to kill. One morning, he decided to kill his mother, but she wasn't around; so he killed his brother instead.

God created a law in man: "For as he thinketh in his heart, so is he" (Proverbs 23:7 KJV). God made man so that he becomes what he chooses to think about. Many misuse this law and fail to benefit from it. But God promises that if we ponder heavenly things, we will mature spiritually; we will grow closer to God. The thought of heavenly things shapes us into the pattern of Jesus.

~ Ryo Fusamae

May 23

A Priceless Gift

The spiritual senses must be matured by continual advancement in the knowledge of heavenly things. Thus the mind would learn to delight in them; and every precept of the word of God would shine forth as a priceless gem. – Sketches from the Life of Paul, pg. 124

Would you like to receive the best gift known to man? What would you be willing to give for such a priceless gem? What would you do if you knew that the gift has already been paid for, and all you need to do is reach out and take it?

Have you ever worked really hard to get a gift for your best friend, only to find your efforts to please them were rejected? Salvation is a gift that God offers to every one of His children. Christ came to this earth and died so that He could offer that gift to us, and it breaks His heart when we refuse to accept what He has worked so hard to give us. He wants everyone to be able to partake of His victory over sin, and He cannot bear to see any of His children go astray.

But, you may ask, "How do I accept this gift?" You must choose to advance continually in the knowledge of heavenly things. I know that the more time I spend in God's Word, the more I will delight in the knowledge gained. We can reach out and take the gift that Jesus offers to us by applying to our lives what we learn from His Word each day.

~ Leighton Sjoren

May 24

God's Power at Work

The refining influence of the grace of God changes the natural disposition of man – Sketches from the Life of Paul, pg. 125

The natural disposition of man is to sin and follow the carnal desires of the heart. However, the grace of God works a change in man's natural disposition. This is a wonderful process that God works out in our lives.

There was once a man who was addicted to alcohol. His family was destroyed because of his evil habit. When the man's sick wife died, he was too drunk to comprehend what had happened, and his two children were left alone and without money. Many prayers were lifted up on behalf of this poor man, and finally, God reached his heart. Because of God's love and power, there was a radical change in this man's life. He went from being a bitter drunk to a joyful son of God.

Today, we face many trials and struggles. People say things that aren't true or do things that aren't right. Many times every day, we encounter obstacles that frustrate and hurt us. Yet, God is calling us to be transformed. God worked for the man in the story and changed his life from one of drinking and sorrow to one of soberness and peace. God is waiting to change our lives too. Let God's power work in your life, and He will change you.

~ Douglas Schappert

May 25

Reflection

When man dies to sin, and is quickened to new life in Christ Jesus, divine love fills his heart… and the light of an eternal day shines upon his path, for he has the Light of life with him continually.
– Sketches from the Life of Paul, pp. 125, 126

A good old fisherman was once asked how he knew there was a risen Savior. He said, "I go fishing on the lake very early in the morning. By and by, I see the glory and brightness of the sunrise reflected in the windows of the homes on the lakeshore. I don't have to turn around and see whether the sun has risen. I know it has risen because I can see the reflection of it. So," he continued, "when I see love, kindness, and thoughtfulness for others shining in the faces of men and women, and being given out in their words and actions, I can tell by the reflection that there is a risen Savior."

What a wonderful thought! Others can tell by the reflection in our lives whether we have the love of Christ in our hearts. Sin is like a dark stain over our hearts, which makes it impossible to reflect love and joy to others. But when we invite Jesus into our hearts, he cleanses us and removes the stains that sin leaves, so that we can reflect Him to a world full of darkness.

~ Rebecca Luchak

May 26

Talents and Smoothies

God has given to each of his messengers his distinctive work: and while there is diversity of gifts, all are to blend harmoniously in carrying forward the great work of salvation. They are only instruments of divine grace and power. – Sketches from the Life of Paul, pg. 126

"For thou art an holy people unto the Lord thy God: the Lord thy God hath chosen thee to be a special people unto himself, above all people that are upon the face of the Earth" (Deuteronomy 7:6 KJV).

To make a good smoothie I need: bananas, strawberries, blueberries, milk, vanilla, and a little honey or sugar. If I just combined these ingredients in a bowl, the smoothie would not taste very good; the ingredients need to be blended together. But they cannot blend themselves; they have to be placed in the blender by a person.

You have a talent; it might be music, cooking, speaking, writing, or just being you! You cannot do anything by yourself; you need God to help you blend your talents with Him. He has chosen you for a special purpose, and if you combine your talents with His strength, you can bear much fruit.

"Herein is my Father glorified, that ye bear much fruit; so shall ye be my disciples" (John 15:8 KJV).

~ Jenny McCluskey

May 27

Watch Him!

The consciousness of being God's servant should inspire the minister with energy and diligence perseveringly to discharge his duty, with an eye single to the glory of his Master...They are only instruments of divine grace and power. – Sketches from the Life of Paul, pg. 126

Everybody was in an uproar. The orchestra members at Ohio College had just been informed that a new conductor was coming to their school, and bad reports were going around about him. People said he was so strict that he had been asked to leave several other colleges where he had worked.

When the first day of rehearsals arrived, the usual pre-practice chatter and rowdiness disappeared; nobody acted foolishly. "From the top please," announced the new conductor quietly. The music began with a grand opening by the trumpets and horns; everything seemed to be going well. Suddenly, the conductor shouted, "Stop, stop!" Some did not notice the call and kept playing. "I said, stop!" He shouted again, louder this time. Everything became silent. "It is obvious that none of you are paying attention to my baton. Therefore, we will quit this rehearsal, and the next time I see you all, you must have the piece memorized completely." The conductor left the room without waiting for a response.

The next rehearsal day arrived. All the orchestra members were nervous and wondered what the conductor would do this time. As soon as the conductor entered the room, he took away all the music stands. "Okay now, that looks much better," the conductor smiled. "I hope all of you know where to look this time." The music began. Since they had memorized the song, their eyes were locked onto the conductor. They had to admit that the music sounded better than ever. When the conductor stopped moving his hand, everybody stopped playing. "Do you see how important it is to watch me? Remember, I am here for you."

Our master is God. When we look up to Him, we will stay in tune with Him. When we lock our eyes on Him, we will play our instruments just like He wants. Look up and keep your eyes focused on God.

~ Ryo Fusamae

May 28

A Humble Servant

His work should be to preach Christ, and studiously to avoid calling attention to himself... – Sketches from the Life of Paul, pg. 126

The renowned black educator Booker T. Washington is an astonishing example of a truly humble servant. Shortly after taking over the presidency of Tuskegee Institute in Alabama, he was walking on the street when a wealthy white woman stopped him. At first sight, she did not know who he was. The woman asked him to chop wood for her. Mr. Washington, without hesitation, proceeded to do the humble chore. After finishing, he carried the logs into the woman's house and stacked them by the fireplace. The woman's daughter recognized him and revealed his identity to her mother.

The next morning, the woman went to see Mr. Washington in his office at the Institute and sincerely apologized. He kindly replied by telling her not to worry, and that it was a delight to work for others. After this event, the wealthy woman persuaded some of her acquaintances to donate thousands of dollars to the Tuskegee Institute.

Mr. Washington's meek and gracious attitude impressed the woman's heart. Even after the woman discovered who he was, he did not bring himself into the spotlight. His position as president did not prevent Mr. Washington from working for others.

That is how Christ worked in this earth. He knew He was going to be the Savior of Mankind; He knew that His teachings would influence millions of people, but instead of asking people to work for His own pleasure, He humbled Himself and became their faithful servant. Doesn't His example motivate you to want to be a humble, faithful servant of God?

~ David Ortiz

May 29

Unburied Talents

God has given to each of his messengers his distinctive work; and while there is a diversity of gifts, all are to blend harmoniously in carrying forward the great work of salvation. – Sketches from the Life of Paul, pg. 126

Have you ever thought that you had no talents? It is easy to look at others and think that they are more blessed than you are. The truth is that God has given each of us different gifts. There may be some talents that stand out more than others, but that does not mean they are better.

In the Bible, there is a story about a man who left some talents with his servants. He had given one man ten talents, the other five, and the last man one talent. The first two men, who received ten and five talents, multiplied them while their master was gone. But the servant, who received only one talent, thought that it was of less importance, so he buried it.

God has given each of us talents and we need to use them. We may feel like we have none because others seem to have more important ones; however God has given us our talents for a special purpose. We just need to fulfill His plan for our lives. You may not even know what your talents are, so take a moment to uncover your talents; and once they're dug up don't bury them again.

~ Melody Hyde

May 30

Paint

...All are to blend harmoniously in carrying forward the great work of salvation. – Sketches from the Life of Paul, pg. 126

With each careful stroke of my brush, the painting became more beautiful. The vivid colors of the flower filled the canvas, and on each petal, the various hues blended together. Deep red-orange blended into coral, which merged into a glowing yellow.

This concept of "blending together" was one that Paul wished to teach His church members. Division was surfacing as some claimed Paul as their leader, while others claimed Apollos as theirs. Some members chose still other leaders (see Acts 18:24-28 and 1 Corinthians 1:12). Paul emphasized the importance of unity—of working together. He longed for them to realize that they were all a part of one "painting": "the great work of salvation." In this work, no one was to stand out as being better than another. In contrast, all were to "blend harmoniously" into the big picture.

God Himself follows this concept. The members of the Trinity always work together in perfect harmony. Jesus proclaimed, "I have no wish to glorify myself" (John 8:50 NLT). Instead of trying to stand out from the others, they blend their individual jobs together into the wonderful plan of redemption.

Do you blend into the "painting"? Or, by your self-reliance, are you causing division? Unity is essential in order to create a beautiful "picture." If you insist on doing your own will instead of God's, your color will eventually be taken off of the canvas. But if you humbly do the work that God gives you, the "great work of salvation" will be carried forward. Allow Jesus to use His brush. He desperately wants you to be a part of the finished masterpiece.

~ Jonathan Sharley

May 31

Be a Christian Everywhere

In the apostles' day, one party claimed to believe in Christ, yet refused to give due respect to his ambassadors. – Sketches from the Life of Paul, pg. 127

Many people, who claim to be Christians, only act like it when they are around other Christians. At home, they're very different people. Even at school, students fake who they really are. They act polite around others and don't grumble or complain when they have to work, because they want to impress their friends. But when they're at home, and Mom or Dad asks them to do the chores, they moan and groan and have a bad attitude. Since their friends aren't there to see, they don't care what kind of an attitude they have.

How would it make you feel if someone commented on how caring and helpful you are at school and that you must be a big help to your family, when you know you aren't like that at home? Wouldn't that make you feel dishonest?

Years ago, my Dad was talking to a lady, who mentioned how well-behaved his kids were in church; they didn't run around or make noise during the service, and she wished her kids had been like that when they were younger. When he asked her what she wished she had done differently to make them better behaved, she said, "I wouldn't go to church and do one thing, and go home and do another."

How do you think Christ feels when He sees that you are more respectful to your friends, but not your own family? How do you think your family feels? They sacrifice so much for you, and you just throw it away. That's how Jesus feels when people claim to be Christians, but only act like it in certain places.

We need to strive to have more respect not only for our friends, but for our family, too. If we love Jesus, and claim to be Christians, we need to act like one everywhere and around everyone.

~ Jennifer Atkins

June 1

Sand and Stone

Then came Peter to him, and said, Lord, how oft shall my brother sin against me, and I forgive him? till seven times? Jesus saith unto him, I say not unto thee, Until seven times: but, Until seventy times seven.
– Matthew 18:21-22 KJV

Long ago, two friends were walking through the desert. During the journey, they talked, laughed, and had a good time. However, one day, they had an intense argument. With impatience, one friend slapped the other. The hurt friend was deeply distressed, but instead of slapping back, he wrote in the sand: "TODAY MY BEST FRIEND SLAPPED ME IN THE FACE."

They kept walking until they found an oasis, where they decided to take a bath. However, the friend who had been slapped became trapped in the sludge and started to sink. In desperation, the drowning friend called for help. Instantly, the other friend came and saved his life. After his recovery, he thanked his friend and wrote on a rock: "TODAY MY BEST FRIEND SAVED MY LIFE." The friend who slapped and later saved his best friend asked him, "After I hurt you, you wrote on the sand; and now, you wrote on the rock. Why?"

The other friend replied, "When people hurt us, we should write it on the sand of forgiveness where it will be blown away; but if someone does something good to us, we should write it on a stone where no winds can erase it." The friend who was slapped never repaid evil with evil, but instead, allowed the winds of forgiveness to carry the evil away. This is the forgiveness that Jesus spoke of.

Have you ever wondered, "How in the world do you forgive someone 490 times?" Whenever someone hurts you, don't *just* forgive him, but let the winds of forgiveness carry those emotions away. Whenever we confess, God covers our sins with the winds of Christ's righteousness. We are so used to sin that we engrave the bad feelings towards others and often erase the good ones. Just as the wind removed the words in the sand, won't you allow Jesus to blow your wicked feelings away?

~ David Chang

June 2

The Man Who Died for Me

By faith, they [Paul's hearers] grasped the atoning sacrifice of Christ, and acknowledged Him as their Redeemer. – Sketches from the Life of Paul, pg. 130

It was late April, 1944. In the Bergen-Belsen concentration camp, the sickening stench of cremated flesh permeated the air. Shots resounding off the concrete walls marked the termination of yet more human lives. Where was God in this time of prevailing hate and evil?

One day, screaming Nazi guards lined a number of prisoners up against a bloodstained wall for extermination. As they were being blindfolded, a single older man approached the commandant and addressed him respectfully:

"Sir, I have no immediate family, and my life is at an end. But that man over there is young and has a family. Please, transfer my upcoming release to him and take my life in place of his." The astonished commandant gave the order to release the young man, and the older man took his place in the line-up. After a countdown, gunfire splattered across the range, snuffing out the lives of those against the wall. With tears of mingled anguish and unspeakable gratitude, the ransomed man walked out of the camp gates completely free. Throughout the rest of his life, he never forgot the man who died for him.

Jesus gave His life so we could live. When we refuse His offered gift of life, we waste His tears and blood. Paul also risked his life to share the awesome love of Jesus, and as a result thousands were captivated by the love of a God who cared enough to die for *them*. The old gentleman faced the sleep of death until the resurrection; Jesus risked death for all eternity so we wouldn't have to. What an awesome God we serve!

~ Jonathan Fink

June 3

Teachable

It was by cherishing a humble and teachable spirit that these brethren gained their precious experience. – Sketches from the Life of Paul, pg. 130

When a breeder chooses a puppy to train as a guide dog, he chooses the most teachable dog. You might ask, what is meant by teachable? Well, it is not the kind of dog that is intimidated by humans, or that barks a lot. It is also not the kind of dog that is very hyper and runs around everywhere. Then, what kind of dogs does the breeder choose?

The breeder chooses the dogs that think first before they act. For instance, most dogs love to play ball. So, the breeder will gather some potential puppies and throw a ball for them to chase. But, some dogs do not chase the ball immediately. They are always one beat slower than the others. Those are the kind of dogs that the breeder chooses as guide dogs. This is because they are humble and smart enough to be taught. The dogs that are one beat slower always think before they decide on a course of action. They are very attentive and vigilant. They have the teachable spirit that breeders look for.

Just like those dogs, if we have a humble and teachable spirit, we can gain a precious experience with God. When we calm ourselves and listen to what God wants to say to us, we are able to hear His voice more clearly.

~ Ryo Fusamae

June 4

Stubborn or Obedient

It was by cherishing a humble and teachable spirit that these brethren gained their precious experience. – Sketches from the Life of Paul, pg. 130

An old sailor repeatedly got lost at sea, so his friends gave him a compass and urged him to use it. The next time he went out in his boat, he took the compass with him. But as usual he became hopelessly confused and was unable to find land. His friends finally rescued him. Disgusted and impatient with him, they asked, "Why didn't you use that compass we gave you? You could have saved us a lot of trouble!"

The sailor responded, "I didn't dare to! I wanted to go north, but as hard as I tried to make the needle aim in that direction, it just kept on pointing southeast."

That old sailor was so certain he knew which way was north that he stubbornly tried to force his own personal persuasion on his compass. Unable to do so, he tossed it aside as worthless and failed to benefit from the guidance it offered. If the sailor had been humble and teachable, he would have easily found his way to land. Instead, he felt self-sufficient, and thought he could not possibly be wrong. In fact, he sincerely believed that there was something wrong with the compass.

Have you ever done what the sailor did? Have you ever been presented with something that you knew was true, but you were too stubborn to change your ways because it went against what you wanted? God wants to give you an infinite amount of blessings, if only you will take the position of a learner and cherish every word He says. Will you be His student?

~ Jeremy Grabiner

June 5

Help Me Help You
Part 1

There are many who make but little progress in the divine life, because they are too self-sufficient to occupy the position of learners.
– Sketches from the Life of Paul, pg. 130

Mrs. Thompson, the fifth-grade teacher, said she loved all her students equally; but that was not true with Teddy Stoddard. He was dirty, smelly, and didn't fit in with the other children. His lazy attitude annoyed her to the point that she almost enjoyed marking his papers with a red "F."

One day, as Mrs. Thompson reviewed Teddy's file, she made a discovery that completely changed her feelings toward him. Teddy had once been an excellent student who was often applauded by his teachers for his hard work and good manners. But after his mother became ill and died, Teddy had declined rapidly. The reports for each year were worse and ended with his fourth-grade teacher's lamentation that Teddy was failing and had withdrawn from his class and friends. After reading this, Mrs. Thompson felt ashamed of her prejudice towards Teddy and changed the way she treated him.

In our society, we often judge people by their looks, their aptitude, and their ability to "blend in." If someone fails in any of these "requirements," we just do not accept them for who they are. We do not attempt to help them improve. Have you not wondered, "Do they have to improve? Or do I, so that I can treat them with love and dignity?"

~ David Ortiz

June 6

Help Me Help You
Part 2

The great work for us as Christians is not to criticize the character and motives of others, but to closely examine our own heart and life...
– Sketches from the Life of Paul, pg. 232

Yesterday, we learned how Mrs. Thompson criticized Teddy due to his appearance, smell, and intellect. Her attitude towards Teddy changed after reading his file, which revealed the story of his rapid decline since the time of his mother's death.

On Christmas day, Teddy presented Mrs. Thompson with a damaged rhinestone bracelet and a half-full bottle of perfume. Silencing the laughter of the other children, she slipped on the bracelet and dabbed some of the perfume on her wrist. As she did so, Teddy whispered, "You smell just like my Mom used to." From that day on, Mrs. Thompson paid special attention to Teddy, helping him with his studies and patiently drawing him out of his depression.

Through the years, Mrs. Thompson received letters from Teddy as he progressed from high school to college, then to medical school. Some time after his graduation as Theodore F. Stoddard, MD, Teddy asked Mrs. Thompson to come to his wedding and sit in the place reserved for the groom's mother. She came, wearing the bracelet and perfume that he had given her. After the ceremony, Teddy thanked her for believing in him and showing him that he could make a difference. With tears in eyes, Mrs. Thompson replied, "You were the one who taught me that I could make a difference. I didn't know how to teach until I met you." Mrs. Thompson had to change her own heart before she could help Teddy and inspire him to improve.

Often, Jesus teaches us not to criticize others, but to examine our own hearts. Though we claim to understand others, we actually do not. We cannot truly know how they are thinking and feeling. Are we willing to have our hearts changed? If so, God will enable us to love others as unconditionally as He does.

~ David Ortiz

June 7

One Step Forward, Two Steps Back

There are many who make but little progress in the divine life, because they are too self-sufficient to occupy the position of learners. They are content to remain in ignorance of God's word; they do not wish to change their faith or their practice, and hence make no effort to obtain greater light. – Sketches from the Life of Paul, pg. 130

Once, when I was a boy, my mom took me to a large shopping mall in a big city. While there, we happened on a wonderfully exciting piece of machinery. There were two long flights of moving stairs, one going up, and the other coming down. As soon as I saw it, I wanted with all my heart to try it out. After she finally consented, I departed immediately for a wild adventure of running up one escalator and down the other. It was after I had tried this many times, that a new idea suddenly popped into my head. Why not try to run up the wrong escalator?

As soon as this idea had popped into my mind, and quite before my mind had thought the idea through, I was already quickly making my way toward the escalator that was coming down. As I jumped onto the escalator, I realized (with a start) that this would be harder than I thought. I had to try much harder just to make the smallest progress, and if I slackened my pace even for a minute, I would end up going backwards instead of forwards.

My escalator experience is much like our Christian walk. We have to try our hardest just to make the smallest progress, and if we stop for even the slightest moment, or even just slow our pace, we start going backwards. Then, it takes even more work to get back to where we were before. Then, from there, if we continually work upwards, never looking back or slowing down, we will reach the goal—the Kingdom of Heaven.

~ David White

June 8

Unity Equals Love

Now I beseech you, brethren, by the name of our Lord Jesus Christ, that ye all speak the same thing, and that there be no divisions among you; but that ye be perfectly joined together in the same mind and in the same judgment. – 1 Corinthians 1:10 KJV

Do you remember the times when you had those day-to-day quarrels with your siblings? I can remember those days when my mother would ask my brother and me if we could pass a day without hissing and growling. I now realize that, even though we fought a lot, I can rarely remember the cause of the squabble. The things that we fought over were really of no significance.

In Paul's time, many of the Jews in Corinth thought that to be accepted in the church, you must be circumcised. Even though the temple veil was rent, signifying the end to the ceremonial laws, the Jews still persisted. Just like I realized that the squabbles with my brother were really of no importance, the Jews didn't realize that they were crippling the church by focusing on the nonessential things.

As modern "Corinthians", we make the same mistake. We tend to focus on the unimportant things and forget the calling of Paul to unite. When we have unity of mind, we will have Jesus' love flowing through our church. When there is unity all the little problems won't matter, for we will have the same goal—to be like Christ.

~ Sharon Jeon

June 9

A Blessing

Whoever will give himself to God as fully as did Moses, will be guided by the divine hand... he may be lowly and apparently ungifted; yet if with a loving, trusting heart he obeys every intimation of God's will, his powers will be purified, ennobled, energized; his capabilities increased... he is enabled to make his Life an honor to God and a blessing to the world. – Sketches from the Life of Paul, pg. 131

We may not all be able to do what seems like, " a great work for God," but if we use every opportunity that God sends our way, He will enable us to be a blessing to all we come in contact with.

As I was on my way to Arizona, I had the opportunity to be a blessing to several people. While we were waiting in line to get our tickets, behind me was an older couple that had a lot of luggage. They were dropping things everywhere, so I offered to pick them up. Then I helped them carry their luggage to the counter. As I sat waiting for my flight, there was another older lady waiting at standby. She was tired and hungry, so I offered to get her some food. These people that I helped were very grateful and surprised. I was filled with such happiness that I didn't know helping others could bring. I hadn't done very much, but the little I had done, totally made my day.

You don't have to be a preacher to share Jesus with others. If He's in your heart, you can't help but let it show. I didn't even have the chance to talk to those people about Jesus, but I used the little opportunity He gave me to help them, and even in this, I was very blessed.

~ Becky Brousson

June 10

Loved and Thus Committed

He may be lowly and apparently ungifted; yet if with a loving, trusting heart he obeys every intimation of God's will, his powers will be purified, ennobled, energized; his capabilities increased.
– Sketches from the Life of Paul, pg. 131

The work of Christ is one that deserves only the best of our efforts. It should receive nothing less than the purest, noblest, and most energetic endeavors that we can offer. So, how do we know that we are giving our best efforts?

When you commit all that you are to Christ, you gain a first-hand experience of His amazing love. The closer you come to Christ and His love, the more joy you find. In finding more joy yourself, you also find that you are even more committed to sharing the amazing gift that you have found.

When you ask yourself the question, "Am I giving my all to the cause of Christ?" The answer is really very simple. Have you committed your will to Him? Do you enjoy thinking and talking about Jesus? Have you found His amazing love and taken it for your own? If you have, He will give you what you need to do His work, and you will be able to give nothing less than your all in return for His all.

~ Leighton Sjoren

June 11

Not Just Knowing

A mere intellectual knowledge of religious truth is not enough.
– Sketches from the Life of Paul, pg. 131

One day a rich young man came to Jesus and asked Him what he should do to be saved. Jesus told him that to have eternal life, he must keep the commandments. "Which ones? he asked. Jesus replied, Do not murder, do not commit adultery, do not steal, do not give false testimony, honor your father and mother, and love your neighbor as yourself" (Matthew 19:18-19 NET). The young man told Jesus that he had done all these things and was wondering if there was anything else. Jesus said to him, "If you wish to be perfect, go sell your possessions and give the money to the poor, and you will have treasure in heaven. Then come, follow me" (Matthew 19:21 NET). But when the young man heard this, he was sad and went away because he had great wealth.

Sometimes we know what we need to do; yet we don't want to make the change. The spirit is willing but the flesh is weak. The rich young ruler knew the commandments and what he should do, but he held onto his own desires. You and I need to make the decision today to take what we know and apply it to our lives daily, because later may never come.

~ Melody Hyde

June 12

Be a Branch

The juices of the vine, ascending from the root, are diffused to the branches sustaining growth, and producing blossoms and fruit. So the life-giving power of the Holy Spirit...imparted to every disciple...brings forth the precious fruit of holy deeds.
– Sketches from the Life of Paul, pg. 131

Jesus gathered His disciples beside a 7/11 gas station and began to teach them a parable: "I Am the gas pump and you are the cars. You may drive around independent of Me, as long as you come back occasionally and fill up your tank. And once in a while, you can stop for a little longer and get an oil change and car wash too." And having been "filled up" for the day, the disciples nodded their heads and left.

Never heard this parable before? That's because I made it up. But sadly, I think it illustrates the attitude of many of us toward our walk with Christ. For myself, I don't really know what it means to abide in Christ. I tend to treat Him like a gas station that I visit for a fast spiritual "fill-up" before zooming into my hectic day. By the end of the day, I'm often running on vapors, if anything is left at all.

In the real parable, Jesus said, "I am the vine, ye are the branches: He that abideth in me, and I in him, the same bringeth forth much fruit: for without me ye can do nothing...As the branch cannot bear fruit of itself, except it abide in the vine; no more can ye, except ye abide in me" (John 15:4, 5 KJV). If the branch wants to live, it must stay connected to the vine 24/7. This is the same with you and me. If we want to be vibrant, fruit-bearing Christians, we must abide in Christ every single moment of the day.

~ Cara Dewsberry

June 13

God's Will

If the followers of Christ were but earnest seekers after divine wisdom, they would be led into rich fields of truth, as yet wholly unknown to them. – Sketches from the Life of Paul, pg. 131

"What is my goal in life?" This is one of the most important questions that you can ever ask yourself because the answer can change your life. In fear of going against God's will, many just lie back and wait for signs from God. Though it is necessary to seek God's will, we should never just wait for God to show us. Instead, we should exert an effort to find our goal.

Moses exhibited this in his life. Living in a palace, he learned how to be a general and a ruler. Though this was not God's final plan for his life, He did not come and tell Moses that; instead, an incident led Moses in a different direction. When he murdered an Egyptian slave master, he thought that Pharaoh would execute him. So he ran and ran until he arrived at the house of Jethro the Midianite. There in the wilderness, the proud and boastful prince became a humble shepherd. This was where Moses learned how to be meek and lowly. Though Moses was content to stay in Midian, God called him to lead the Israelites to the Promised Land. Moses was called from prince to shepherd and finally to the leader of God's people. Do you think that the prince of Egypt ever thought that he would lead the Israelites out of captivity? No!

It seems that too often we do not grasp God's will for us right away. Just as God led Moses from place to place, even when he was off track, God will do the same for you. If you start wherever you are by seeking God, He will use you mightily and lead you to truth that is "wholly unknown" to you.

~ David Chang

June 14

Seek after Wisdom

If the followers of Christ were but earnest seekers after divine wisdom, they would be led into rich fields of truth, as yet wholly unknown to them. – Sketches from the Life of Paul, pg. 131

A young man seeking for wisdom once approached Socrates. Socrates could tell that this man did not have his whole heart dedicated to this pursuit and decided to teach him a valuable lesson. He led the young man to a local river and shoved his head under water for thirty seconds. Socrates let the young man up, and then asked him what he wanted in life; gasping for breath, the young man answered, "Wisdom." Socrates proceeded to dunk his head under for longer periods of time, and each time the young man came up, his answer was still the same: "Wisdom." After the third time, the man flung himself out of the water, and Socrates asked him the same question, "What do you want?" Choking on water, the young man exclaimed, "Air!" Socrates then replied, "You will have wisdom when you desire it as you desire the very air you breathe."

God states that this is the same level of desire that we must have for Him. In the book of Jeremiah we find, "When you seek me…you will find me…If you seek me with all your heart" (Jeremiah 29:13 NET). When you seek after God, God will provide you with wisdom for He "gives to all generously" (James 1:5 NET) and "from his mouth comes knowledge and understanding" (Proverbs 2:6 NET). Jesus promises us this gift for, "Ask, and it will be given to you; seek, and you will find; knock, and the door will be opened for you" (Luke 11:9 NET). God will endow us with wisdom beyond our understanding; all we have to do is seek.

~ Luke Gonzalez

June 15

Unseen

The Author of this spiritual life is unseen, and the precise method by which it is imparted and sustained is beyond the power of human philosophy to explain. It is the mystery of godliness.
– Sketches from the Life of Paul, pg. 131

Once upon a time, a young man who didn't believe in God was traveling on a ship to England. Also on the ship was a godly old minister. One day they got into a conversation, and the young man ridiculed the idea of anybody believing anything they hadn't seen.
"You believe many things you haven't seen." said the minister.
"No, I don't!" the young man snapped back.
"You believe in a country called England, don't you?"
"Of course!"
"But you haven't seen it."
"No, but others have."
"Oh, I see," said the old man. "Then it's only the things that you have seen or that someone else has seen that you believe exist?"
"That's it," said the young man confidently.
The old minister looked at him with a half smile on his face and said, "Have you ever seen your brain?"
"Well... umm..."
"Has anyone else ever seen your brain?"
"No, but..."
"Do you believe you have a brain?" asked the old minister. The young man went away feeling very uncomfortable.

We only need to look around us at the beautiful world of nature to realize that there is a God who created all the marvelous wonders we see. But even more amazing is the wonderful change that takes place in the human heart when it is surrendered to Christ. This was dramatically apparent in the life of Paul, who went from a persecutor to a preacher of the gospel. I want it to be as dramatically apparent in my life. How about you?

~ Rebecca Luchak

June 16

Excuses

The honest seeker after truth will not plead ignorance of the law as an excuse for transgression. – Sketches from the Life of Paul, pg. 133

Once a woman asked her pastor, "Pastor, I'm deeply troubled about the sin I cherish. It is exaggeration. Every time, I get up on a pulpit the devil tricks my brain and enlarges my testimony until it is all distorted." Then the pastor answered, "Let's talk to the Lord about it." She began to pray, "Dear Jesus, you know I tend to exaggerate—" Suddenly the preacher interjected by saying, "Ma'am, call it lying, and you may get over it." In that moment, the woman began to weep, because she knew he was right. She had been trying to make "lying" acceptable, and her excuse making had made results from prayer nearly impossible.

Many Christians like to cover up their sins by giving them a "polite name." A bad temper is called "righteous indignation" or lying is labeled "harmless exaggeration." However, why do we do this? We do it because we want to hold on to our sins and look like "saints." Ellen G. White said, "The honest seeker after truth will not plead ignorance." She hints that if we try to cover up our sins, we are not genuine Christians. Think about it, I'm sure the Pharisees covered their sins with "polite names." Then, what did Jesus called them? He called them "whited sepulchers"! (Matthew 23:27 KJV). The Pharisees were hypocrites. In reality, when we label our sins and cover them, we are just like the Pharisees. In this world, there is only good and bad. If whatever we are doing is not good, it is bad. If you are still struggling with covering your sins, why don't you get rid of your "polite names" and confess your real sins to Jesus who will change any who will accept His aid?

~ David Chang

June 17

What's Filling You?

"We adjure thee by Jesus, whom Paul preacheth." But the evil spirit answered with scorn, "Jesus I know, and Paul I know; but who are ye?" – Sketches from the Life of Paul, pg. 136

Have you ever taken a balloon and blown it up? After many huffs and puffs, you finally get it big and looking really nice; but then you let go of it, and it just flutters and sputters uncontrollably through the air before dropping to the ground. However, if you fill your balloon with helium, and tie it off, when you let go, it will fly high in the sky.

Now this is how it is in our lives. When we blow ourselves up with pride and think that we are the best, we are like balloons full of hot "human" air; and we can't even float, much less fly. However, when we allow God to fill up our lives with His Holy Spirit, we will always keep rising just like a balloon filled with helium.

The seven sons of Sceva were full of themselves; they did not have the Spirit of God in their hearts. When they tried to cast out the demon, the demon knew that they were full of their own "air" and did not truly represent Christ or have His power. But, Paul had the "helium" of God's Spirit, and the demons fled at his command.

We may not be flying high for Jesus right now, but we can ask Him to start filling our "balloon hearts" today.

~ Melody Hyde

June 18

His Name is Sacred

The discomfiture and humiliation of those who had profaned the name of Jesus soon became known throughout Ephesus, by Jews and Gentiles… Terror seized the minds of many, and the work of the gospel was regarded by all with awe and reverence. – Sketches from the Life of Paul, pg. 137

In 2 Kings 2: 23, 24 there is a story that has a very important lesson for us. In this story, some young men were taunting Elisha. "Go on up, baldy!" they shouted. They thought they could treat him rudely and call him names, but they would discover that by making fun of Elisha, they were making fun of God. Finally, God sent two female bears, which ripped all forty-two young men in pieces.

In the story of the rude young men, there is a lesson for me. God does not just punish people for the sake of punishing them, because His character is to save. But, when we dishonor His name, we too will have to face the consequences. God's work is something that we take far too lightly. Maybe we don't go to the extreme those young men did, but we have to always remember that He is someone to respect, honor, and worship. He alone is truly holy, and we should always treat the name of God with the utmost reverence.

~ Becky Brousson

June 19

Taking God's Name in Vain

Unmistakable proof had been given of the sacredness of that name, and the peril which they incurred who should invoke it while they had no faith in Christ's divine mission...the work of the gospel was regarded by all with awe and reverence. – Sketches from the Life of Paul, pg. 137

God wrought special miracles through Paul. By the touch of his handkerchief, people would be healed of their diseases, and evil spirits would be dispelled. The seven sons of Sceva thought that the name of Jesus was a charm, which anyone could use to perform miracles. So, they tried using this "charm" on a demon-possessed person, but the demon scornfully replied, "Jesus I know, and Paul I know; but who are ye?" (Acts 19:15 KJV). Then the possessed man beat and bruised the seven brothers. This was quite a shock to them because they thought that by saying these magical words, the charm would work instantly. But the demons could only be cast out by a true follower of Christ.

"Thou shalt not take the name of the Lord thy God in vain," (Exodus 20:7 KJV) doesn't simply mean, do not swear or cuss. If God's name is spoken carelessly, it can harm you like it did the seven brothers. God allows this because He wants you to realize what an awesome God you serve. God wants His followers to realize His love for man, so they may have a relationship with Him. If you take the name of Jesus and don't know Him, wouldn't it be like taking God's name in vain? Would you be acting like the seven brothers? Do you claim things that you don't really know? Take time to get to know Jesus and the power of His name.

~ Sharon Jeon

June 20

The Myths

The manifestation of the power of Christ was a grand victory for Christianity in the very stronghold of superstition. – Sketches from the Life of Paul, pg. 137

Every year in Japan, on New Year's Day, many people visit the shrines and temples all over the country. Sometimes, the temples will be filled with up to ninety million people. They go to the "god of safety" to ask for safe travel throughout the year. They go to the "god of wealth" to ask for a wealthy life throughout the year. They go to the "god of education" so that they will be able to pass their exams. They buy a strange looking ball of glass from the temple to keep as a charm.

In the village where I came from, a certain day is set aside for the worship of the "mountain god." It is considered to be the most holy day of the year. Everybody in the village will rest that day and go to the temple to worship the "mountain god." "My grandfather went to work on the day of 'mountain god' once," one of my friends said, "and he ended up cutting one of his fingers very badly." Another said, "A friend of ours went to work on this holy day, and he lost his working tools in the forest."

Who created these myths and why? There are many more superstitions in the world. For over six thousand years, humans have been creating thousands of myths and false gods. As Christians, we know that only Jesus is "the way, the truth, and the life" (John 14:6 KJV). While humans create false gods, the Word of God stands as the ultimate and undeniable truth and teaches of the true God. In the end, any kind of false god, false myth, or false belief will be clearly exposed as foolishness that humans themselves have created. The power of Christ has always been stronger than what humans have created, and it will remain that way forever.

~ Ryo Fusamae

June 21

The Frontlines of War

The visible and the invisible world are in close contact. Could the veil be lifted, we would see evil angels employing all their arts to deceive and destroy. – Sketches from the Life of Paul, pg. 140

Take a moment to imagine you are at the frontlines of a brutal war. Above you, planes screech past dropping their deadly bombs, while tanks on the ground discharge their heavy shells. Enemies on each side are constantly firing at each other, barely giving you a second to breathe. You can hear the footsteps of the running soldiers as they charge at their enemies.

Back to reality, this war is happening right now, in a spiritual sense. This war is just as tense as and even more life threatening than a real war. It is a picture only seen through the eye of faith.

God has given us the two weapons we need for this spiritual battle: prayer and God's Word. God's angels are waiting for our prayers. Each time we pray, they gain strength to fight off the enemy. Also, prayer makes Satan tremble, for it connects us with our power source, God. God's Word is the sword mentioned in Ephesians 6:18. Without your sword, how can you conquer the enemy? Just like Jesus overcame Satan by saying, "It is written" (Matthew 4:4 KJV), we need to use the sword of God's Word every time we are attacked.

This war is brutal and hard. But unlike any other war, your fate is marked by whose side you stand on. God's side means victory, while Satan's side means defeat. We are in the heat of the battle where not even one mistake can be permitted. We cannot sleep in a battle so fierce and so tense. Every day, we must depend on our weapons to gain the victory over our enemies.

~ Sharon Jeon

June 22

Courage

His courage was in keeping with the occasion. He was ever ready to press to the front in the battle for his Master. – Sketches from the Life of Paul, pg. 143

One morning as he fixed his breakfast, Ray Blankenship glanced out the window just in time to see a small girl being swept away in the rain-flooded drainage ditch beside his home. He knew that farther downstream, the ditch disappeared underneath a road and then emptied into the main culvert. Mr. Blankenship rushed out of the door and raced along the ditch, so he could get ahead of the helpless girl. Hurling himself into the deep water, Mr. Blankenship was able to grab the child's arm. Three feet away from the culvert, Mr. Blankenship's free hand felt a rock on the bank. He clung desperately to the boulder, but the immense force of the water attempted to yank both of them away. Struggling, he hung on until help came. By the time rescuers had arrived Mr. Blankenship had pulled the girl to safety. Immediately, both were taken to medical care. On April 12, 1989, Ray Blankenship was awarded the Coast Guard's Silver Lifesaving Medal. Mr. Blankenship had been at even greater risk than most people knew. He did not know how to swim.

When serving God, Satan will throw challenges in your way. And when those challenges come, do not be afraid of them; confront them. God will not let Satan shatter the efforts that you have made in His name. Even though those challenges might seem overwhelming, God will give you strength that you never expected to find.

~ David Ortiz

June 23

Angels Watching Over You

Angels of God were sent to guard the faithful apostle. His time to die a martyr's death had not yet come. – Sketches from the Life of Paul, pg. 143

While Paul was carrying out the work of God, he constantly had to hide from the murderers trying to track him down. But God always sent His angels to protect Paul whenever he was in danger. When the angels would spare Paul's life, he knew his time to die had not come yet; so he continued to trust in God while doing his work.

A number of years ago, my grandma was worrying over personal problems so much that she was getting hardly any sleep. One night, she prayed more earnestly than usual: "I really need Your help, Lord. I can't do it by myself. Please help me in my work." That night, after sleeping an hour or so, she woke up at 12:30 a.m. She turned over and faced the wall in her dark room. Suddenly, she saw a beautiful white-robed being beside her bed and a hand extending down from the fold in his garment. In astonishment she said, "Oh, Lord, thank You for being with me. I know now You will help me."

Just then, she heard two hard pounds on the side of her house. She said out loud, "What is going on outside?" Realizing that it must be Satan trying to scare her, she prayed and thanked God for being with her and protecting her. In this visible way, God let my grandma know that He cared for her and would always be near her.

If you're ever in danger and feel that you're alone, always remember that your guardian angel is right there beside you.

~ Jennifer Atkins

June 24

Stay Connected

So then faith cometh by hearing, and hearing by the word of God.
– Romans 10:17 KJV

    Have you ever wondered what would happen if we treated our Bibles like we treat our cell phones? What if we carried them around in our purses or pockets, and turned back to go get them if we forgot them? What if we used them to receive messages from the text, and treated them like we couldn't live without them? What if we gave them to our kids as gifts? What if we used them when we traveled and in case of emergency?

    God wants us to be as connected with Him as we are with those we call. Unlike our cell phones, we don't have to worry about our Bibles being disconnected because Jesus already paid the bill.

    Many people live in countries where the Bible is prohibited by law, and they have to go through great effort to find a Bible. In North America, we have Bibles everywhere; we find them in book stores, hotels, churches, schools, and in almost every home. But are we as connected to Christ as we should be? Would we rather hear God speak through His Word than talk to our friends on our phones? God has given us His word in abundance, so let's stay connected. Can you hear God now?

~ Rebecca Luchak

June 25

The Foundation

Amid the constant storm of opposition, the clamor of enemies, and the desertion of friends, the intrepid apostle at times almost lost heart.
– Sketches from the Life of Paul, pg. 148

Every day we encounter various trials, decisions, and problems that affect our emotions. Admit it or not, all of us are affected and even sometimes driven by them. And this happens every day! For instance:

Day 1: Weather: Bright and Sunny!
              Family: Doing well—just came back from a picnic.
              Mood: Happy, Satisfied.

But then the weather changes…

Day 2: Weather: Dark and cloudy.
              Family: Became irritable—arguing.
              Mood: Aggravated, Stressed, Depressed.

Paul went through a lot! The weather was the least of his worries; every day he encountered difficulties threatening to drive his ministry and even his life literally into the dust. In the face of all these trials, Paul was sure to be discouraged from time to time, but he never lost heart because his faith was anchored in the words of Scripture: "I, the LORD, do not change" (Malachi 3:6 NAS). Paul lifted his eyes and beheld the Christ, the firm foundation on which he could stand through any storm. We too can stand on this foundation. Though situations and circumstances may change around us, let's not lose heart. Nothing can break down the firm foundation on which we stand.

~ Robby Folkenberg

June 26

Look to Calvary

Amid the constant storm of opposition, the clamor of enemies, and the desertion of friends, the intrepid apostle at times almost lost heart. But he looked back to Calvary, and with new ardor pressed on to spread the knowledge of the Crucified. – Sketches from the Life of Paul, pg. 148

Have you ever felt discouraged? When trials come, do you feel disheartened and unable to bear what life throws your way? During Paul's ministry he faced many discouragements. He endured the clamor of his enemies, constant storms of opposition, and even the desertion of his friends. At times Paul almost lost heart, but still he pushed onward through difficulty; in Paul we find a prime example of how to deal with the tribulations that are thrown our way.

Paul, when feeling weighed down with discouragement, looked to Calvary. He saw how Christ had endured the very same things and had thus set the standard, giving him hope. Christ's strength on Calvary encouraged him and gave him strength to overcome the circumstances he met.

When you face trials, take the example of Paul and turn your eyes upon Calvary. Christ walked in this world to be our divine example. When you have trials that seem unbearable, look to Christ, for He has surely overcome them all, and because He overcame them, He can give you the strength to do the same.

~ Leighton Sjoren

June 27

At the Cross

But he looked back to Calvary, and with new ardor pressed on to spread the knowledge of the Crucified. – Sketches from the Life of Paul, pg. 148

> "At the cross, at the cross,
> Where I first saw the light,
> And the burden of my heart rolled away;
> It was there by faith I received my sight,
> And now I am happy all the day!"

During November 1850, a revival meeting was being held at the Thirtieth Street Methodist Church in New York City. Among the people who attended each evening was a man named Jed Crosby who twice sought to find peace at the altar. However, it was not until one particular evening that Mr. Crosby found peace. As the light dawned upon Mr. Crosby, he arose and went to the altar alone. A prayer was offered, and the congregation began to sing the consecration hymn, "Alas, and did my Saviour bleed, and did my Sovereign die?" By the time they had reached the fourth stanza, which reads, "Here Lord, I give myself away," his very soul was touched by the Spirit of God. Springing to his feet he cried out "Hallelujah!" It was then that he realized for the first time that God had not been the center of his life. He had been trying to hold the world in one hand and the Lord in the other, and he praised God for showing him his need.

We often try to have both the world and God at the same time. However, the inspired Scriptures tell us clearly that we cannot serve God and the Devil at the same time. It all comes down to what Mr. Crosby faced. While his heart was divided, he had no peace: he was being convicted by the Holy Spirit. Once he had surrendered all to the Lord, he was happy and at peace.

Search for the Lord today, and you will find Him. Give Him all, and peace will pervade your soul.

~ Douglas Schappert

June 28

Power Tools

All power is given unto me in heaven and in earth.
– Matthew 28:18 KJV

Dr. Helen Roseveare, a missionary to Zaire, told the following story:

"A mother at our mission station died after giving birth to a premature baby. We tried to improvise an incubator to keep the infant alive, but the only hot water bottle we had was beyond repair. So we asked the children to pray for the baby and for her sister. One of the girls responded. 'Dear God, please send a hot water bottle today. Tomorrow will be too late because by then the baby will be dead. And dear Lord, send a doll for the sister so she won't feel so lonely.'

That afternoon a large package arrived from England. The children watched eagerly as we opened it. Much to their surprise, under some clothing was a hot water bottle! Immediately the girl who had prayed so earnestly started to dig deeper, exclaiming, 'If God sent that, I'm sure He sent a doll too!' And she was right! The heavenly Father knew in advance of that child's sincere requests, and five months earlier He had led a ladies' group to include both of those specific articles."

Prayer is a powerful tool for us when used in the right way. The book, *E. M. Bounds on Prayer*, states, "Prayer can do anything that God can do." Jesus furnishes us with all power in heaven and on earth. So, with all heaven at your disposal, is there anything you can't do?

~ Jourdain Smith

June 29

Not of This World

The good seed sown by him had seemed to promise an abundant harvest; but tares were planted by the enemy among the wheat, and ere long these sprung up, and brought forth their evil fruit.
– Sketches from the Life of Paul, pg. 149

If you were around Paul for just a few moments, you would have a better acquaintance with Jesus. His fervent prayers and unswerving faith strikingly reflected the character of Christ. While Paul ministered at Corinth, the new converts ever thirsted after Jesus. They saw the love of their Savior in Paul and understood that to be like Jesus should be their ultimate goal. However, when Paul left the city, the believers began to fall apart. Not able to see their living example, they began to compromise little by little, until they had returned completely to the world.

Jesus calls us to be "not of the world" (John 17:14 KJV). Paul was in this world, but not of this world. His purpose in life was to ever bring honor to God! Paul was like an evergreen tree. No matter what season it was, Paul always kept his beautiful leaves of Christ. On the other hand, the Corinthians were like deciduous trees. They kept their leaves beautiful when the weather was good; but when the season changed their "Christ-leaves" shriveled up, and they became like the world. For us today, it is easy to be spiritual when everyone around us is too. However, when the world goes against God it gets difficult to stand for the truth. Paul never left his faith because he was firmly grounded in Christ. When the world is trying to seduce you, are you going to be a deciduous or an evergreen tree?

~ David Chang

June 30

Little by Little

It is not in a day that the education and habits of a life are to be overcome. – Sketches from the Life of Paul, pg. 150

Once, there was a young man who had a strong desire to become a Christian. After studying and learning about Christianity, this young man was baptized. At first, Christianity seemed to be all about fun! He loved hanging out with other Christian people and still being able to do the same things he had done before. But then he began studying his Bible and realized that many of the things he had done before he was a Christian, were not acceptable in God's sight.

After that, he tried and tried to be that "perfect Christian" whom he had visualized, but it didn't seem to work. Even when he tried his hardest to be perfect, he would fail again and again. Then came discouragement. This young man became more and more depressed because of his failure in being the "perfect Christian". He felt like God would probably give up on him because of his failures! Finally, he talked to a friend about his discouragement, and his friend reminded him to keep his focus on God instead of his many failures.

Sometimes, in our Christian walk, we try to overcome all of our bad habits at once. Then we become so obsessed with our problems, that we lose sight of God. But, if we keep ourselves focused on God and try to overcome our faults with His help, little by little we will overcome our old habits and become more and more like Him, our Ultimate Example.

~ Dave White

July 1

Because the Bible Tells Me So

Some practiced iniquity in secret, others openly, and with a spirit of bravado, perverting the Scriptures to justify their course. – Sketches from the Life of Paul, pg. 150

"Thou shalt not judge!" the young woman exclaimed, attempting to quote Luke 6:37. "That verse always gets abused," I responded as I walked into the room. I had no idea what was going on, but I knew that Scripture was being twisted. The lady loved her sin and would not let it go, so when the rebukes came, she always responded by quoting that verse. Over the years, she had been researching how to safeguard her sin, always reading only what protected her view. I was witnessing the only fruit that Scripture twisting can ever produce: more Scripture twisting. When such people do this type of "research," they do so to "their own destruction" (2 Peter 3:16 NET).

By twisting the Scriptures, they are trying to twist the image of God. They are removing God from their lives and replacing Him with their own ideas and theories, which is nothing more than idolatry. Such people cherish the sin in their lives and love it more than the plain teachings of God. Paul talked about this type of men in his letter to the Romans, which states, "Although they fully know God's righteous decree that those who practice such things deserve to die, they not only do them, but also approve of those who practice them" (Romans 1:32 NET). It is clearly a fearful thing to ignore the words of God. When you hear and obey the Word of God, you "will prosper and be successful" (Joshua 1:8 NET). God will bless you, but most importantly, He will guide you for "you will hear a word spoken behind you, saying, 'This is the correct way, walk in it,' whether you are heading to the right or the left" (Isaiah 30:21 NET).

~ Luke Gonzalez

July 2

Ever Upward

He reminds them of…their duty to make continual advancement in the Christian life, that they may attain to the purity and holiness of Christ. – Sketches from the Life of Paul, pg. 152

Henry Wadsworth Longfellow wrote a poem entitled "Excelsior," which means "ever upward." In the poem, a young man, bearing a banner embroidered with the word "Excelsior," struggles up a steep mountain. Though the climb is arduous, he continually presses forward allowing nothing to stop him. Many things tempt him to halt his climb, from the inviting warmth of a cozy village, to an old man's warning of dangers ahead, to the love of a fair maiden; but he ignores them all. He knows that if he is to reach the top, he must keep moving forward.

We also have a goal to reach—the "purity and holiness of Christ," and it is only by daily advancement that we will reach this goal. If you start out on a journey, but never go farther than the first stoplight, how can you ever expect to reach your destination?

It's the same with our Christian experience. We are called to walk the narrow way. Step by step, we are to advance each day, growing more and more like Christ. Nothing must hold us back—not the pleasures of this world, the arms of loved ones, or the bitter winds of trial that assail us. We must hold up the banner and cry, "Excelsior! Always upward to heaven!" Start climbing today—and keep climbing. The only way to attain perfection in Christ is to press ever upward. Excelsior!

~ Cara Dewsberry

July 3

Uni-Mind

Now I beseech you, brethren, by the name of our Lord Jesus Christ, that ye all speak the same thing, and that there be no divisions among you. – 1 Corinthians 1:10 KJV

Have you ever played the game "Jinx"? In case you don't know, this is how it goes: when two or more people say a word or phrase at exactly the same time, the first person to say "Jinx" freezes everyone else that said the same word or phrase at the same time. The frozen person can only talk once someone else removes the jinx by saying his or her name. The reason I mention this is because this game wouldn't be too much fun if nobody ever said the same thing at exactly the same time. People saying or thinking something in unison (without prearrangement, of course) is really not that uncommon. In fact, it happens a lot.

We really are made to be of one mind after all. So how come it is so hard to get along and agree on things that matter? It's one of those questions God throws at us to get us to wake up and live our lives His way. I was asking myself that same question recently. Why is it that we can get each other the same Christmas gift without either of us knowing, but can't decide after much discussion in a church board meeting what color the new blinds should be?

Let us come together on the foundations of unity upon which our church was built! This doesn't mean that we should all be carbon copies of each other; God created and loves our individuality, but there are things in which we should be absolutely as one. Christian love is one of these things. Without it, we are nothing and cannot minister to anyone. Are you going to be "Uni-minded?"

~ Jonathan Fink

July 4

A Strong Foundation

Paul had now been working in the Gentile quarry, to bring out valuable stones to lay upon the foundation, which was Jesus Christ, that by coming in contact with that living stone, they might also become living stones. – Sketches from the Life of Paul, pg. 154

As Paul was, we are also called to work in the quarry to bring valuable stones to lay on the Foundation—Jesus Christ. Before we can do this great work, however, we ourselves need to become precious stones that may be laid upon this holy Foundation.

Through humble obedience, prayer, and patience we may become stones polished by the grace of God. We cannot, however, become refined and polished through our own efforts; we must be built upon the True Foundation. Those that do not set themselves upon the True Foundation will find themselves to be merely stubble that will fall away in the end. The only way to become living stones is to come into contact with The Living Stone.

Once we have laid ourselves upon the True Foundation, we will find in ourselves love and the desire to bring in as many other stones "whether large or small, polished or unhewn, common or precious to be connected with the living foundation-stone" (*Sketches from the Life of Paul*, pg. 156). True love and the character of Christ are shown when we desire to show those around us the way to life more abundant and free.

~ Leighton Sjoren

July 5

Crash or Stand Fast

"If any man build upon this foundation, gold, silver, precious stones, wood, hay, stubble, every man's work shall be made manifest; for the day shall declare it." Some ministers, through their labors, furnish the most precious material, gold, silver, and precious stones, which represent true moral worth in those gained to the cause by them. The false material, gilded to imitate the true,-- that is, a carnal mind, and unsanctified character, glossed over with seeming righteousness,-- may not be readily detected by moral eye; but the day of God will test the material. – Sketches from the Life of Paul, pg. 155

Jesus told a parable about two men who built houses. One man built on a rock, and the winds blew and beat on that house, but it stood fast because it had a firm foundation. The other man built his house on the sand, and when the winds blew and beat on his house, it fell with a great crash. The first man in this story had a good foundation, and he built a good character on top of it.

Christ has laid the foundation, and it is up to us to build on it the right way. We cannot build with the wrong materials; we need the polished, precious stones instead of hay. We polish our stones or our characters by a careful, prayerful study of God's word.

Have you built on the right foundation? Have you used the right material? There is a storm coming; will you be able to stand?

~ Jenny McCluskey

July 6

Worthless Rocks

From worldly policy, many endeavor, by their own efforts, to become as polished stones; but they cannot be living stones, because they are not built upon the true foundation. – Sketches from the Life of Paul, pg. 155

An older man stopped at a jeweler's shop in Chicago. In his hand he held a queerly colored, rough rock. Nervously, he walked up to the counter. The medical bills for his wife, the traffic accident, and the increased cost of living were weighing heavily on his shoulders. At the glass counter, he pulled the rock out of his pocket and set it on the tabletop.

"I came across this red rock in a box of stuff I was goin' through. It's been pushed around my family for a few generations. Might it be worth anything? It's awfully pretty." The appraiser was dumbstruck. He just kept staring at the stone in the man's hand.

After a while, he exclaimed, "Sir, this is an uncut pigeon's blood ruby! These are very rare, and when it is polished, it will be worth over $250,000." The man had the answer to his financial troubles in his hand the whole time and didn't even know it!

We are precious to God, but sometimes we don't realize or care what we're worth to Him. Even when we're "in the rough", we're worth everything to Him. The difference between gems and us is that our Maker gave us a choice as to whether or not we are going to let ourselves be polished. Paul had been working for the Gentiles because he saw "uncut gems" glimmering in the mire of superstition and paganism. God feels the same way about you. He thinks you are valuable, and He has already paid your ransom. Let God take you out of the mine and into His workshop!

~ Jonathan Fink

July 7

Don't Bring Your Swimsuit

There hath no temptation taken you but such as is common to man: but God is faithful, who will not suffer you to be tempted above that ye are able; but will with the temptation also make a way to escape, that ye may be able to bear it. – 1 Corinthians 10:13 KJV

Once there was a boy whose father told him not to swim in the canal. The son promised that he wouldn't, and then went his way. When the boy returned that evening with a wet swimsuit in hand, his father questioned him, "Where have you been?"

"Swimming in the canal," answered the boy.
"Didn't I tell you not to swim there?" asked the father.
"Yes, Sir," answered the boy.
"Why did you?" he asked.
"Well, Dad," he explained, "I had my bathing suit with me, and I couldn't resist the temptation."
"Why did you take your bathing suit with you?" his father questioned.
"So I'd be prepared to swim, in case I was tempted," the boy replied.

Often, our lives are like this boy's; we know what we should and shouldn't do. But we allow ourselves to be brought into situations where we know that we are weak. Then we fall. Yet, God can take away our desire to lead ourselves into temptation. Also, God has promised that He will not allow us to be tempted in areas where He does not have a way of escape for us. So, when you feel that there is no way out, remember that "God is faithful" and He is always with you to be your strength.

~ Melody Hyde

July 8

Perfect Notes

Paul laid himself upon the true foundation, and brought every stone, whether large or small, polished or unhewn, common or precious, to be connected with the living foundation-stone, Christ Jesus.
– Sketches from the Life of Paul, pg. 156

"I must tell you something," my violin teacher stopped my playing as if she heard something disappointing. "There is no such thing as 'almost perfect sound.' If the note that you played was not the note that was on the musical score, then it is a wrong note no matter how close it was to the right one." I had to agree. I just been playing and thinking, "Oh, that didn't sound perfect, but it was close enough." And I kept playing. Once again, she prodded me saying, "Okay, start again from the same place."

If the note that was produced from my performance was wrong, then it was wrong. My violin teacher was trying to emphasize the fact that there is no such thing as an "almost perfect note." It's either right or wrong, nothing between the two.

Ellen White tells us that Paul gathered every single stone to lay a firm foundation and was "connected with the living foundation-stone, Christ Jesus." None of the rocks were missing out of his foundation.

God expects us to be perfect. If a man is lost in one area, he is lost in everything. Paul warns us that God requires "holiness, without which no man shall see the Lord" (Hebrews 12:14 KJV). Holiness is "wholeness" in the service of God. There is no such thing as an "almost holy Christian". God expects us to be wholly surrendered to Him.

~ Ryo Fusamae

July 9

Watch Out!

Many who wrought as builders of the temple of Christ's church could be likened to the builders of the wall in Nehemiah's day: "They which builded on the wall, and they that bore burdens, with those that laded, every one with one of his hands wrought in the work, and with the other held a weapon." – Sketches from the Life of Paul, pg. 157

The world is in the midst of an invisible controversy. If we could see the unseen beings around us, we would realize just how perilous this war really is. Because we can't see the forces that are ever seeking to harm us, we often forget that they are present. But, we cannot afford to be off guard. If the enemy can catch us when we least expect it, we'll fall right into the trap.

I have my learner's permit, and I'm learning how important it is to watch my blind spots, look out for pedestrians, and watch the road ahead to make sure I drive safely. If I take my eyes off the road, even for an instant, I could crash. I must be focused on my destination, but also be alert of the dangers along the way.

We are called to be "builders of the temple of Christ's church." We all know that builders are supposed to build. But the builders of the wall in Nehemiah's day did something strange. They worked on the wall with one hand and held a weapon in the other. We too must be constantly on the lookout for lurking temptations, traps, and fallacies. While focusing on building with all our might, we are also to be fighting against sin.

~ Melissa Butler

July 10

Transformed

God will not accept the most brilliant talent or the most able service, unless it is laid upon the living foundation stone, and connected with it; for this alone gives true value to ability, and makes the labor a living service to God. – Sketches from the Life of Paul, pg. 158

While Israel was in apostasy, the great prophet Isaiah courageously defended the truth. However, like any human, he had a flaw: he thought of himself too highly. He was proud of the fact that he was a brilliant orator and prophet of God. Because Isaiah didn't see his need of God, God sent him a vision.

In his vision, Isaiah saw God's throne surrounded by seraphims singing, "Holy, holy, holy, is the Lord, the whole earth is filled with His glory" (Isaiah 6:3 KJV). On the throne sat the Alpha and Omega. "His head and his hairs were white like wool, as white as snow; and his eyes were as a flame of fire...and his countenance was as the sun shineth in his strength" (Revelation 1:14-16 KJV). Although Isaiah always preached God's messages to others, he sometimes overlooked applying them to himself. His heart wasn't changed until he saw God in His glory. The marvelous sight of God made him realize that he was as much a sinner as the people he condemned! This revelation forced him to exclaim, "Woe is me! for I am undone; because I am a man of unclean lips, and I dwell in the midst of a people of unclean lips: for mine eyes have seen the King, the LORD of hosts" (Isaiah 6:5 KJV). When Isaiah saw Jesus, he realized that it was not his talents that made him a great servant of God, but his connection with Jesus Christ.

It is not talents or intelligence that qualifies a person to defend the truth. But those who are contrite in heart and who have God as their utmost desire will be the ablest defenders of truth. This was the key to success for the apostles and prophets, and this can be the key for you and me. Isaiah was changed when he saw Jesus. Why don't you pray that Jesus will clearly reveal Himself to you and change your heart?

~ David Chang

July 11

We Are the Same

He strove to lay aside his personal feelings, and to bear with the prejudices of the persons for whom he was laboring. – Sketches from the Life of Paul, pg. 160

As Paul labored in Ephesus, the vulnerable church of Corinth worsened. The church shattered into factions; false teachers arose who brainwashed the people. The doctrines of the Gospel and its ordinances were perverted. Pride and idolatry increased within the church of Christ. But despite their blunders, Paul helped the Corinthian church to rise from the ashes. He recognized himself as a sinner just as they were sinners and helped them in their predicament.

Perhaps the church in India needed a leader like Paul to teach them humility. During his student years, Mahatma Gandhi, the famous peace activist, read the Gospels and almost converted to Christianity. He believed that the teachings of Jesus could provide a solution to the caste system that was dividing the people of India.

One Sunday, he decided to attend services at a nearby church and speak to the minister about becoming a Christian. However, when he entered the sanctuary, the usher refused to give him a seat and suggested that he worship with his own people. Gandhi left the church and never returned. "If Christians have caste differences also," he said, "I might as well remain a Hindu." The usher's prejudice not only misrepresented Jesus, but also turned a person away from trusting Jesus as his Savior.

When ministering to the needs of people, remember that you are not different from them. All of us are children of God, with the same promise of mercy and salvation. Are you willing to be judged by the same standard you use to judge others?

~ David Ortiz

July 12

Paul and the President

He would not mislead the Jews nor practice deception upon them; but he waived his personal feelings, for the truth's sake. With the Gentiles his manner of labor was different. – Sketches from the Life of Paul, pg. 161

Paul's life was devoted to the spreading of the gospel message to the Gentiles. But as he traveled he often encountered Jews who had not heard the good news either. If Paul approached the Jews with Christ's fulfillment of the ceremonial law and its uselessness to them now, many Jews would immediately reject Christ. With the Gentiles he could be more open about the subject, but with the Jews he had to use tact. Not that he didn't speak the truth; he merely crafted the truth to fit the truth-seeker.

"Speak softly and carry a big stick." Theodore Roosevelt spoke these words as Vice President of the United States, only twelve days before President William McKinley was shot and killed. Soon the new Mr. President was using this slogan at the head of a country bound to be the superpower of the modern world. If there is ever a job that demands more tact than is demanded of the vice president, then being president is it! Roosevelt negotiated peace worldwide while tactfully building a powerful nation to defend its peace-loving position. He went as far as sending sixteen new battleships from the Atlantic Fleet on a world cruise to show off America's power, so all could see who they were up against in case they sought to destroy the peace.

Tact is important in everything, not just when you're the president. Comments can be misunderstood if the speaker does not consider the sensitivities of his audience. Forgetting someone's background could lead you to spout out some otherwise inoffensive language. But speak with tact, and you can speak with anyone.

~ Robby Folkenberg

July 13

Fifty Percent

It was when the children of Israel sat down to eat and drink, and rose up to play, that they threw off the righteous fear of God which they had felt a short time before as they listened to the law from Sinai.
– Sketches from the Life of Paul, pg. 169

The accounts of the children of Israel were recorded to show us an example. From these stories, we see that entertainment distracted their minds from the fear of God. The commandments that God had set up only a short time before were quickly forgotten. They became caught up in creating a golden calf to worship right after God had spoken specifically about graven images. The indulging of their appetite and pleasure had caused them to sin against their God.

In pleasing self, my mind is led away from God. I have two choices: will I please self or God? "No man can serve two masters" (Matthew 6:24 KJV). This was the error of the Israelites. There is no such thing as a fifty-percent Christian. I must be fully devoted to Christ if I am to be a Christian at all. This calls for a close examination of my heart. I cannot let the imperfections that keep me from drawing close to Christ remain in my heart. If I decide to place my life in harmony with God, then it must be sincere and heart-felt.

Never lose your connection with Christ. Cherish not the things of the flesh that would separate you from an awesome God. He loves you. Would you turn away from Christ's open arms waiting to give you a hug? Today, choose to serve Him fully.

~ Buddy Taylor

July 14

Penny-Pinchers

This [Philippian] church could not be prevented from making donations to the apostle for his support while preaching the gospel.
– Sketches from the Life of Paul, pg. 173

Imagine it's Friday morning, and you're at the mall trying to decide which of the hundreds of products available you want to buy. Shelf after jam-packed shelf beckons for you to sample its wares. You see something you want and check the price—OUCH! It's pretty expensive, but you have enough money for a little splurge.

The next day in church, an old deacon gets up and gives the offering call. As he asks for contributions to the dwindling church budget, you're busy thinking about the purchase you made the day before: yeah, it was a bit expensive, but it's going to be so great to have. Suddenly, you realize the offering plate is coming down your row. When it reaches you, you look away and pass it on—you just don't have the money to spare for offering today.

What's wrong with this picture? You had enough money to buy stuff that you really didn't need, but not enough to support the work of God. The Philippians couldn't be stopped from giving to the Gospel, but we can hardly bear to part with a penny for offering. Isn't it sad that we are so wrapped up in self that we won't even sacrifice for the cause of our dear Lord? I don't want to be so selfish, and I'm sure you don't either. I want Jesus to change me today and make me willing to give my all to His cause. How about you?

~ Cara Dewsberry

July 15

Gifts of Value

The Philippians did not hold their small earthly possessions with a tenacious grasp, but considered them as theirs only to use in doing good. – Sketches from the Life of Paul, pg. 175

These Philippian brothers freely offered their assistance to Paul. Instead of keeping their possessions, they provided them to support the church at Jerusalem. They realized that their possessions were gifts from God. After all, the Father is the giver of all good gifts. So, the Philippians used these and returned them to the service of God, not worried about losing them.

Likewise, we have been granted many gifts. What are we doing with them though? Do we understand their value? Often, one of the problems with gifts is that we don't realize their presence. One of these is the gift of time. I've been trying to imagine what my day would be like if I used my time in doing only good. But, to use my time wisely, my objective must be to meet other people's needs. This is often the hardest part for me, for I would rather hoard that time for myself. Our most beloved possessions aren't even ours though. They are God's, to be used in His service.

You have been given gifts as well. If you don't see them, then search deeper. Every gift comes with an opportunity to discover it. Once you have found a gift, do not hesitate to use it. For in sharing your gifts, they will be strengthened. God will place in your life chances for you to strengthen your gifts. Take hold of them, for once an opportunity is past you cannot get it back. Don't hold back your gifts. Today, use your gifts for the good of someone. The opportunity is yours.

~ Buddy Taylor

July 16

Giving

The Philippians did not hold their small earthly possessions with a tenacious grasp, but considered them as theirs only to use in doing good. – Sketches from the Life of Paul, pg. 175

A little girl received six dollars from her grandma for her birthday. With a bounce in her step and joy on her face, she ran to her room. She had six dollars to spend however she chose! Several days later, she asked her grandma to take her to the Dollar Store. She wanted to spend four of her six dollars to replace items in the gift box at church. Her grandma was pleased with her decision and took her to the store.

At the store the little girl could not decided on what to get. She loved everything. She would put something in the basket, and then change her mind. Finally, she narrowed her decision down to six items. The little girl had a perplexing look on her face, she wanted to get six items but she only had $ 4.00 to spend. After a while, she slowly took two items out of the basket. Suddenly her eyes lit up! She told her grandma that she would just use all of her six dollars to give to the gift box at church.

This little girl amazingly understood the principle of giving, and that God would take care of her needs. So many times, I fail to grasp this lesson so clearly presented. I do not feel like helping others because all I think of is myself. God wants to give you and me a new heart; He's ready and waiting to perform the surgery. Will you decide to have this heart transplant?

~ Jeremy Grabiner

July 17

Serving or Being Served

And whosoever shall exalt himself shall be abased; and he that shall humble himself shall be exalted. – Matthew 23:12 KJV

Exhausted from their travels, Jesus and the disciples sat down around the table. Jesus' time of crucifixion was drawing near, and he wanted to spend one last Passover with his disciples. At these gatherings, it was the custom for the servants to wash the guests' feet, but there were no servants at this feast. Who would perform this act of servitude? Pride filled the disciples' hearts, preventing them from moving. They sat as if glued to their seats, and then One stood among them. As they looked up, their gaze rested upon their beloved Master. He, Master of heaven and earth, knelt down to wash their dirty, stinky feet. Stupefied, the disciples watched. All feelings of pride and self-centeredness slithered away. Jesus' silent rebuke struck at their hearts. If they wanted to be served, they must be willing to serve.

Many times, we go through life, trying to find ways in which we can esteem ourselves better than others. This is illustrated in the poem "I."

"I gave a little tea party this afternoon, at three.
T'was very small, three guests in all—I, myself, and me.
Myself ate all the sandwiches while I drank all the tea.
T'was also I who ate the pie and passed the cake to me."

In this little poem, we see the self-centeredness exhibited by the speaker, yet many times we too exhibit this same trait. Jesus showed us that by humbling ourselves, we would be blessed. Are you going to serve or be served?

~ Jourdain Smith

July 18

Gifts to be Given

It is more blessed to give than to receive. – Acts 20:35 KJV

Dark, chilly, and wet would be excellent descriptions of the conditions in the cave that quiet afternoon. Francis Bernardone, who lived in the city of Assisi, was using this cave to get away from the world's stresses and to spend some time with God. "Lord, what would you have me do?" He asked. For a while, all he could hear was the fluttering of bats' wings and the splashing of water droplets on the cave floor. Then, out of the recesses of his mind, the thought came "Blessed are the poor in spirit, for theirs is the kingdom of heaven" (Matthew 5:3 KJV).

Hmmm, he thought, *What's that supposed to mean? Maybe if I go to the church, I'll there understand what he wants me to do.* As he passed the poor beggars who gathered outside the church in hope of receiving a hand out from some kind soul, the words again passed through his mind: "Blessed are the poor in spirit, for theirs is the kingdom of heaven." Suddenly, he knew what he had to do. He traded clothes with a filthy beggar and sat there for the rest of the day, begging for alms. He went on to give away all he had and live as a poor man, preaching wherever he went.

How often are we unwilling to give just a small amount to God? I know I don't use what I have as if it was a gift from God, for me to use to help others. God gave us our talents, money, personality, and everything else so that we can better glorify him and help others. Will you use your gifts to further God's work today?

~ Dave White

For the Good of Others

July 19

The Philippians did not hold their small earthly possessions with a tenacious grasp, but considered them as theirs only to use in doing good. – Sketches from the Life of Paul, pg. 175

Have you ever stopped to focus on just how blessed you are? Whether or not you are literally wealthy, God has blessed you with spiritual wealth in this world. He has given the chance of eternal life to you.

The things that we call our possessions in this world are not actually ours; whether many or few, they are all loaned to us by the grace of God. These things, which we cherish so much, are given to us so that through them we may bless others.

Christ came to earth for the purpose of dying on the cross. The God of the universe lowered Himself so far as to come into this repulsive world. He left His riches and honor, not only degrading Himself to our level, but also showing His amazing love for us by redeeming us on Calvary.

Christ took everything He had in Heaven and sacrificed it all to show us how much He really loves us. Is this love too amazing to show to others? Christ asks that we do something in return for what He did for us. Take all that you have, all the blessings that have been given to you, and use them for the good of those around you.

~ Leighton Sjoren

July 20

Give
Part 1

The revelation of the gospel should lead all who accept its sacred truths to imitate the great Exemplar in doing good, in blessing humanity, and in living a life of self- denial and benevolence.
– Sketches from the Life of Paul, pg. 175

In a little one-room apartment lived a little boy, Jimmy, and his sister, Lisa. They were very poor children and had hardly anything; but the one thing they did have was love. You see, Lisa was a very sick little girl, and every day Jimmy would take care of her. One day, as he was walking down the street, a nice woman stopped him and asked if he would like to come to a Christmas party. He wanted his sister to go too, but the woman said only one person per family was allowed to go. Finally, Jimmy decided to go to the party and told his sister that he would try to bring back something for her.

After playing games and eating dinner it came time for the gifts. There was a big Christmas tree with all sorts of wonderful things on it. Jimmy's eyes grew big. On the tree was a bright red fire engine. He had wanted one all his life, but never had the money to get one. Then his eyes caught sight of a beautiful doll. His sister had never had anything so pretty. Finally, his turn came and he went up to the tree.

Jimmy could have been thinking about himself and what he wanted the whole time, but no, he was thinking of his sister. Jesus' life was one of service and self- denial, and He was always thinking of the people around Him. Don't you want to be like that too?

~ Becky Brousson

July 21

Give
Part 2

I have shewed you all things, how that so laboring ye ought to support the weak, and to remember the words of the Lord Jesus, how he said, It is more blessed to give than to receive.
– Acts 20:35 KJV

Jimmy walked up to the tree, but instead of getting the red fire engine that he wanted, he reached for the doll. The other children started to snicker. "He's getting a doll, sissy, sissy," they taunted. His face started to turn red, and quickly he left. Inside himself, he felt happy with his decision. As he turned up the street to their apartment, his steps quickened. He opened the door to his sister's room and held the doll out to her. Her face lit up. "Is it for me?" she cried. Just then, there was a knock at the door. Jimmy went to open the door and was surprised to see the woman from the party standing there. She apologized for the other children's behavior and handed him a package. "The others didn't understand the situation, but they do now, and they wanted you to have this," she smiled. He excitedly opened the package and right inside there was the red fire engine he had wanted!

The thought of how much his sister would love the doll, overruled the insults coming from the other children. Today, why not experience Jimmy's selflessness and give to someone else, even when it seems like you might be missing out. Instead of missing out, you will experience more joy and the true meaning of the words of Christ, "It is more blessed to give than to receive."

~ Becky Brousson

July 22

The Widow Woman

They therefore, in their poverty, felt called out to help other churches more needy than themselves. – Sketches from the Life of Paul, pg. 175

A widow woman heard missionaries asking for funds. How she wished she had money to give. She prayed, "God, I will give you everything above my basic needs." When she went to work, she told her boss that she would pray for his business while she cleaned his house. After work, he went to her and asked, "Did you pray for me?"
"Yes," she replied.
"It's amazing! We made the best deals today! Pray for me every day!" Then he handed her a tip, and she tucked it away for the missionaries.

When another employer gave her money for a new coat, she gave that money to the missionaries also. Then her employer, wondering why she did not buy the new coat, came to the conclusion that her family must be starving. So, he went to the grocery store and requested that all her bills be charged to his account. When the widow discovered that her groceries were paid for, she sent the grocery money to the missionaries too.

When the missionaries came on furlough, they asked, "Who is the wealthy family that is supporting us every month?" The local pastor asked whose name was on the check, and the missionaries gave him the name of the widow. The pastor had a hard time believing this. Over the years, eight missionaries came and asked about the widow. The pastor calculated that she had given twenty thousand dollars a year to missions.

This widow found real joy in giving. Christ has said, "It is more blessed to give than to receive" (Acts 20:35 KJV). Try giving, and your joy will be full.

~ Jenny McCluskey

July 23

What are You Giving?

It is more blessed to give than to receive. – Acts 20:35 KJV

In the latter part of the 17th century, German preacher August H. Francke founded an orphanage to care for the homeless children of Halle. One day when Francke desperately needed funds to carry on his work, a destitute Christian widow came to his door begging for a ducat, a gold coin. Because of his financial situation, he politely but regretfully told her he couldn't help her. Disheartened, the woman began to weep. Moved by her tears, Francke asked her to wait while he went to his room to pray. After seeking God's guidance, he decided to trust the Lord to meet his own needs and gave her the money. Two mornings later, he received a letter of thanks from the widow. She explained that because of his generosity she had asked the Lord to shower the orphanage with gifts.

Later on the same day he'd received the letter, Francke received twelve ducats from a wealthy lady and two more from a friend in Sweden. He thought he had been amply rewarded for helping the widow, but he was soon informed that the orphanage was to receive five hundred gold pieces from the estate of Prince Lodewyk Van Wurtenburg! When he heard this, Francke wept in gratitude. In sacrificially providing for the needy widow, God had enriched him, and not allowed him to be impoverished.

At times, giving may seem impossible because of the position we are in, just like with August Francke. But our God will not leave us destitute, and if He asks us to give to someone less fortunate than ourselves, He will bless us in return. Paul tells us that it is better to give than to receive. Are you giving as God leads?

~ Jourdain Smith

July 24

Solace

But, amid all his persecutions and discouragements, he could rejoice in the consolation which he found in Christ. – Sketches from the Life of Paul, pg. 179

When having a bad day, have you ever felt vulnerable? Have you been stung by loneliness? Do you wonder if anybody understands your predicament?

Paul expressed, in his Second Epistle to the Corinthians his hope that the Corinthian church would not be forsaken in trials without consolation. He also related the desperation that he felt amidst the dangers and fears that he himself had faced. But, despite challenges, he found solace in God's comforting love enabling him to continue in his ministry.

During Queen Victoria's reign, the wife of a common laborer had miscarriaged, thus losing the baby. After hearing of the mother's loss, the Queen felt moved to express her sympathy. The Queen, who had experienced deep sorrow herself, later called on the grieving mother and spent some time with her. After the Queen left, the neighbors asked the mother what the Queen had said. "Nothing," she replied. "She simply put her hands on mine, and we silently wept together."

When days are bleak and upsetting, don't think that you are struggling alone. God is always there for you to comfort you with His unending love. In days when trials bombard your life, when you feel that nobody understands your struggles, go to the God who will always provide solace and strength.

~ David Ortiz

July 25

Can I Trust You?

His testimony had been straightforward, uniform, and harmonious and exemplified by his own life. – Sketches from the Life of Paul, pg. 181

Has someone you truly admired ever disappointed you? Imagine you met an apparently devoted Christian. You quickly became friends and were soon able to share almost anything with each other. Your new friend seemed so sincere and spiritual, and talking together just made all problems fade away.

Then, one day on your way to church, you had to take a detour through the slums of town. As you nervously drove down the road, you saw a group of disheveled people surrounding a rundown bar. Suddenly, you saw a familiar figure in the group, and as you looked closer, you realized that it was your dear friend staggering about in a drunken stupor. As you passed by, your eyes filled with tears, while the trust you had for your friend melted away.

Your friends here on this earth are only human. They don't always live up to what they preach. Jesus is the only One whom you can fully trust. Who He is today is who He will be tomorrow because He says, "I am the same, yesterday, today, and forever" (Hebrews 13:8 KJV). There is no "shadow of turning" with Him (James 1:17 KJV). Why don't you join me in asking God to help you live up to what you preach?

~ Melody Hyde

July 26

Your Call

Paul had been an ardent opposer of the gospel, but he had been conquered by light from Heaven, and had yielded himself a captive of Christ. – Sketches on the Life of Paul, pg. 182

Through the pitch-black night a sea captain saw a light dead ahead on a collision course with his ship. He quickly sent a signal: "Change your course ten degrees east."

The light signaled back: "Change your course ten degrees west."

Angry, the captain sent: "I'm a navy captain! Change your course, sir!"

"I'm a seaman, second class," came the reply. "Change your course, sir."

The captain became furious. "I'm a battle ship! I'm not changing course!"

There was one last reply. "I'm a lighthouse—your call."
The big navy ship slowly turned west and headed back out to the open sea, saving the captain and his men.

While Paul was zealously opposing the gospel, God had been sending him His "signals" to change course. Although at first Paul was proud and wouldn't recognize where the signals came from; when a light shone from heaven and Christ revealed Himself to Saul, he had a change of heart and altered his course.

God sends you and me signals as well, warning us of danger and encouraging us on our Christian walk. All we need to do is listen for His voice and act on the advice He gives. Won't you join me as I attempt to obey those signals today?

~ Rebecca Luchak

July 27

Reflect and Repent

He had delayed his coming, to give them time for reflection and repentance. But now all who continued in their course of error and sin, must be separated from the church of Christ.
– Sketches from the Life of Paul, pg. 184

Paul had heard of the struggles the Corinthian church was having. Many had strayed from the church, and some weren't truly converted to Christianity. Paul wrote them a letter in which he rebuked them, and this brought about reform in the church. Then he wrote another letter to them in which he commended them on their changed lives. In this second letter, he mentions that he had been planning to visit them again before going on to another city, but God had told him to wait a bit longer.

Why had it not been in God's time for Paul to visit them when he was planning to? Because the Corinthians were not ready to have him in their presence. It would have added more problems to the ones they already had. Because Paul waited until God said it was okay, they had their time of change and repentance.

It is kind of the same today as in Paul's day. There is a lot of trouble in this world and even in our church. Christ is delaying His return because we aren't ready for Him. We need to have a time of reflection, repentance, and consecration of our own hearts. This will lead to us being more determined to spread the gospel, which will help Jesus to come sooner because everyone will be ready for Him. It all starts with our own lives. Will you take the time and effort to reflect and repent?

~ Amy Windels

July 28

Metamorphosis

How widely different the appearance, purposes, and spirit of Saul and Paul! – Sketches from the Life of Paul, pg. 185

On a warm summer's day, a brightly colored caterpillar crawled along a branch. In just two short weeks it would eat many times its own body weight in milkweed pods. Its goal was to leave behind its cumbersome body in exchange for another. At last, it finds a branch to spin its home (called a chrysalis) for the next two weeks. At the end of this metamorphosis stage, the caterpillar emerges as a mature, beautiful butterfly. Possessing a marvelous pair of orange and black wings, it can now be free to fly to places it only dreamed of before.

When Saul found Jesus, his entire being was altered, and the difference between Saul, the persecutor, and Paul, the apostle, was as drastic as night and day. His priorities, motives, speech, and attitudes all gave way to the pervading influence of the One he formerly persecuted. Even his appearance was "widely different." Once Paul became the new creature God wanted him to be, the freedom to soar to new heights opened to him, and he couldn't stop telling others about it!

"Metamorphosis" can be defined as "a change of physical form, structure, or substance *especially by supernatural means*." God takes everything we are, and gives us something better in its place. With God's help, we become stronger and more beautiful. Our perceptions of who we are and our capabilities of what we can accomplish are heightened. So, crawl into the chrysalis. It may be dark, cramped, or get us into "sticky" situations, but when you emerge, you'll be able to spread your new wings into the breeze and derive flight from the transformation.

~ Jonathan Fink

July 29

At All Times

It is only by maintaining a close connection with God that his servants can hope to meet judiciously the trials and difficulties that still arise in the churches. – Sketches from the Life of Paul, pg. 190

The only way Paul was able to endure the trials he went through was by keeping his close connection with God. Paul talked to God daily and prayed earnestly for His help. He knew he didn't have the strength to face any trials on his own; no one does. If you have a close connection with God, He will give you the strength you need for whatever trials you may face.

There once was a family who had been memorizing Psalm 34:1 with their church family. The verse reads, "I will bless the Lord at all times: His praise shall continually be in my mouth." Sometime later, while they were traveling, this same family had a tragic car accident, leaving only the husband and his wife alive. Later, in the hospital, the man reached over, took hold of his wife's hand, and with tears in his eyes, said, "I *will* bless the Lord at all times: His praise shall continually be in my mouth."

If tragedy occurs in your home, whether a family member dies, or your best friend gets into a serious car accident, remember that you have a sympathizing Friend whom you can call on to comfort you and give you the strength you need to carry on.

~ Jennifer Atkins

July 30

A Cross to Bear

But when Christ was revealed to him, he at once renounced all his prospective honors and advantages, and devoted his life to the preaching of the cross. – Sketches from the Life of Paul, pg. 191.

"So likewise, whosoever he be of you that forsaketh not all that he hath, he cannot be my disciple" (Luke 14:33 KJV).

When a rich man came to Jesus and asked what he should do to enter into the kingdom of heaven, Jesus told him to sell all he had and give the money to the poor, and he would have treasure in heaven. After he had done this, he was to go and follow Jesus. The rich young man left because he was very wealthy and was not about to sell all he had to give to the poor. This man gave up the treasures of heaven for the rust of this earth. He was not willing to bear the cross.

I, personally, want to be nearer to God. As the song says:

"Nearer, my God, to Thee, nearer to Thee!
E'en though it be a cross that raiseth me,
Still all my song shall be, nearer, my God, to Thee."

God has a plan for you and me; He wants to give us all the wonderful things of heaven, but so many times we only want the things that are temporary. God has prepared a mansion just for you, with all your favorite colors. He has made a crown with you in mind. All He asks is for you to give him your heart. Will you give it today?

~ Jenny McCluskey

July 31

Too Great a Sacrifice

Such a religion required too great a sacrifice. – Sketches from the Life of Paul, pg. 192

Gideon's story is an inspiring one—one of victory through self-sacrifice and trust in God (Judges 6-8). When Gideon asked God for a sign, God answered his prayer to the very last detail. Gideon then set out with 32,000 men, but God knew that Israel would take all the credit if all these men went to fight. So God told Gideon to send thousands of the warriors home. Gideon couldn't quite comprehend how they would win with only three hundred men, but his faith was growing. Self was being sacrificed. As Gideon learned to trust God, he relied less on himself.

Paul came across many people who heard the words of truth, but rejected this truth because it "required too great a sacrifice." Being a Christian does require a great sacrifice, but it is not impossible. Heaven is not unreachable. God is extending to us a free gift of salvation, and it is completely attainable if we but trust Him. That's where the catch is. We can't do it by ourselves, so we have to learn to let God come into our lives and lead us. It might not always be comfortable. Dying to self is a painful procedure. Like Gideon, we might not understand what God is doing in our lives, but we can trust Him because He can see the bigger picture. Do not be discouraged! Being a Christian is a sacrifice, but it is not "too great a sacrifice." One day soon, you will look back at your time on earth and say, "Heaven is cheap enough!"

~ Melissa Butler

August 1

New Friends

Paul greatly desired to reach Jerusalem before the passover, as he would thus have an opportunity to meet the people who came from all parts of the world to attend the feast. – Sketches from the Life of Paul, pg. 194

When young people visit my church, they sometimes join my youth class. Unfortunately, the tendency for me is to smile, politely say hello, and then ignore them for the rest of the time. I don't really want to leave my comfortable circle of friends and reach out to the "strangers."

Paul was completely the opposite. He wanted to join in the Passover at Jerusalem for the exact purpose of meeting new people and developing friendships with them. He wasn't afraid to leave his comfort zone because he knew that these friendships could yield eternal results; those people that Paul befriended and won to Christ could return to their home countries and share the Good News with thousands more.

When visitors come to see Fountainview, we students try to develop a friendship with them and make them feel at home so that they'll come here for school. Why don't we do this for Christ? We should be developing friendships with the strangers that cross our paths so we may draw them to the Savior. Are you ready to make some new friends? The effort and apparent discomfort will be worth it!

~ Cara Dewsberry

August 2

In the Face of Opposition

His strong statement, "There is neither Greek nor Jew, circumcision nor uncircumcision," was regarded by his enemies as daring blasphemy. – Sketches from the Life of Paul, pg. 195

If there were two things that characterized Jews around the time of Christ, their hang-ups on legalism and Jewish superiority would top the list. Paul openly challenged both of these. This was an exceptionally daring move, considering the violence most Sanhedrin members showed towards fledgling Christians. Paul ultimately gave His life for stating the truth in the face of opposition.

Paul demonstrated a great example of speaking truth despite opposition. This is more than just standing up for what is right. He publicly announced to the world that they were all wrong! And look at the change he made. Without these people of standing throughout history, today we'd all be sitting back and going with the flow. The world would either be locked in Judaism, the Dark Ages, or in a dictatorship.

Dead fish go with the flow—but I'm not dead yet. And neither are you. Speak out for what is right. Other's apostasy is no excuse for your silence. Maybe no one will listen. Maybe no one will care. They wouldn't anyways if you hadn't mentioned it. But maybe, just maybe, your determination will become the catalyst for a needed change. And maybe, like Paul, you will shake the world.

~ Robby Folkenberg

August 3

Commune with God

But Paul, passing through the affrighted company, clasped him in his arms, and sent up an earnest prayer that God would restore the dead to life. The prayer was granted. – Sketches from the Life of Paul, pg. 197

Since you are reading this devotional book, I'm going to assume you pray. Generally a non-praying person would also be a non-devotional-reading person. So by the end of the day, let's assume that you will have prayed five times. Once when you got out of bed or had morning worship, once at each meal, and once at evening worship or just before you went to bed. That's five times in a day that you will have talked to God! When you look at it from the perspective that you've communicated with the Creator of everything five times a day, you realize what an incredible privilege it is!

Heaven's gates are always opened for incoming prayers. We serve a King who loves to commune, not just communicate, with his subjects! So, from this perspective, why pray only five times a day? Why not pray ten times a day? If God loves to commune with us, let's spend our whole day with Him. If only our lives were constant teleconferences with heaven, instead of just quickly dropping a line now and then.

When Eutychus fell out of the window and died, Paul sent up an earnest prayer to the God he was so connected with, and God granted his prayer! Christ longs to commune with you and assist you today. He's hurt when He gets left outside the door of your heart, or when you invite him in, but shove Him in the corner for most of the day. It's time for you to get to know your guest.

~ Robby Folkenberg

August 4

Brought Back to Life

Trouble not yourselves, for his life is in him. – Acts 20:10 KJV

While awaiting fair weather for his journey to Troas, Paul spent time with his Christian brothers. The grim news of his coming departure brought together a large crowd of devoted believers.

There was a young man by the name of Eutychus who attentively listened to the teachings of Paul, but as the night drew on he began to tire. While slumbering in the windowsill, he slipped into a deep sleep and suddenly fell from the window into the courtyard below. Finding him dead in the court, Paul sent an earnest prayer to God to restore life to the young man, and by the power of God he was restored to life. Over the sound of mourning and lamenting, Paul's voice was heard saying, "Trouble not yourselves, for his life is in him."

This story is one that is often the story of our Christian walk. We start out fresh and vitalized, ready to hear and do the will of God. Then, as time goes by we find ourselves falling asleep and drifting ever so slowly away from Christ. Then, we fall. We are taken as dead, but we have the promise of life from the only One who can give it. He will pick you up off the ground and breathe the breath of life into you again.

~ Leighton Sjoren

August 5

Lame to Limber

The minister of Christ is not to present to the people those truths that are the most pleasing, while he withholds those which might cause them pain. – Sketches from the Life of Paul, pg. 200

On a bus tour in New Zealand, excited passengers gazed at hundreds of sheep crossing the road ahead. A shepherd ran here and there, trying to keep all the sheep together and making sure that none got lost. However, one little lamb kept trying to run away from the flock. Every time the shepherd would guide it back to the others it would take off across the plains. The tourists were shocked and outraged to see the shepherd finally grab the lamb and snap its foreleg in two. The bus driver restrained them by saying, "Wait! You see this pain that has just been caused; but while the animal's leg is healing, the shepherd carries it everywhere with him. For two months, it does not leave his shoulders. He splints the leg and comforts the lamb and when it's finally healed, it is the closest to the shepherd of all the sheep."

Paul, in his church building endeavors knew that ingesting only the sweet things of the Word caused "truth" decay. There are hard and painful truths in the Christian walk, and sometimes God has to allow hurtful things to get our attention and devotion. We won't be able to get along without Him so He carries us, and when the ordeal is over, we'll be closer to Christ. Does He do this because He hates us? No, but rather because He loves us. With His tender love, we go from crippled to leaping, attached to the One who loves us so much.

~ Jonathan Fink

August 6

Stolen!

It is while the husbandman sleeps that tares are sown; while the shepherds are neglecting their duty, the wolf finds entrance to the fold. – Sketches from the Life of Paul, pg. 201

Years ago, there was a family who went to Disney World on vacation. While enjoying the fascinating scenes around them, the parents turned their backs on their baby in the stroller. When they turned around again, their baby was gone. The family was terrified and searched everywhere, but to no avail. Heartbroken, they finally decided to go back to their motel. When they arrived, an older couple came up to them and said, "You look worried. Is there anything wrong?" When the distraught couple informed them that their child had been kidnapped, the other couple replied, "Oh, no! Would you like us to watch your kids for you while you go and search some more?" Unfortunately the couple accepted the offer and left their kids while they went in search of their baby. When they got back to the motel, they found no older couple and no kids. In watching the news the next morning, the family found that they were not the only ones suffering from the loss of family members.

It is when the shepherd turns his back on his flock that the wolf snatches a lamb. The shepherd must be watching his flock at all times, for the wolf comes when he least expects it. Your flock is your family, friends, neighbors, church family, and work or school associates. Don't let the devil distract you and cause you to turn your back on your "flock."

~ Jennifer Atkins

August 7

Firm Foundation

But let every man take heed how he buildeth thereupon. For other foundation can no man lay than that is laid, which is Jesus Christ.
– 1 Corinthians 3:10-11 KJV

The Leaning Tower of Pisa in Italy is going to fall. Scientists travel yearly to measure the building's slow descent. They report that the 179-foot tower moves about one-twentieth of an inch a year, and is now seventeen feet out of plumb. They further estimate that by the year 2011 the 836-year-old tower will have leaned too far and will collapse onto the nearby ristorante, where scientists now gather to discuss their findings. Quite significantly, the word "Pisa" means "marshy land," which gives some clue as to why the tower began to lean even before it was completed. Also, its foundation is only ten feet deep!

In the Bible, Jesus shares a story about two men who had to choose where to build their houses. One man chose to build his house on the sand. When the rains and the floods came, his house was washed away, because he didn't build it on a firm foundation. Whereas the other man built his house on the rock, and it stood when the floods and the rains came.

The Tower of Pisa took 177 years to complete; yet it was still defective when completed. The tower's shallow foundation of only ten feet, combined with the unstable soil, led to its current state.

Our spiritual foundation needs to be solidly rooted in the Rock of Ages. Are you going to be firmly grounded in Christ or shallowly grounded in this world? Where does your foundation lie?

~ Jourdain Smith

August 8

True Representative

As representatives of Christ, they are to maintain the honor of His name. – Sketches from the Life of Paul, pg. 201

One day, a lady was running late for work. She came to a stoplight and found herself behind an old man. When the light turned green, the old man did not move. The lady started to honk her horn, but the old man did not move. She became increasingly angry and, rolling down her window, started to yell at the old man. Finally, the old man heard some noise, realized that the light had turned green, and he slowly drove through. What the lady did not realize was that there was a police officer behind her, observing her every action. The police officer pulled her over and told her that she was being arrested. When she asked why, the police officer said that she was in a stolen car. She protested that this was really her car. The police officer said that there was a sticker on her bumper that read, "Honk if you are a Christian." He said that if it were her car, she would be acting like a Christian, just as the sticker said she was. How embarrassing this must have been for the lady, to be shown that she was not acting like the kind of person she said she was.

We do the same thing as this lady. We claim to be "Christians," yet you cannot tell the difference between us and other people. Our actions and our words are no different from those of non-Christians. If you are Christ's representative, you will not want to bring dishonor to His name.

~ Jeremy Grabiner

August 9

A Willing Captive

But the same Spirit which had warned him of afflictions, bonds, and imprisonment, still urged him forward, a willing captive. – Sketches from the Life of Paul, pg. 203

With this warning, God showed the intense love He had for His servant, Paul. Yet in spite of the warning, Paul held fast to the Holy Spirit's leading. Though his heart was filled with anxiety and sadness for the brethren he left behind, he pressed on to Jerusalem. Imprisonment did not scare him because he was following Christ. He exhibited a humble, submissive spirit to the Holy Spirit's direction.

We too need to cultivate in our hearts this compliant spirit. As God's will is clearly shown to us at each crossroad, we must choose to follow the signs. This will mold and shape our characters after Christ. My problem has been being willing to be placed in the mold. Sometimes, I feel like the shape I'm in is the way I want to be. At other times, I feel that I am too impure to be set in the mold. My greatest fear, though, is the fiery furnace, the trials and difficult circumstances that, like Paul, we must face. The truth is, we need to be willing to be made willing. When we place our lives in the crucible, we will be purified and refined. We will no longer fear for we will not be alone. Christ is leading us.

Christ has a plan for your life just as He did for Paul's. If you want that plan to be unveiled, then give your will to God. He has a crucial message for you to share. Do not harden your heart while God is trying to melt it. Jesus has demonstrated His love and care for you through the life story of Paul. The Holy Spirit will burden your heart with a mission if you will but lay your life down. Become a willing captive to God.

~ Buddy Taylor

August 10

Giving All for Christ

...One by one they laid at the feet of James the offerings which the Gentile churches had freely given, although often from their deepest poverty. – Sketches from the Life of Paul, pg. 209

Ever since I can remember, I liked material things. When I was little, it was little things. I loved to pore over the "Wish Book" Christmas catalog and tell my mommy all the things I longed to have. The things I desired grew bigger and more expensive as I grew older. I wanted a remote-controlled airplane, an iPod, brand-name clothes, an apple computer, a mountain bike, snowmobile, car, and the list went on. E-bay became my wish book catalog. I pored over things for hours. My dad and mom wisely didn't get me everything I desired but sometimes gave me things that were not exactly what I wanted, because they cost less. I tried to be grateful, but inside I still wanted the real thing! Often getting what I wanted fed my desire for looking for something better.

When I read about the early Christians, whose only desire was to see the church grow instead of to buy things for themselves, I think, *Man, I have tons of stuff. Why can't I give up some things for Christ?* It was in their deepest poverty that the believers freely poured out offerings. Their love for Jesus Christ was so great, that they didn't even consider things for themselves. They were willing to sacrifice all for others. The first clue that the Holy Spirit was in their lives was when they took their eyes off themselves and looked to see how they could fill the needs of others. Wouldn't that be cool if all of us could do that too? Think of all that would get accomplished. Let's give all for Christ.

~ Joey Heagy

August 11

Tangible Proof

Here was tangible proof of the love and sympathy felt by these new disciples... – Sketches from the Life of Paul, pg. 209

Imagine that you have a friend who claims to love you dearly. However, as your friendship progresses, you begin to see a pattern in your friend's treatment of you. When you ask your friend to do you a favor, he ignores your request; but if you ask him not to do something, he does it anyway. He also expects you to do him favors even though he won't do anything for you. When in public, your friend claims to love and value you; but you start to wonder if he really means it. After all, he isn't giving you any proof that he is really your friend.

Do you realize that God deals with this very problem? So many who claim to be Christians do not give any proof of it in their lives. I find myself requesting many things of God; yet when He asks something of me or commands me not to do something, I try to squirm around His words and find a way of doing what I want anyhow.

We are saved by faith in Christ; but if there is no concrete evidence of our faith, what is the point of having it? James says, "Even so faith, if it hath not works, is dead, being alone" (James 2:17 KJV). I want God to change my heart and help me give "tangible proof" of my love for Him through obedience and submission to His will.

~ Cara Dewsberry

August 12

Multiplied Money

The liberal contributions from the new churches he had raised up, testified to the power of the truth. – Sketches from the Life of Paul, pg. 211

My family and I knew we where going to India, but did not have all the funds for the tickets. Although our church had given much, it was still not enough. We needed five thousand dollars; we only had three thousand. Our travel agent called my mom and asked her if she had the money for the tickets. My mom said, "Yes, but I don't know what pocket God has it in."

The agent told her to come quickly to his office to pay for the tickets. All the way to the office, my mom was praying that God would provide. When she arrived, she started counting. She would count, and then the agent would count. One thousand, two thousand, three thousand…then her heart began to beat faster. She reached into her purse and found more money! She kept counting…four thousand. She reached into her purse, and again there was more money. It all added up to $4,950. Then my mom prayed, "God, why did you stop?" The travel agent asked, "What church do you belong to?"

"I'm a Seventh-day Adventist!" my mom replied.

"Your church is very generous! You should stay with it. Don't worry about the last fifty dollars, tomorrow God will provide."

The next day, the rest of the money arrived in the mail.

Whether you give time, money, or talents to God, He will use it in a powerful way.

~ Jenny McCluskey

August 13

Past Mistakes and Present Benefit

Now was the golden opportunity for these leading men to frankly confess that God had wrought through Paul, and that they were wrong in permitting the reports of his enemies to create jealousy and prejudice against him. – Sketches from the Life of Paul, pg. 211

When Oliver Cromwell ruled England, a shortage in currency occurred. There was no silver to make more, so Cromwell sent representatives out into all the country to procure the needed silver. Soon the report came back. The only silver left was contained in cathedrals, in the statues of saints. To Cromwell, the answer to this predicament was a no-brainer. It was time for the saints of old to be melted down and made into currency!

You see, sometimes you have to get rid of the relics that serve no good purpose, that gloomily decorate the courtyard of your life. Let me illustrate it this way. Being wrong about something is usually difficult to admit to. My brother and I love birding, and when my brother saw a Mountain Bluebird the other day, it dominated our discussions. I insisted that it was a Lazuli Bunting, but Randy refused to budge. Eventually he proved to me the accuracy of his identification, and I had to sheepishly own up to his superior birding capabilities.

Being wrong is a phenomenon, that if I'm not mistaken, we will all go through at some point in time. Praise God that when we sin, He can take the situation and use it for His glory anyways. Like those statues in Cromwell's day, our sins too often litter our pasts, because we have not, in humility, made confession. If we would but bring them before God, He could take those mistakes and cash them in for His glory.

~ Robby Folkenberg

August 14

Pencils

Though some of these men wrote under the inspiration of the Spirit of God, yet when not under its direct influence they sometimes erred.
– Sketches from the Life of Paul, pg. 214

Once there was a shop that was well known for its woodcarvings. Each day, the carpenter would cut and chisel formless trees into gorgeous furniture. One day, the carpenter decided to carve two beautiful pencils and give them to two fine artists, so that they might use the pencils to draw uplifting pictures. So, with this idea in mind, the carpenter started to work. Selecting only the best materials, he chiseled and cut the wood. Though it was hard and intricate work, the carpenter finally finished. In excitement, he mailed one pencil to each artist. As the carpenter expected, one artist used the pencil to sketch drawings that uplifted the sad and healed the broken hearted. However, the other artist used his pencil to sketch drawings that crushed and disheartened others.

Often times in our society, we get so caught up with the work we have to do that we forget there is a battle being fought because of us. The angels of light and darkness encompass you every moment, each desiring possession of your heart. Though both sides are desperate to possess you, they can't do that until you allow them to enter through your words or actions. Do you realize that whenever you lie, steal, or hurt other people, you are actually being controlled by Satan? We are just pencils, who sketch according to the artist we allow to hold us. So, will you let Satan bring down people through you? Or will you let Jesus uplift people through you?

~ David Chang

August 15

Insecure

I will praise thee; for I am fearfully and wonderfully made: marvellous are thy works; and that my soul knoweth right well.
– Psalm 139:14 KJV

I grew up in Africa from the time I was four until I was fourteen, when we moved to Tennessee. I was scared about moving, going to a new place, and making new friends. What would they think of me? Would I fit in or would I be an outcast? These questions flooded my mind. I started to care a lot about what other people thought about me. I focused all my attention on what I looked like and what I did. I was insecure.

One day I came upon this verse (Psalm 139:14), and I realized how ridiculous I was acting. I had not been aware that God made me the way I was for a purpose. I spent all my time trying to impress other people, and I did not focus on my relationship with God. That day, I asked God to help me to focus my attention more on Him and less on what other people thought of me.

Many people are unhappy with themselves. They try to find happiness by being like someone else. The secret to happiness is accepting yourself. If you want to be happy, be grateful with who you are and how God made you. You are "fearfully and wonderfully made."

~ Jeremy Grabiner

August 16

Rejected!

Priests and people were actuated by the same Satanic spirit that moved them thirty years before to clamor for the blood of the Son of God. From the staircase and from the crowd below again echoed the deafening shout, "Away with him! Away with him!" – Sketches from the Life of Paul, pg. 218

Have you ever felt like you were unwanted, or that nobody cared about you? Have you ever thought that people didn't want you around because you were so different from everyone else?

There was a man that went to church one Sabbath dressed like a homeless person from off the street. His clothes were dirty, and his face was unshaven. No one welcomed him or even offered him a seat. When the service was over, he got up to leave, but a lady stopped him and invited him to her house for lunch. When she did, the man told her that he was her pastor. He had not gone to the church for a while, and when he did, he disguised himself to see how the church members would treat him.

When Paul was doing the work of God, priests and people wanted him dead. They hated him for who he was. But Paul kept his focus on Christ and the example that He gave when He was on earth. Christ did only good, but still people rejected Him.

Christ never promised that our Christian walk would be easy. If you stand up for Him, people will reject you. But don't let that discourage you; after all, Christ could have rejected you, but He didn't. Will you stand up for Christ?

~ Jennifer Atkins

August 17

Be Still

Be still, and know that I am God. – Psalms 46:10 KJV

    Imagine with me a scene in which you are standing alone in the middle of New York City. All of a sudden, the whole crowd of people in the street starts rushing towards you screaming and yelling. How would you feel? You have no clue why these people are mad at you or what you did wrong to them. Could you stay calm if that happened to you?

    The whole crowd was rushing towards one old man. Anger, frustration, jealousy, bitterness, hatred… Their evil faces appeared like the face of Satan, and it was he who was leading the crowd. They were determined to kill Paul; they were not going to miss the chance. If the Roman soldiers had not been there to stop the crowd, Paul would have been torn in pieces. But the hand of God was with Paul, and Paul knew that the "angels of Heaven were about him." His mind was with God, and God's spirit was upon him. Paul remained calm, though crowds of angry people were running towards him.

    We are so fragile without God. We cannot even feed ourselves without His mercy. Yet, our recognition of our need of God is incredibly poor. We may have lots of money; we may have a place to live; we may have jobs to provide for ourselves. But, if we were put in the situation where we would have to stand alone just like Paul, could we stay calm? How much do we need the power of God? "Be still, and know that I am God: I will be exalted among the heathen, I will be exalted in the earth."

~ Ryo Fusamae

August 18

Assurance

In the midst of the tumult the apostle remained calm and self-possessed. His mind was stayed upon God, and he knew that angels of Heaven were about him. – Sketches from the Life of Paul, pg. 218

Once there was a boy named Joe. He went to work on a farm for the summer, and when he was hired, he told his manager, "I can sleep through windy nights." The manager wondered what he meant, but didn't really think anything about it. Then one night, it was extremely windy. The farmer woke up worried and went to check the barn, to make sure everything was okay. To his surprise, he found all the animals safe and everything in its place. When he got back to the house, he went to check on Joe to see if he had woken up with all the noise. However, to his surprise, he found him sound asleep. In the morning, he asked Joe about it. Joe told him that, because he knew he had made sure everything in the barn was safe and secure before he went to sleep, he knew everything would be okay, no matter what happened.

When the winds of life seem like they will blow us over, if we believe that Jesus is in control, we will not be afraid. No matter happens, we can have the assurance that Jesus will be with us through any trial, any circumstance. Joe knew that he had made everything secure, and he didn't have to worry. If we know that we are right with God, even the thought of death will not frighten us. Don't you want to have the same serenity Joe had? You can. Give your life fully and completely to Jesus and trust in Him.

~ Becky Brousson

August 19

Ruling Peace

The apostle's bearing was calm and firm. The peace of Christ, ruling in his heart, was expressed upon his countenance. But his look of conscious innocence offended his accusers... – Sketches from the Life of Paul, pg. 222

We are told that, during the time of the end, we will face many persecutions and trials for the name of Christ. Just as Paul was, we might be arrested and brought before the Council, but we have the same assurance that he did. When we come into trials we can look to Paul's example, which mirrors the example of Jesus, and thus we may set our standards.

Paul's appearance was calm, steadfast, and showed no trace of fear. He calmly supported his position by stating facts rather than by showing emotion. This upset his accusers so much that the high priest ordered him to be smitten upon the mouth. Being under the influence of the Holy Spirit, Paul exclaimed, "God shall smite thee, thou whited wall, for sittest thou to judge me after the law, and commandest me to be smitten contrary to the law?" (Acts 23:3 KJV). This rebuke was similar to the prophetic denunciation pronounced by Jesus at the hypocrisy of the Jews, and bystanders viewed it as one of the greatest insults possible to the high priest.

Where is your loyalty? Do you submit to Christ, or do you submit to the taunting of Satan through the voice of men in high places? When you trust in God, your confidence will show through, and you can be assured that this confidence is one that cannot be defeated.

~ Leighton Sjoren

August 20

A United Front

The two parties began to dispute among themselves, and thus the strength of their opposition against Paul was broken. – Sketches from the Life of Paul, pg. 223

As Paul stood there, in front of that vast, murderous throng of "religious" leaders, one could see a slight smile creeping over his face. Then "he shouted out in the council... 'I am on trial concerning the hope of the resurrection of the dead!'" (Acts 23:6 NET). The whole council went into an uproar, "For the Sadducees say there is no resurrection" (verse 8) while the Pharisees confess that there is. This caused hatred between the two parties that was so strong that they lost sight of their goal. By squabbling, they lost their one greatest opportunity to destroy their strongest opponent. By losing their united front, they lost everything.

We are part of a community of believers, and we too have a united front to maintain. By bickering among ourselves, we give opportunity for non-believers to justify their rejection of the truth. Paul exhorts us to "agree with one another" and to "live in peace" with our fellow believers (2 Corinthians 13:11 NET). Whenever you squabble over petty differences and cultural ideas, you lose sight of the main goal. Differences of opinion and rebuking of sins are to be done in private, while the gospel is to be proclaimed openly. God's truth gains priority over all of the opinions of men. Learn to love the weaker brother and always remember your main goal, "to seek and to save the lost" (Luke 19:10 NET).

~ Luke Gonzalez

August 21

Light

The future seemed enveloped in darkness. – Sketches from the Life of Paul, pg. 224

Bruce Olson was a missionary among the Motilone people in Columbia. They were a primitive tribe. He lived among them, winning their confidence and teaching them better health principles, agricultural practices, and naturally, the gospel. One of his close friends, Bobby, became a Christian. It looked like their work was advancing. Then, Bobby was murdered by farmers who wanted to take over the Motilone land. When they gave Bobby a funeral, the village came out at night and prayed. They expressed how dark it was, how a beautiful fruit and flower was destroyed. It took Bruce several weeks before he could leave the area, as the murderers were hunting for him as well. However, it turned out that instead of ending their work, this tragedy expanded it. They began teaching dozens of warring tribes in the area, and having a tremendous impact on the people. Bobby's death became a catalyst for encouraging other Motilone to use their talents for God's work.

If you are going through a difficult place right now, and it feels like your future is bleak, and God is far away, be assured that He is standing in the shadows. Just as He knows about the sparrow, He knows all about you and He cares. If you commit and trust your life to God every day, He will be a light that leads you out of darkness.

~ Jeremy Grabiner

August 22

God is Always There

The Lord was not unmindful of his servant. He had guarded him from the murderous throng in the temple courts, he had been with him before the Sanhedrim council, he was with him in the fortress and was pleased to reveal himself to his faithful witness. – Sketches from the Life of Paul, pg. 224

Do you remember the last time you felt all alone? The last time for me was the summer of 2008. I missed the spiritual setting at Fountainview Academy, and I felt very discouraged. Like a person blind in darkness, I was groping along. Finally, I just plopped down on the empty ground. This is a picture of how I felt during that moment. When we feel the most discouraged or lonely, that is when God draws nearest. Although I felt so alone at that time, I know as I look back that God was right there beside me.

Paul, a mere human being had the escort of the King of Kings. Whether he felt it at the time or not, God was with him. As Paul was standing up for God, God was standing up for His faithful servant. Everyone will have one or more moments of despair and loneliness, but the God of Paul will always be there. Does it sound too good to be true? Try standing up for Him, and He will keep His promise to stand up for you.

~ Sharon Jeon

August 23

Time Won't Wait

It was important that no time be lost. – Sketches from the Life of Paul, pg. 227

Have you ever taken the time to calculate that each normal year contains 31,536,000 seconds, or 525,600 minutes, or 8,760 hours, or 365 days, or 52 weeks, or 12 months? You may never have realized that what your year consists of is really seconds; and that even a little moment makes a great difference.

For Paul it was important that "no time be lost." He needed to escape before his adversaries captured him; so, he had not a moment to waste. We also have enemies who lurk around every corner. I have found for myself that the devil knows that I'm easily distracted, and if he can't get me distracted, then he will do all in his power to keep me busy doing things that have no eternal value.

We need to realize that the devil is trying to get us to waste our time and not spend it with Jesus. For example, if you were to waste five minutes everyday for a year, you would have lost about thirty hours. Imagine what you could do with all that time! We never will know exactly when our time will come to an end, so we need to realize the importance of the time we have and maximize our opportunities.

~ Melody Hyde

August 24

In the Light

The widow of Sarepta and Naaman the Syrian had lived up to all the light they had. Hence they were accounted more righteous than God's chosen people who had backslidden from Him, and sacrificed principle to convenience and worldly honor. – Sketches from the Life of Paul, pg. 229

The other day, I was reading the fine-print instructions of a test I was about to take. If I violated any of the rules, I would get a score of zero. I was very careful, while taking the test, not to look at my classmate's paper or do anything else that might cause me to fail.

If I was so careful to follow the rules for a test, I should be so much more careful when it comes to heavenly matters. I should be even more vigilant when following God's rules because they are a life and death matter. God holds us accountable for the light that we receive. If we have never heard about the Ten Commandments, He does not require us to keep them, for it would be impossible to know what He expects of us. But the Bible is clear concerning what He does require of us; we must live up to all the light we have. 1 John 1:7 tells us that "…If we walk in the light as He is in the light, we have fellowship with one another, and the blood of Jesus Christ His Son cleanses us from all sin" (NKJV). The widow of Sarepta and Naaman were heathen people, but they lived up to every ray of light they had. You, most likely, have been given more truth than they were. Are you living up to it?

~ Melissa Butler

August 25

The Rose

He declared his mission to comfort, bless, and save the sorrowing and the sinful… – Sketches from the life of Paul, pg. 229

    Once there was a little seed planted in a garden. Eventually, the seed sprouted, put out leaves, and became a gorgeous rose. The rose had a lovely fragrance that attracted many bees and butterflies. But, one day, a mighty storm tore through the garden. The wind whipped the trees in every direction, and all the animals hid in fear. Helplessly, the rose stood against the fury of the wind and miraculously the rose survived.

    However, the storm made a bigger impact on the rose than it thought. Slowly the rose started to grow thorns, and what was once a resting place for bees became dangerous ground for them. The thorns were sharp, piercing, and caused pain to any animal that came too close. So, one by one, the animals and insects left the rose until it was all by itself. The rose wept bitterly because the thorns continued to grow, and it couldn't do anything about it. All hope seemed to have disappeared. Then, one day, in the midst of despair, a gardener came and showed love to the rose. He willingly allowed the thorns to pierce him so he could get close to the rose. The gardener continued to manifest his love for the rose until the rose had lost all its thorns and had become perfect again.

    Like the gardener who acted so lovingly towards the rose, Jesus has the same affection for you. Whenever you feel like you have messed up, just remember, though you have pierced him, He has no evil thoughts towards you. He looks past your thorny, sinful heart and sees the beautiful, perfect person you can become.

~ David Chang

August 26

To be Trusted

God sent Elijah to the widow of Sarepta, because he could not trust him with Israel. – Sketches from the Life of Paul, pg. 230

What a tragedy! A man of God could not find refuge among the professed people of God. What was the cause? It was a matter of trust. God's children had broken the trust of their Father. If they could not be trusted by God, how then could they be trusted with His appointed servant?

Humans have a desire to be trusted. But if we are not trustworthy with those around us, how can we be called "trusted of God"? Trust does not come from words but from actions. Failing to carry through from what we say to what we do, breaks trust. In our lives, we must have a commitment of fulfillment. By being a child of God, we have entered into a covenant with God. We have given Him our word. But when we do not follow through on our word, we are breaking our covenant. This was the state of the Israelites. They had broken their covenant with God and thus lost the trust of their Maker.

The beauty however, is that God never breaks His side of the covenant. He always fulfills His commitments to us; and one of these commitments is to love us, even while we are still untrustworthy (Romans 5:8). There is then hope for you to regain the trust of God and to be trusted with His blessing. While we cannot force others to trust us, we may live our lives worthy of being trusted. This may not always cause human beings to trust you, but God will never hold His trust back when you have committed your life to Him. Today, renew your promise to live a life of trust through the power of God.

~ Buddy Taylor

August 27

Who Am I?

The great work for us as Christians is not to criticize the character and motives of others, but to closely examine our own heart and life…
– Sketches from the Life of Paul, pg. 232

    I looked with disgust in the direction of a teenage girl, whose entrance into church had made quite a stir. She was wearing huge pearls around her neck, and her bright red toenails peeked out from five-inch heels. Her lipstick matched her toenails, and her hair was half black and half blonde. She was covered in tattoos and piercings. I didn't want to talk to her, and no one else in the room made a move to welcome her either. *Why does she even come?* I wondered.

    I had lost the focus of Christianity: Christ. This girl had come to church to worship, and who was I to judge her? *My* business was to worry about my own heart. I should have been asking myself why *I* kept coming to church. Jesus warned that we should take the plank of wood out of our own eye before we try to point out the speck in another's eye. It's a sobering thought to think that her problems may have been specks while mine were planks.

    The Bible tells us that even though we may look at the outside, God looks at the heart. It's not my place to criticize others' intentions because I cannot see into their hearts. My work is not to dissect their every move and motive, but rather to examine my own heart and life. My sole purpose is to make sure that I am in close connection with Jesus. What is your purpose today?

~ Melissa Butler

August 28

Thomas, Thomas

Satan is constantly working through his agents to dishearten and destroy those whom God has chosen to accomplish a great and good work. They may be ready to sacrifice even their own life for the advancement of the cause of Christ, yet the great deceiver will suggest doubts... – Sketches from the Life of Paul, pg. 232

Let me meet you on the mountain, Lord,
Just once.
You wouldn't have to burn a whole bush.
Just a few smoking branches
And I would surely be ...your Moses.

Let me meet you on the water, Lord,
Just once.
It wouldn't have to be on White Rock Lake.
Just on a puddle after the annual Dallas rain
And I would surely be...your Peter.

Let me meet you on the road, Lord,
Just once.
You wouldn't have to blind me on North Central Expressway.
Just a few bright lights on the way to chapel
And I would surely be...your Paul.

Let me meet you, Lord,
Just once.
Anywhere. Anytime.
Just meeting you in the Word is so hard sometimes
Must I always be...your Thomas?

God has a work for each of us to do, but sometimes we doubt God's power. We allow the devil to destroy our hope and courage. God has promised in His word, "I will never leave thee, nor forsake thee" (Hebrews 13:5 KJV). If we remember God's promises when we are ready to doubt, He will lead us through. "All His biddings are enablings" (Christ's Object Lessons, pg. 332). Are you going to let God enable you?

~ Jourdain Smith

August 29

Love Your Neighbor as Yourself

The great work for us as Christians is not to criticize the character and motives of others, but to closely examine our own heart and life, to jealously guard ourselves against the suggestions of Satan. We should bear in mind that it is not the hearers of the law that are justified before God, but the doers of the law. – Sketches from the Life of Paul, pg. 232

Has anyone ever put you down or criticized you for anything? Maybe it's because you move more slowly than they do, or are not as smart. How does it make you feel?

Well, I know how it feels, because I've experienced it. I've had someone tell me that I was slow and stupid. I already thought that about myself, so it made me feel even worse when someone actually told me. You don't realize how much you can impact someone's life by saying unkind words to them, unless you've experienced it yourself. If you're ever unkind to someone, remember that you're not only hurting that person, but Christ; for He says in Matthew 25:40, "Inasmuch as ye have done it unto one of the least of these my brethren, ye have done it unto me" (KJV).

You might think it's the person who is treated unkindly that will hurt the worst, but in the end, it is really the one who did it who will hurt the worst. So, make it your goal to treat everyone in a kind and loving way, for that is how Christ treats us.

~ Jennifer Atkins

August 30

Character Development

Every one has a work to do to learn the lessons of justice, humility, patience, purity, and love. These traits of character are more precious in the sight of our Lord than offerings of gold or silver. They are more acceptable to him than the most costly sacrifice. – Sketches from the Life of Paul, pg. 233

For some reason my mom or dad could always tell when I was grumpy, and they would never let me stay that way for long. They had what they called a "grizzly run," which covered a long distance trail of ups and downs throughout our acreage, and I had to run this trail to get rid of all the "grizzlies" in my heart. My parents hoped that I would get to the point of exhaustion and be open to letting God help me choose to have a different attitude. This was one of their ways to ensure character development in their children. They told me that my character was the only thing I could take with me to heaven. But, what is the character? It is actually very simple; it is our private thoughts and feelings.

My mom told me about her friend who claimed it was easy being a Christian on the outside but impossible on the inside. But, the inside is where Jesus resides. When we cooperate with Him, He changes our characters on the inside, and the results automatically flow to the outside. Getting ready for Jesus to come is the process of divine character development. My mom's friend may have thought that it was easy to look like a Christian, but it is in a crisis that our true characters are revealed. If she had been subjected to a crisis in her life, the bad fruits she developed in her private thoughts and feelings would be opened to the whole world.

God chose for us this special work of developing our characters while here on earth. He knows that it is the only way to guarantee us lasting joy and happiness. My desire is to have the fruits that will stand through a crisis and show the whole world of my love for Jesus.

~ Joey Heagy

August 31

God's Grade School

Every one has a work to do to learn the lessons of justice, humility, patience, purity and love. These traits of character are more precious in the sight of our Lord than offerings of gold or silver. They are more acceptable to him than the most costly sacrifice. – Sketches from the Life of Paul, pg. 233

Every Christian needs to learn in God's grade school. In this school there are grades or steps: "And beside this, giving all diligence, add to your faith virtue; and to virtue knowledge; and to knowledge temperance; and to temperance patience; and to patience godliness; and to godliness brotherly kindness; and to brotherly kindness charity" (2 Peter 1:5-7 KJV). Every step is essential to have a character like Jesus'. Every day we need God to be our teacher. "For if these things be in you, and abound, they make you that ye shall neither be barren nor unfruitful in the knowledge of our Lord Jesus Christ" (2 Peter 1:8).

Without these different steps in our lives, we cannot have a full knowledge of God. It is vital to cultivate these traits in our character. "But he that lacketh these things is blind, and cannot see afar off, and hath forgotten that he was purged from his old sins. Wherefore the rather, brethren, give diligence to make your calling and election sure: for if ye do these things, ye shall never fall: For so an entrance shall be ministered unto you abundantly into the everlasting kingdom of our Lord and Saviour Jesus Christ" (2 Peter 1: 9-11 KJV).

Without God's perfect character in you, you cannot graduate from God's school and enter into heaven.

~ Jenny McCluskey

September 1

It is in Our Nature

There is the same disposition to lean toward the world and to follow its mocking shadows. – Sketches from the Life of Paul, pg. 233

A frog was hopping along in the forest when, suddenly, she came upon a small river. The frog was about to leap into the water, when she heard a voice, "Is there any chance that you can help me across this river?"

The frog turned to see a scorpion moving towards her. The frog became frightened and trembled as she asked the scorpion, "If I help you across the river, will you promise not to sting me?"

The scorpion answered, "If I sting you, we will both drown, and who wants that? Besides, I only sting for self-defense. Please help me!"

The frog crouched down and let the scorpion jump onto her back. She then hopped into the river with the scorpion on her back and began swimming. When they reached the middle of the river, she felt a pinch.

"Ouch!" said the frog. "What was that?"

"I just stung you," said the scorpion.

As the poison took effect, it became harder for the frog to swim. "Why did you do that? Now we will both drown!" the frog cried.

But it was too late. As they began to sink, the scorpion answered, "I am a scorpion; it's in my nature."

Ever since Adam fell, the scorpion of sin has been stinging away at our souls. There are times when we feel that the "mocking shadows" of sin seem to envelop us in darkness, but there is still hope! That hope can be found in God, who erases the evil within us.

~ David Ortiz

September 2

Dead Sea to Living Spring

The presence of ambitious, selfish, time-serving members is imperiling the church, whose greatest danger is from worldly conformity. – Sketches from the Life of Paul, pg. 233

Between the countries of Israel and Jordan, there rests a body of water that has been called the Dead Sea since before the time of Jesus. With 33.7% salinity, it is one of the saltiest bodies of water in the world. It is 8.6 times as salty as the ocean, and people can easily float on their backs because the high sodium content exponentially improves their buoyancy. Also, the mud is believed to be medicinally helpful; so, international tourists migrate to the lowest point on earth to find healing. With current climate changes, the Dead Sea is gradually receding. The only inlet into it is the Jordan River, flowing down the Jordan Rift Valley. This is the reason for the sea's lack of life. There is no outlet to be seen anywhere, even from space. Thus, all the minerals brought into it stay there even after the water has evaporated. The sea becomes increasingly crusty and acidic because it always takes, and never gives. It is called the Dead Sea because it only takes for itself and never gives in return.

What about us? Our church today, as in Paul's day, is struggling with being like the world. Our actions of always taking are causing it to "recede" in its effectiveness. When we take only for ourselves and don't serve the needy people we come in contact with, we become acidic, callous, and eventually "dry up." Let Christ be your outlet, let Him change your heart; start giving yourself up, and watch how the Lord constantly replenishes you with a never-ending stream of life. Change from a dead sea to a living spring.

~ Jonathan Fink

September 3

A Promise

...He has said, I will never leave you nor forsake you.
– Hebrews 13:5 ESV

In 1982, a devastating earthquake rocked the country of Armenia. A father thought immediately of his son who was at school. He remembered a promise he had made to the boy that he would always be there for him, no matter what. He rushed to the school where his son was and found it a heap of rubble. There was no sign of life. But the father started to dig through the rubble anyway. Other parents were also there looking for their children. The fire chief arrived along with the police. They told the father, "Why don't you just go home? There's nothing you can do. We're very sorry."

But the father kept digging. He had to keep his promise. He was going to find his son, dead or alive. After digging for thirty-eight hours, he moved a boulder and heard his son's voice. "Armand!" he called.

"Oh Dad, I knew you would come," came the answer. "I told all the other kids that you promised you'd always be there for me. We weren't worried because I knew you'd come." The courageous boy, along with fourteen of his classmates, had been trapped underneath the rubble, but they were miraculously unharmed.

It's the same way with God, except even better. He promises that He will always be there for you, no matter what. He won't give up on you. He will search until He finds you because He can't imagine life in Heaven without you. He assures us: "I will never leave you nor forsake you," and He always keeps His promises.

~ Melissa Butler

September 4

Barren or Full

Like the barren fig-tree, they were clothed with pretentious leaves, but destitute of the fruits of holiness; "having a form of godliness, but denying the power thereof." Filled with malice toward a pure and good man, seeking by every means to take his life, and extolling a vindictive profligate! – Sketches from the Life of Paul, pg. 236

As Jesus returned from Bethany, He and His disciples passed through an orchard of fig trees. Because the trees were full of leaves, they thought there would be fruit, and they decided to gather some. To their surprise, when they searched the trees, Jesus and his disciples found no fruit. Why was this? A fig tree with so many leaves should have borne its fruit already, but there was no fruit. It appeared as a fruitful tree, yet there was no fruit.

Jesus saw this as an opportunity to teach His disciples a lesson. The Jewish nation carried the name of God and professed to follow and obey Him, but they really didn't. Just like the fig trees, they appeared to have fruit, but didn't have any. They made a pretentious show of holiness and uprightness, yet on the inside they were filled with "dead men's bones" (Matthew 23:27 KJV). Because they were hypocrites, this outward show caused them to despise everyone who truly followed Christ; their defects and faults were becoming fully exposed.

Do we let others believe we bare fruit when we are just growing leaves? Do we put on an outward show of godliness? Jesus said that if we glorify God, we will bare much fruit (John 15:8). Do you want just leaves, or good fruit? It's your choice.

~ Jourdain Smith

September 5

To Save Sinners

A cruel and licentious Roman governor and a profligate Jewish princess were to be his sole audience... [The Gospel] is addressed to all mankind who feel their need of its gracious invitations.
– Sketches from the Life of Paul, pg. 240

"Who then can be saved?" (Luke 18:26 KJV). Throughout all ages, this question has haunted millions of minds. God has told us in His word that every son of Adam may have everlasting life; but we insist on second-guessing God. After all, there must be some restrictions on who can be saved—aren't some people just too sinful? Perhaps you have felt this way about yourself.

Let's look at who was given salvation in the Bible. David, an adulterer and murderer, sought repentance and received pardon. Peter, who had denied His Lord three times, was forgiven and became one of the strongest defenders of the faith. The thief on the cross received salvation in his dying hours. Paul himself had been a murderer of God's people, but Jesus made him a shepherd of the flock. Now Paul found himself witnessing before two of the wickedest people he had ever met. Felix was a corrupt murderer and tyrant. Drusilla, his "wife," was an adulteress, who had left her former husband to be with Felix. But Paul did not think them too low to hear the saving message of the Gospel. He understood Jesus' words, "They that are whole need not a physician; but they that are sick. I came not to call the righteous, but sinners to repentance" (Luke 5:31, 32 KJV).

Are you a sinner? Then Jesus died to save *you*. Don't let His sacrifice go to waste.

~ Cara Dewsberry

September 6

Today's Opportunity

Paul considered this God-given opportunity, and he improved it faithfully. – Sketches from the Life of Paul, pg. 240

Mongol emperor, Kublai Khan, sent a message to Pope Gregory X in 1269 asking for missionaries. He longed for one hundred Christian missionaries, whom, he said, would convert him and from there, his whole kingdom, which covered a large portion of Asia. If the opportunity had been fully used, the history of Asia and probably of the world would have been very different. But instead of one hundred, two friars were sent. Neither even reached Khan, because they both turned back in Armenia.

Paul was also faced with an opportunity, but He responded to the God-given task quite differently. When he was before the Roman governor Felix and his wife, Drusilla, Paul knew that though these two had the power to put him to death, he had the opportunity to win them to Christ. Others were intimidated by the violent Felix, but Paul saw Felix as, yes, a man of great power, but also a man of great influence who could potentially reach many with the truth. Paul took the opportunity given him and worked fearlessly to capitalize on it.

Today you will encounter great opportunities. God purposely puts them in your path so you can make the most out of them, glorifying God! When you think of it that way, today *is* an opportunity given to you by God. Wasting it is not an option.

~ Robby Folkenberg

September 7

Don't Be Selfish

...Forgetting all selfish considerations, he sought to arouse them to the peril of their souls. – Sketches from the Life of Paul, pg. 240

Paul had a genuine love for everyone. In fact, he loved people so much that he cared about *their* future. As Paul stood before Felix and Drusilla, he told of his Friend Jesus. He shared "about righteousness and self-control and the judgment to come" (Acts 24:25 NLT). He boldly shared the truth despite the many reasons he could have come up with to remain silent or water the message down. He could have compromised the truth in order not to offend his worldly audience. After all, Felix had the power to kill Paul if he wished. The apostle could have selfishly wanted to impress the ruler and his wife so that they would set him free. Also, he could have been worried about what this influential couple might think of him. But this was not what Paul did; "...Forgetting all selfish considerations, he sought to arouse them to the peril of their souls."

How often do we, because of our selfishness, disregard the fact that someone is headed for eternal ruin! Instead of caring about their well-being, their future, we care only for ourselves. We pass up opportunities to lead them to Jesus because we are too worried about what they might think of us.

Jesus gives all of His followers a message of salvation. It is our job to share it with others. We cannot be silent or water it down, for these actions are rooted in selfishness. When we do this, we are saying, "I don't really care if you go to Heaven or not." Ask Jesus to help you to disregard all selfish considerations. Let your life tell of Jesus' love so that others may also experience eternal joy.

~ Jonathan Sharley

September 8

Which Path?

The gospel message admits of no neutrality. It counts all men as decidedly for the truth or against it; if they do not receive and obey its teachings, they are its enemies. – Sketches from the Life of Paul, pg. 240

On the road of life, there are only two pathways. One leads to eternal happiness and the other to destruction. The road that leads to destruction looks inviting. It is easy, straight, wide, and well traveled. The way that leads to eternal happiness doesn't seem to look nearly as inviting. It is up-hill, narrow, windy, and steep.

In the book *Pilgrim's Progress*, the pilgrim, Christian, is traveling to the Celestial City. He is supposed to travel on the straight and narrow way, but he is constantly being tempted to travel on the easy, well-traveled path. There were times when he went the wrong way, but if he called out to God, He would always help him get back on track again.

Each of us is traveling on just one of those paths. We cannot walk in two different directions at the same time. If we love Jesus and want to follow Him, we will choose the way that leads to eternal happiness. If the world looks too inviting, we might try to walk on both paths, but our lives will show in reality which road we are on.

Don't try to fool yourself. If you are not following Jesus, you are automatically on the road that leads to destruction. Which path will you take?

~ Becky Brousson

Something Better

Delight yourself also in the Lord and He will give you the desires of your heart. Commit your way to the Lord, trust also in Him and He shall bring it to pass. – Psalm 37:4-5 NKJV

Have you ever asked God for something, and He didn't seem to answer your prayer? I have, but God has been teaching me to trust Him in every situation. God is omniscient, and if He decides not to answer my prayer, it's because He has something better in mind.

When my sister was in college, she had an entry-level job as a secretary at an apartment complex. As she was praying for a better paying job, the assistant manager's position opened up, and my sister applied for the job. Much to her disappointment, someone else was chosen for the position. She couldn't understand why God hadn't answered her prayer. A couple of weeks later, her boss asked her to be the manager of the complex. Now she understood why she had been turned down to be the assistant manager: God was reserving the manager's position just for her.

God loves to give you the "desires of your heart." Sometimes, it's hard to understand the way He answers your prayers. Maybe you have asked Him for health, but you are an invalid. Maybe you have asked for wealth, but you are in want. Even though it's hard to understand, He answered your prayer in the way that is absolutely best for you. When you look back on your life, you will see that God's way was better than yours.

~ Melissa Butler

September 10

Standing in the Storm

The dark passions that lie hidden from the sight of men, the jealousy, revenge, hatred, lust, and wild ambition, the evil deeds meditated upon in the dark recesses of the soul, yet never executed for want of opportunity—of all these God's law makes a record. Men may imagine that they can safely cherish these secret sins; but it is these that sap the very foundation of character; for out of the heart "are the issues of life."– Sketches from the Life of Paul, pg. 242

It is dangerous for us to cherish small sins in our hearts. If we haven't given everything to God, the little things we think are insignificant will start growing, just as seeds germinate in the dark earth where no one can see them. As these small sins continually develop, we may think that we can hide them from others. But we can't hide them from everyone; the Holy Spirit will prick our consciences telling us that we should give up these things.

Before I was born, my parents had a large tree in their yard; they really enjoyed the shade and beauty it gave. One spring, they went to visit my grandparents for the weekend. On their way home, they were driving in a very heavy rainstorm and when they arrived at home, they saw their big, beautiful tree had fallen and smashed their other car. As they surveyed the damage, they saw the core of the tree had rotted away, and it wasn't able to withstand the wind and rain of the storm. This more fully brings out my point; although the outside of the tree had appeared strong and stately, the inside was hollow and worthless.

Sooner or later there is going to be a storm in each of our lives. If we have allowed some small sin to rot the core of our hearts, we will not be able to stand, even if we look like beautiful Christians on the outside. When Jesus appears in the clouds, the brightness of His coming will destroy sin. We must have all of our sins covered by His blood, or they will consume us. Let's get rid of those secret sins that are rotting our cores, so that when Christ comes we will be ready.

~ Joey Heagy

September 11

Death within Salvation's Reach

But instead of permitting his convictions to lead him to repentance, he eagerly sought to dismiss these disagreeable reflections. – Sketches from the Life of Paul, pg. 243, 244

Years ago, an international team was climbing Mt. Everest, the Nepalese top of the world. One of the climbers was stranded on a ledge in a region called the Death Zone. Rising 29,029 feet from sea level, the tallest mountain in the world has a terrifying space spanning 23,000 to 26,200 feet, whose oxygen-deprived atmosphere hampers the decision-making capabilities of the climbers in its clutches. In these conditions, climbers make irrational decisions, some of which cost them their lives. The stranded climber had been there for two days in extreme pain from broken bones, which he sustained from falling down a cliff face. A Search and Rescue team located him in a blizzard. The only way to extract him was by means of a harness that was let down over the side. However, he never would grip the hook. Barely audible above the wind, he said, "I'm not going to reach for it. I feel warm, and I just want to go to sleep." None of the efforts made by the team could change his mind. He died on that ledge, his frozen body a mute testimony to the power of wrong choices.

When Felix heard the words of Paul, he knew he was hearing the message of salvation, but he felt comfortable where he was. Sin had clouded his mind and judgment, hampering his decision-making processes, so that when his opportunity for salvation came, he let it slip right through his fingers. He never had another opportunity to accept Christ, and history tells us he died in his state of indecision. Don't pass up the opportunities God sends you. Allow yourself to see your faults; that is the only way you will feel your need of the Savior.

~ Jonathan Fink

September 12

A Matter of Necessity

The interview with Paul was cut short. "Go thy way for this time," he said, "when I have a convenient season, I will call for thee."
– Sketches from the Life of Paul, pg. 244

Felix felt the conviction of the Holy Spirit as Paul preached a message that moved him to his core. For the first time, Felix saw the sins that he had committed, crimes against his fellow men. Yet, despite the strong sense of conviction, he chose to cut the message short. In essence, he turned away from God, shutting the pleading of the Holy Spirit out of his life. He thought he could have religion whenever it best suited him. He did not see that it was a necessity to have God in his life.

Could it be that we, like Felix, might seek God only when it is convenient? Do we search for Him only when there is, in our view, nothing better to do? Or do we take advantage of every opportunity to know God better?

One summer, while I was on a mission trip in the Dominican Republic for the purpose of presenting health talks, I was asked to preach the Sabbath morning sermon. This took me by surprise, as I had not intended to preach on that trip. So I declined the invitation, and as a result, the door closed. I said no because it was a slight inconvenience, and I missed out on a blessing from God.

Don't miss out on God. "Seek ye the LORD while he may be found, call ye upon him while he is near" (Isaiah 55:6 KJV). Felix lost his opportunity for salvation because he cut short the voice of the Holy Spirit. You, however, still have time; don't make the same mistake. Realize that you need God. He's not just a person to summon in a moment of desperation. Your need of Him is constant. It is a matter of necessity.

~ Buddy Taylor

September 13

A Bold Claim

The Jewish inhabitants…claimed the city as theirs, because their king had done so much for it. – Sketches from the Life of Paul, pg. 245

If you were to look upon the city of Caesarea, you would see a beautiful metropolis filled with amazing architecture and art. The city was known as a bustling center of commerce; and all of this was because of the first Herod. While Caesarea was known for its pagan temples, the Jews laid claim to this city. They could make this claim since it was their king who had paid the price for the scenery, harbor, and magnificent buildings. Even though they did not pay for it, they walked with their heads high and claimed the city as their own.

We as Christians have a lot to learn from these people. While Christ has not given us a temporal dwelling or an earthly kingdom, we can lay claim to heaven through the power in His blood. Paul writes in Hebrews that we can "confidently approach the throne of grace…whenever we need help" (Hebrews 4:16 NET), and Jesus says, "Forceful people lay hold" of the "kingdom of heaven" (Mathew 11:12 NET). While you are not to be arrogant, as if you were the one that brought about your salvation, you are to be "bold" upon the claims of forgiveness. Christ has purchased your salvation, and His blood is your key into heaven. This is a "free gift" (Ephesians 2:8 NET). You can have confidence that there is "a place for you" in heaven (John 14:2 NET).

~ Luke Gonzalez

September 14

Some Other Time

A ray of light from Heaven had been permitted to shine upon this wicked man... That was his Heaven-sent opportunity to see and to forsake his sins. But he said to the Spirit of God, "Go thy way for this time; when I have a convenient season, I will call for thee." ...He was never to receive another call from God. – Sketches from the Life of Paul, pg. 246

There is a story told of a Persian prince who, when he grew to manhood, divided his future life into four periods: ten years for travel, ten years for government work, ten years for pleasure, and ten years for God. He thought his plan was a good one, but the problem was he died during the first ten years! If only he had known, how much more wisely he could have planned.

How sad that Felix closed his mind to Paul's appeal and hardened his heart against the Holy Spirit. Felix not only rejected the apostle's message, but also turned his back on God. Just think what an awesome witness for the gospel he could have been if only he had surrendered his life to Christ. But instead, he continued on his wicked course until he was finally removed from office because of the extreme injustice with which he treated his subjects. "His days were ended in disgrace and obscurity" (*Sketches from the Life of Paul*, pg. 246).

Today, many of us say to ourselves, "I'll do what I want today and surrender to Christ tomorrow." I have been tempted by these same thoughts, but I strive to remember that today is all I have, and tomorrow may never happen. So, let's make the most of our "Heaven-sent opportunity" and give all to Christ!

~ Rebecca Luchak

September 15

Integrated Integrity

But Festus was not a man who would sacrifice justice to gain popularity. – Sketches from the Life of Paul, pg. 247

As professional golfer Ray Floyd was getting ready to tap in a routine 9-inch putt, he saw the ball move ever so slightly. According to the rulebook, if the ball moves in this way the golfer must take a penalty stroke. Yet, consider the situation. Floyd was among the leaders in the tournament offering a top prize of $108,000. To acknowledge that the ball had moved could mean he would lose his chance at big money.

Writer David Holahan describes as follows what others might have done. "The athlete ducks his head and flails wildly with his hands, as if being attacked by a killer bee. Next, he steps back from the ball, rubbing his eye for a phantom speck of dust, all the while scanning his playing partners and the gallery for any sign that others have detected the ball's movement. If the coast is clear, he taps the ball in for his par." Ray Floyd, however, didn't do that. He assessed himself a penalty stroke and wound up with a bogey on the hole.

Many times, doing wrong seems convenient, and its pros might outdo the cons; but, will we sacrifice doing right for the "pros" of doing wrong? Will we let feelings of momentary gain outdo God's moving on our hearts?

~ Jourdain Smith

September 16

Who's Controlling Your Heart?

He looked with disgust upon the scene before him, the Jewish priests and rulers, with scowling faces and gleaming eyes, forgetting the dignity of their office…he turned to Paul, who stood calm and self-possessed before his adversaries… – Sketches from the Life of Paul, pg. 249

I have three distant cousins, two of whom are twins. These guys grew up in a non-Christian home, and through this influence, developed many bad habits and were constantly getting into trouble. They always had terrible attitudes and behavior. When they were older, the twins both committed crimes and ended up in jail. While they were in jail, their grandfather visited and prayed with them. After their release they agreed to attend some evangelistic meetings with him, and soon after the meetings, they were both converted. Following their conversion, they tried sharing their faith with their other brother, but he didn't want anything to do with their religion.

Over the next couple of years, the twins drew closer and closer to Christ with both of them studying for the ministry, while the third brother continued his worldly life. Recently, one of the twins married a lovely Christian girl. At the wedding, the other twin was the best man and the third brother was a groomsman.

The contrast between the twins and the third brother was startling. The twins were smiling and had a peaceful, joyful radiance; Christ was clearly in their hearts. But, the third brother had a scowl and throughout the ceremony was grumbling and cursing. The twins had acted just like that before their conversion, but their time with Jesus had made a huge difference. Standing beside their brother, the contrast was very obvious.

Even the worldly can see if God has made a difference in our lives. If our lives are full of peace and joy, or if we gripe and grumble when things don't go our way, it shows who controls our hearts. Why not let Christ control your heart?

~ Joey Heagy

September 17

Is Your Drain Clogged?

All who would fearlessly serve God…will need moral courage, firmness, and a knowledge of God and his word, to stand in that evil day. – Sketches from the Life of Paul, pg. 251

Has your sink ever been clogged? When the filth gets inside, it's next to impossible for the water to drain properly. However, when you pour Drain-O© down the sink, it will flow unblocked once again. We need to realize the importance of guarding our minds so they won't be filled with garbage. When we have the filth of this world clogging our drain, it's hard for the Holy Spirit to flow through us. But if we let it, the "Drain-O©" of God's word will cleanse our hearts.

Last year I experienced this problem; every time I would take a shower in the dorm, the water would just keep rising, and it took hours after the shower for it to finally go down. It got to the point where I could not handle it any longer, so I told one of the maintenance workers all about it. A couple of days later, he told me to come see the "rat" that he had taken out. And what I saw was the biggest, grossest, slimy wad of hair. I did not have tools or the knowledge to remove the wad; however, he did and I would not have been able to remove it alone. I then realized the importance of having help from another source. In other words, I was struck by how much I needed God to clean up my slimy life of sin.

We all want to stand with firmness in the last days. To do that, we need to be filling our minds with God's word and guarding them from the things of this world. So, let's remove the gunk that is in our hearts and fill them with the pure and true knowledge of God.

~ Melody Hyde

September 18

Fog

Then Satan will work with all his fascinating power, to influence the heart and becloud the understanding, to make evil appear good, and good evil..."insomuch that, if it were possible, [he should] deceive the very elect." – Sketches from the Life of Paul, pg. 251

Fog is a dreaded hazard in the world of aviation. It deceives pilots and causes them to make fatal miscalculations.

During WWII, the U.S. Army Air Corps chose a foggy hilltop about forty-five minutes from my house as the testing site for fog dispersal techniques. This airfield eventually became the Arcata/Eureka airport—one of the foggiest airports in the world. Flights into Arcata are often cancelled, delayed, or rerouted because of the thick fog that rolls in from the sea.

Right now, Satan is creating his own fog to cloud our minds so that we can't see that we're on a crash course. Sadly, unlike planes, we can't reroute the course of our lives to avoid Satan's foggy deceptions; we must fly straight through them. But Jesus wants to give us guidance instruments that will safely navigate us through the mist. He says, "Put on the whole armor of God, that ye may be able to stand against the wiles of the devil. For we wrestle not against flesh and blood, but against...the rulers of the darkness of this world" (Ephesians 6:11, 12 KJV).

It's your choice whether to use the instruments God has provided to guide you safely to life, or to attempt to fly through on your own, which will inevitably result in a collision with death. Which will you choose?

~ Cara Dewsberry

September 19

A Star in Your Crown

Henceforth there is laid up for me a crown of righteousness, which the Lord the righteous judge, shall give to me at that day: and not to me only, but unto all them that love his appearing.
– 2 Timothy 4:8 KJV

A teenage girl was dressing for a party. Carefully she adjusted on her head a beautiful little crown decorated with stars. Her little sister, Carrie, was watching the procedure intently. When the tiny miss climbed up and touched the crown, the older sister reprimanded her.

"I was just looking. I was thinking about something else," little Carrie explained.
"What were you thinking about?"
"Well, my Sabbath School teacher told us that for each soul we win, we will have a star in our crown. I wish I could win one."

The older sister went to the party, but all evening she kept thinking of Carrie and the star she wanted in her crown. The dancing and other frivolous entertainments seemed strangely hollow.

When she retuned home, she tiptoed over to her little sister's bed, stooped over and kissed her. "Bless your heart, little sister; you have won your star tonight!" That night the older girl knelt by her own bedside and surrendered her heart to the Lord.

Often we don't realize what an influence we can have on people just by a few words. We can bring people close to Christ, or we can push them away. I'm going to try to bring someone nearer to Christ today. I want to be able to say with Paul, "Henceforth there is laid up for me a crown of righteousness, which the Lord the righteous Judge, shall give to me at that day: and not to me only, but unto all them that love his appearing."

~ Rebecca Luchak

September 20

Ready?

God would have his people prepared for the soon-coming crisis.
– Sketches from the Life of Paul, pg. 252

Have you ever been afraid about what the future holds? Or has the thought of a "great tribulation, such as was not since the beginning of the world to this time" (Matthew 24:21 KJV) ever scared you? A "soon-coming crisis"—a "time of trouble" (Daniel 12:1 KJV)—will occur before Jesus comes back. But there is wonderful news; there is hope! God wants us to be ready for any trial that comes; He "would have his people prepared." What an encouraging thought: Jesus wants me to be prepared for whatever happens. We do not serve a God who is trying to catch us off guard. On the contrary, He is doing everything He possibly can to make us ready for the future.

In Matthew 28:18, Jesus tells us "All power is given unto me in heaven and in earth" (KJV). This means that He even has the power—the ability—to prepare us for the troubles that are coming. However, He cannot prepare you if you do not let Him. Jesus will not force anything on you.

You do not have to be worried about what the "end times" have in store for you. If you allow Him, Jesus will lead you into a relationship with Himself. This relationship will prepare you for whatever hardships might arise.

~ Jonathan Sharley

September 21

Prepared or Unprepared

God would have his people prepared for the soon-coming crisis. Prepared or unprepared, we must all meet it. Only those whose characters are thoroughly disciplined to meet the divine standard will be able to stand firm in that testing time. – Sketches from the Life of Paul, pg. 252

Many years ago, an artist was asked by the Japanese Emperor to paint him a picture of a bird. The artist agreed and went his way. Weeks turned into months, months turned into years, and the painting was still not brought to the palace. The Emperor became impatient, and he went to visit the artist. Upon arriving, he demanded an explanation for why he had not yet gotten his painting. Instead of making excuses, the artist placed a blank canvas on the easel. In about an hour or less, he had completed a magnificent masterpiece, exactly what the Emperor wanted. Stunned by his masterful performance the Emperor asked why he had taken so long to complete it. Leading him to the closet, the artist showed him the many, many canvases that had been used to practice drawing feathers, wings, heads, and feet. The artist told the Emperor that he had to research and study so that he could create such a beautiful painting.

Being prepared is completely dependent upon our priorities. Like the artist who carefully studied all of the details in order to paint a beautiful masterpiece for the Emperor, are you making sure that all of the details of your life are surrendered to Christ? Will your life look like a beautiful picture of the character of Christ when He comes? The King is coming. Are you prepared?

~ Jourdain Smith

September 22

Shining Light

When the darkness is deepest, then the light of a noble, Godlike character will shine the brightest. – Sketches from the Life of Paul, pg. 252

"Hey, look, Ryo's lunch is pretty interesting today!" Everybody in my elementary school knew that I was a vegetarian. I brought my own lunch while the school provided food for the kids, and I hated being different than everybody else. When lunchtime came, my friends competed with each other to see what my lunch would be for that day.

One day, I complained to my mother about how awful it was at the lunch table and begged her to let me eat the same things that my friends ate. "Try thinking this way, Ryo," my mother answered. "Being different, like you are right now, makes your faith shine brighter in your school. In this way, you can be more effective in witnessing about the truth to others." I brought my own vegetarian lunch until the very end of my elementary school years. As a result, I found out that many of my friends and their families gained a knowledge of the health message. They once thought I was weird, but now they realized that vegetarian food was healthier.

My elementary school was located in a little village. Only 1,800 people lived there. Most were atheists and had no idea what Christianity was all about. They never had seen a Christian before they saw me. It was spiritually dark in that village. The lesson that my mother taught me was right. By bringing my own vegetarian food, I was shining because people in that village knew nothing about the health message. Thus, I was able to witness to those who were in the dark.

~ Ryo Fusamae

September 23

Stars in the Night

And those who are wise shall shine like the brightness of the sky above; and those who turn many to righteousness, like the stars forever and ever. – Daniel 12:3 ESV

Stars shine all the time. Even though they aren't noticeable during the day, at night you can see them clearly. Only in the darkness can you really see them shine. Many people profess to be Christians when everything is bright and going well, and it can be difficult to tell who the true believers really are. But, when times of dark trials come, then it will be seen who the real Christians are, for they will shine as brightly as the stars on a moonless night.

In Paul's life, we see that he always focused on Jesus, even when he was in the deepest pit of despair. Paul shone through the darkest nights, not just the brightest days, and his faith was an example for others to follow.

This is the same for you and me. When trials come and the sun isn't shining, people see who I really am. It is very important that my character be like Jesus' and Paul's, shining even when darkness is all around. For it's in the dark that you see who the real stars are.

~ Melody Hyde

September 24

Messenger

Yet this man, apparently without friends or wealth or position, had an escort that worldlings could not see. Angels of Heaven were his attendants. – Sketches from the Life of Paul, pg. 254

Bound with chains, Paul sat in the prison cell. Why was he in there? It was because of the Jews' hatred against him. The dungeon was as dark as a moonless night so that the prisoners could not tell whether it was day or night. The brutal soldiers mocked and ridiculed Paul. However, one day he was able to meet King Agrippa II. Agrippa wanted to see Paul for entertainment, but when he was called in, the king could see that there was a sharp contrast between himself and this prisoner. King Agrippa appeared before Paul with the pomp and splendor of royalty, followed by richly dressed nobles. On the other hand, Paul was chained, pale from the days without sun, and sick from poor sanitation. Though he was in such miserable condition, Paul had more power and riches than Agrippa.

Why do you think Paul was more powerful than Agrippa? It was because he was a messenger of God. When Paul spoke, he was giving an infallible message from God. Furthermore, if Agrippa tried to kill him, God could send His angels to protect His servant. Paul had all the angels on his side. Isn't that exciting? Guess what: this could be for you too. This can only be possible through complete submission to God. God longs to speak through you. Will you allow yourself to be a messenger of God?

~ David Chang

September 25

Heaven's Definition of "Popularity"

But because they possessed, in a limited degree, power and position, they were the favorites of the world...Yet this man, apparently without friends or wealth or position, had an escort that worldlings could not see. Angels of Heaven were his attendants. – Sketches from the Life of Paul, pg. 254

Have you ever wished that you were the popular kid in school? The popular kids have name-brand clothes, many friends, and a lot of confidence. It seems like they have "the life." Do you think they have happiness? Well they might, but their happiness won't last if it's based on temporary things. Money, position, friends, and honor aren't everything, but Satan tries to deceive us into thinking they are. What really matters is that we have a relationship with Jesus.

When brought into the assembly to be tried, Paul was pale from sickness, long imprisonment, and exhaustion. His clothes were shabby, his face unshaven. Nevertheless, amid the pomp and splendor of royalty, he was not deterred from his purpose. He was there to tell them about the crucified and risen Savior. What he wore or how he looked in comparison to them, did not matter. Angels of Heaven were his attendants, and he was there for a purpose.

Knowing Jesus as your personal Savior will bring you more happiness than anything this world has to offer. So, even if you are not the most popular kid in school, that doesn't matter. Paul wasn't the most popular person either, in "worldly terms"; but in "heavenly terms" he was. Angels attended him everywhere he went. Don't you want to have that same experience? You can. Just give your life to Jesus.

~ Becky Brousson

September 26

Does It Really Matter?

The apostle knew of how little worth are the outward circumstances of worldly wealth and position, and he was not disconcerted by the brilliant display or the high rank of that titled audience. – Sketches from the Life of Paul, pg. 255

I have visited some incredible dwellings. I've toured Windsor, a castle home of the Queen of England; Versailles, the palace of Louis the IV of France; The Forbidden City, a vast complex once inhabited by Chinese royalty; as well as Monticello and Mount Vernon, Presidents Thomas Jefferson and George Washington's plantation havens in Virginia. I'm amazed by the immensity and grandeur, but when it comes right down to it, how much do earthly possessions really matter?

When viewed in the light of eternity, these temporal things of the world are worthless. This is how Paul stood undaunted in the face of earthly brilliance and royalty. The things of the earth just weren't important to him anymore.

A few weeks ago, I visited a home I had always viewed with amazement. This time, however, it just didn't appeal to me anymore. As my walk with Christ has strengthened, my ties with this world have weakened. Though I have a lot of growing left to do, I'm beginning to realize that things of the world will burn up someday; why get so attached to them? Instead, let us hold fast to what really matters, trusting in God to provide and care for us. Martin Luther puts it beautifully. He said, "I have held many things in my hands and I have lost them all; but whatever I have placed in God's hands, that I still possess."

~ Robby Folkenberg

September 27

A Personal Touch

Paul again related the familiar story of his conversion from the stubborn unbelief of a rigid and bigoted Pharisee to faith in the Jesus of Nazareth as the world's Redeemer. – Sketches from the Life of Paul, pg. 256

Paul was before some of the strongest and most powerful men of the city. He would have only one chance to convert these men, only one chance to tell them of Christ's love. It was at this opportunity that Paul used one of the strongest arguments in favor of the gospel: his personal story of conversion. Paul began to tell them of the Savior's love to a wayward sinner and about how the former murderer had become a disciple of the Prince of Peace. This argument was so strong it prompted Agrippa, one of the local rulers and a Jew himself, to say, "In a short time you will make me a Christian" (Acts 26:28 NET margin). It was at this point that Agrippa was the closest he would ever get to know the Savior of the world.

Every man and woman has a story, a personal testimony to tell the world. "You are a letter of Christ" (2 Corinthians 3:3 NET); you have a life lesson that someone would benefit from. A man can hear about the crucifixion a thousand times and still not truly know Christ. It may be that only when you tell of your renewal in Christ that the Savior of the world will appear as he truly is: a *personal* Redeemer.

~ Luke Gonzalez

September 28

Contagious Energy

And he could but be affected by that burning zeal which neither stripes nor imprisonment could quench. – Sketches from the Life of Paul, pg. 259

Do you know someone who is really fun to be around? They have a positive outlook on life, plenty of energy, and most likely a good sense of humor. Their zeal for life is contagious. As you hang out with them, you cannot help but long to live life like they do.

Paul was such a person in a spiritual sense. As he stood before King Agrippa, he testified of Jesus and the plan of salvation. His life radiated a "burning zeal" for the truth that the monarch had not seen before. Paul was so "on fire" for the Gospel that Agrippa could not help but be affected by his presence. The spiritual energy given to Paul by the Holy Spirit was so inspiring that the king desired to be like him. The vibrancy of Paul's relationship with Jesus made Christianity an attractive option to others.

Can you imagine what would happen if we were always filled with the "burning zeal" that Paul had? With such a zeal motivating our lives, others will not help but be affected. As they see the fullness of a life submitted to God, many will long for this spiritual energy in their lives.

Ask God to invigorate you; ask Him to fill you with His energizing zeal. As you become more and more excited about your Savior, others will look at what you have and want to be like you.

~ Jonathan Sharley

September 29

Almost a Christian

...Seeing only the humble prisoner standing as God's ambassador, he [Agrippa] answered involuntarily, "Almost thou persuadest me to be a Christian." – Sketches from the Life of Paul, pg. 259

For a moment, the glittering splendor and pomp of the crowded audience room faded from King Agrippa's sight. He saw only the bent, haggard form of the captive Paul and heard only his life-giving words. A strange longing for what the apostle had gripped the king's heart, and he opened his lips to declare his belief in Christ. Suddenly, a snicker from another onlooker brought Agrippa back to the present. Wait! He was a king. How could he degrade himself before all his noble friends to be a follower of some crucified Galilean? Trying to regain his haughty air, but with his eyes still betraying the longing of his soul, Agrippa addressed Paul, "Almost thou persuadest me to be a Christian."

Last week was a week of prayer at Fountainview. In one of the sermons, the speaker stressed that simply wanting God is not enough. We must act on that desire and choose to surrender ourselves fully to Him. If I always sit around wanting to improve on my violin, but never practice, will I get better? No. In fact, I'll lose the skills I have.

You can't just *want* to be a Christian; you must actually *choose* to be one. Agrippa almost became a Christian—he *wanted* to be one; but to be "almost but not wholly saved, means to be not almost but wholly lost" (*Christ's Object Lessons*, pg. 118). When your name comes up in the judgment, will it be marked "A Child of God"? Or will it say "Almost a Christian"?

~ Cara Dewsberry

September 30

He Gave His Life

And now abide faith, hope, love, these three; but the greatest of these is love. – 1 Corinthians 13:13 NKJV

Rena had been in a serious accident and lost a lot of blood. She was rushed to the hospital, and a call was made to the family to come and give her some blood. After tests were taken, it was found that six-year-old Danny had the same blood type as Rena, and he manfully agreed to give his blood to save his sister's life. The transfusion was given; Rena was operated on and soon was out of danger. But Danny lay in a bed, white as a ghost, looking almost scared to death. "You saved Rena's life, Danny. Don't you feel proud of that?" asked a nurse as she tried to cheer him up. But he could only say yes in a small squeaky voice that could hardly be heard.

A little later the supervisor tried to cheer him up. "We think you were very brave, Danny. You have done a beautiful thing for your sister." But Danny slid down under the covers and wouldn't say a word; they could tell he was crying. "Doctor, please come and try to cheer Danny up," said the supervisor. "He's acting so strangely."

So, the Doctor came in. "Hello there, son. What's the trouble?" he asked as he pulled the covers off the boy's face. When Danny saw the doctor, he swallowed hard and asked,

"Doctor, when am I going to die?"

"You die? Danny, you're not going to die. You'll be fine in just a little while. Then you can go home." Danny blinked and looked so relieved that suddenly the doctor understood. "Didn't anyone in this whole hospital tell you that giving blood wouldn't hurt you?" he asked.

"No. I thought I was giving my life," Danny answered.

At Calvary, Jesus not only gave His blood—He gave His life! And He did it because He loves you!

~ Rebecca Luchak

October 1

Almost, but not Quite

But to be almost persuaded means to put aside the proffered mercy, to be convicted of the right way, but to refuse to accept the cross of a crucified Redeemer. – Sketches from the Life of Paul, pg. 260

Although he was a Jew, King Agrippa held a position of great importance. He knew firsthand the meaning of being under Roman authority. Nero required Agrippa to follow his every dictate, thus making Agrippa a puppet of the Roman government. King Agrippa received, as did Nero, a simple presentation of truth and the way of salvation from Paul. However, these proud monarchs would not accept the extended gift of God. Given a small window of opportunity, Agrippa carelessly passed it by with the response, "Almost thou persuadest me to be a Christian" (Acts 26:28 KJV). That day Agrippa rejected truth, and it is doubtful that truth ever knocked on his heart again. Agrippa was almost a Christian. He saw the light; but the things of this earth drew him away.

This same situation is repeated today. God places His witnesses in the paths of lost souls. These lost ones are offered the opportunity to respond to Christ's call. However, so many turn away from the call for temporary pleasure. They reject the call of mercy saying, "Someday when it pleases me I will become a Christian" or "Someday when it benefits me, I will come to Christ." For many souls, it is too late. The door of mercy has forever closed, and they will never see the kingdom of heaven.

Friend, do not let this be you! God is still offering salvation for all who are willing to accept it. Let Him come in to your heart today, and you will never regret you did. Heaven's joy will be your reward.

~ Douglas Schappert

October 2

Ask God *Before* the Mud Puddles

Cause me to hear thy loving kindness in the morning; for in thee do I trust. Cause me to know the way wherein I should walk; for I lift up my soul unto thee. – Psalms 143:8 KJV

Keyboards typing, people chatting, brain cells working...This is the computer lab, and I'm brainstorming over my assignment. Then, I suddenly realize that my computer has just frozen. I ask myself in frustration, "Why didn't I save my work while I had the chance?" There are many times in our lives when we ask similar questions. Why didn't I ask before? Why didn't I talk to that person before? Before, before, before...You've probably asked those types of questions a lot; but what about, "Why didn't I ask God for help *before* I stepped in the mud puddles?" God desires us to ask Him *before* trouble comes, not only when we are in it.

You may ask, "How do I know when trials are coming?" The simple answer is, you don't. Only by spending time with God can He show you how to face them. In the morning, *before* you get muddy, spend that bonding time with God. By doing this, you can avoid regret and gain victories with God.

~ Sharon Jeon

October 3

Almost

"Almost thou persuadest me to be a Christian"…But to be almost persuaded, means to put aside the proffered mercy, to be convinced of the right way, but to refuse to accept the cross of a crucified Redeemer. – Sketches from the Life of Paul, pg. 259, 260

Agrippa was a very wicked man who had committed unspeakable crimes. During his interview with Paul, he was convicted of truth. He felt a deep pull in his heart. But he refused the offer and rejected the absolutely free gift of salvation. He confessed, "Almost thou persuadest me to be a Christian." There is a quote that says, "Almost but not wholly saved means to be not almost but wholly lost" (*Christ's Object Lessons*, pg. 118). When it comes to salvation, "almost" is not good enough.

Imagine with me that we are going to go skydiving together. Our plane soars through the skies right to the place where we must jump out of the plane. We realize that the time has come to take the leap. As we watch others around us putting on their parachutes, we *almost* put on ours as well, but at the last minute, we decide against it and leap out of the plane. What an exhilarating experience! Our whole group is falling through the sky together; but then we see parachutes popping open all around us. It's too late for us. Our parachutes are still up in the plane. Without a parachute, there is no hope for us.

John 12:35, 36 says, "…A little while longer the light is with you. Walk while you have the light, lest darkness overtake you; he who walks in darkness does not know where he is going. While you have the light, believe in the light, that you may become sons of light" (NKJV). Have you had an opportunity to put your parachute on, but didn't take it? I urge you to accept God's free gift while you still have the light.

~ Melissa Butler

October 4

Smoke Signal

And we know that all thing work together for good to them that love God, to them that are the called according to His purpose.
– Romans 8:28 KJV

A ship was wrecked in the Pacific Ocean, and only one survivor was washed ashore on a small island. He made a little hut out of the wreckage he found on the beach, put a blanket on a tall poll (hoping to attract some passing ship) and prayed every day that God would send a ship to rescue him.

The days dragged into weeks. Still, he hoped and prayed. Then, one day as he returned from hunting sea birds' eggs and wild yams, he was horrified to find his little hut going up in flames! You can only imagine his discouragement; he had been praying every day hoping for deliverance, and now his only comfort was gone. But, in a few hours a ship appeared in the distance! It came closer and closer! A dinghy came to the shore, and sailors took the stranded man aboard. The captain said, "We saw your smoke signal and figured it must be someone in distress after the recent wreck!" Of course, then man's eyes were opened, and he thanked God many times for burning up his little hut.

When disappointment comes to you, and you can't see why things are the way they are, ask God to open your eyes, and he will show you that "all things work together for good to them that love God"!

~ Rebecca Luchak

October 5

Just Two Choices

One, at least, had been almost persuaded to accept of grace and pardon. But to be almost persuaded, means to put aside the proffered mercy, to be convinced of the right way, but to refuse to accept the cross of a crucified Redeemer. – Sketches from the Life of Paul, pg. 260

As the governor stared at the piles upon piles of letters, an overwhelming sense of love and awe overcame him. All the letters were concerning a convict on death row. They were all calling for his release. The governor, with tears streaming down his face, grabbed a pen and paper and wrote down "Full Pardon." With the paper in his hand, he disguised himself in a preacher's robe and started out the door of his office to meet this man face to face.

As the governor entered the jail and started to walk to this man's cell, feelings of joy and excitement swelled within him. He charged into the cell and proclaimed, "Man, I have good news for you!"

The man stared back at him, and in a cold, dark tone, told him, "Preacher, I have no need for you or for God. Please leave me alone."

The governor emphatically responded, "But sir, you don't understand!"

"Get out!" the convict screamed back. The governor turned around, shredded the paper and left the cell.

Right then, a guard came into the cell and asked the convict, "So, how was your conversation with the governor?"

On the day of his execution, the prisoner was asked for his final words. He replied, "I am not dying today for a crime I've committed, but for the grace I refused." This is how our eternal destiny works. All you need to do is receive Christ into your heart and let Him live through you. Accept Christ and you will live.

~ Luke Gonzalez

October 6

Crowd Followers

The centurion decided to follow the judgment of the majority.
– Sketches from the Life of Paul, pg. 264

    The season for safe navigation was already coming to an end when Paul's ship left for Rome. On a stop at Fair Havens, the question was raised whether to stay where they were or to try to reach a more favorable place to spend the winter. Since Paul was a trusted prisoner, they asked his advice on the matter. Paul's advice was to stay at Fair Havens for the winter. However, the centurion decided to follow the judgment of the majority of the passengers who wanted to keep searching for a better harbor. Because of the centurion's decision, the ship later sank.

    Following the majority is frequently the easiest way to go; however, the majority is often wrong. In the world, people follow the popular musicians, actors, politicians, and athletes. Entertainers make millions of dollars and video stores are always crowded. Fifty to sixty thousands people spend hundreds of dollars to cram into huge stadiums to watch twenty-two guys chase a pigskin around a field, while churches are losing people and becoming empty. It takes more strength to stand up for what is right when everyone else is doing things that are wrong. Standing up for your beliefs is a lot harder than you might think; but with God, you can do anything (Luke 18:27).

~ Joey Heagy

October 7

Great Day!

In the midst of that terrible scene, the apostle retained his calmness and courage. – Sketches from the Life of Paul, pg. 266

Once there were twin boys; one was an optimist, the other a pessimist. The parents were concerned about how different their children were, and finally took the boys to see a psychologist. The psychologist observed them a while and concluded that they could be easily helped.

The pessimist was placed in a room filled with all the toys a boy could want. The optimist was left in a room filled with horse manure. The doctor and the parents observed both boys through one-way mirrors. The pessimist continued to be a pessimist, complaining that he had no one to play with. When they looked in on the optimist, they were shocked to find him digging through the manure. The psychologist stormed into the room, asking what the boy was doing. The dirty boy smiled and replied, "With all this manure, I'm sure there must be a pony in this room somewhere!"

What optimism this young boy exhibited! No matter how bad the circumstances were, the boy did not stop seeing the bright side! Unfortunately, we don't tend to look on the positive side most of the time. The apostle Paul stands as a perfect example to follow. Even though the shadow of death loomed above the ship he was traveling in, the apostle did not succumb to despair. He remained optimistic, believing that God would protect him from danger. This optimism revived hope within his fellow passengers, which helped them to survive the storm.

So, when a storm darkens your day, remain optimistic! Don't give up on looking at the bright side! Don't give up on trusting God! This hope will help you overcome your trials. Just look up and shout, "It's going to be a great day!"

~ David Ortiz

October 8

Joy

Notwithstanding he was physically the greatest sufferer of them all, he had words of hope for the darkest hour, a helping hand in every emergency. – Sketches from the Life of Paul, pg. 266

Have you ever known someone who had a reputation for always helping others? I have such a friend, whom I will call Peyton. He is one of the most helpful and self-sacrificing people I have ever met. It doesn't matter what someone needs, he's always there to help. If you need someone to stay back to clean up, you can count on him being there. He just loves to assist in any way he can. He is also one of the happiest people I know.

I think Paul was similar to Peyton. No matter what the situation, he was always thinking of the people around him, even when he was weak and feeble himself. He was never focused on self. If Paul had been focused on himself, the whole ship and those on board would have been lost.

I think we have all heard the saying, "**J**esus first, **O**thers second, **Y**ourself last." What does that spell? JOY! It's so true. When you are thinking of others instead of yourself, you will experience true happiness. Instead of always thinking of what you need, want, or don't have, try thinking of what you can do to make the life of those around you better. You will find that helping others not only brightens their day, but it will brighten yours as well. People will want to be around you because you have the love of Jesus in your heart. Try being a blessing to someone today, and you will understand the true meaning of JOY.

~ Becky Brousson

October 9

Invincible

Paul had no fears for himself; he felt assured that he would not be swallowed up by the hungry waters. – Sketches from the Life of Paul, pg. 266

Paul was destined for Rome. He had been called by God to give his testimony before Caesar, and he knew that nothing could stop him along the way. As his escort was in terror, the ship being tossed to and fro by a ruthless Mediterranean squall, Paul had no fears! He was invincible! He could not be stopped! Imagine the confidence that must have radiated from his being; imagine the witness he must have been to those frightened soldiers accompanying him!

Jesus commands us in Matthew 28:19-20 to spread the gospel to the world. Then, in Revelation 14, He tells us to spread the Three Angel's Messages as well. These two mandates fit together, overlapping in order to cover our God-given mission. Considering these orders are from our Savior, we should never take them lightly. We are to go! On our mission we may encounter squalls, storms, maybe even a hurricane or two! But, never fear, God has everything under control, and we cannot be beaten if we're fulfilling the mandate given to us. Just like Paul, we are invincible! For that very reason, we should be confident as we go about our work. Amid the confusion of this world, we can stand on the Rock and show others how they can be unshakable too!

~ Robby Folkenberg

October 10

The Cure for Cancer

Therefore, if anyone is in Christ, he is a new creation; old things have passed away; behold, all things have become new.
– 2 Corinthians 5:17 NKJV

    Cancer is a devastating disease and is often very hard to cure because it spreads so easily. When a person has leukemia, they often undergo radiation, which kills all their bone marrow. Then comes a stem cell transplant where another person donates new bone marrow to the patient. I find it very interesting that if the donor is the patient's twin, the transplant won't be successful. Twins are just too much alike. However, the donor has to be enough like you for your body to accept the transplant. It's difficult to find a donor who is enough like you and yet different enough for the transplant to be effective.

    I hope that you will never have to endure leukemia, but I know you have encountered the cancer of sin. It's the worst kind of cancer in the world; but it has the *easiest* and most abundantly available cure. Christ fully became a man and is also still fully divine. So, He is a lot like us and yet He's also different enough to do a stem cell transplant and save us from death. He first has to get the sin out of our lives and then He can transfer His bone marrow to us. Often times, in a stem cell transplant, the person's blood type changes to the type of the donor. Wouldn't you like your "blood type" to change to Christ's? What a beautiful picture! When the Great Physician does a stem cell transplant, we are totally changed. If left to spread, the cancer of sin will destroy you. Will you seize this opportunity to be cured?

~ Melissa Butler

October 11

Think of Others

For even Christ pleased not himself; but, as it is written, The reproaches of them that reproached thee fell on me.
– Romans 15:3 KJV

More than eight thousand Union soldiers lay dead or wounded on December 14, 1862, on the battlefield at Fredericksburg, Virginia. The cries of the dying for help and water were chilling. Nineteen-year-old Sergeant Richard Kirkland of the Second South Carolina Brigade had seen and heard enough. Kirkland went to Confederate General Joseph Kershaw.

"General," he said, "I can't stand this! All night and all day I hear those poor Federal people calling for water, and I can't stand it any longer. I ask permission to go and give them water."

Kershaw shook his head sympathetically. "Sergeant," he replied, "you'd get a bullet through your head the moment you stepped over the stone wall onto the plain."

"Yes, sir," answered Kirkland, "I know that, but if you let me, I'm willing to try it."

The General responded, "The sentiment which prompts you is so noble that I will not refuse your request. God protect you. You may go."

Quickly Kirkland hurdled over the wall and walked calmly toward the Union lines until he reached the nearest wounded soldier. Kneeling, he took off his canteen lid and lifted the enemy soldier's head to give him a long, deep drink of cold refreshing water. Then he placed a knapsack under the head of his enemy and moved on to the next. He returned again and again to the lines where his comrades handed him full canteens. Both sides stood there in awe as they watched this unselfish act.

So many times I follow my own agenda above the one my heavenly Father has set out for me. It is so easy to be selfish, yet it requires great faith in God to be a servant. We should strive to serve God and others in every possible way we can.

~Jeremy Grabiner

October 12

Caught in a Storm

And now I exhort you to be of good cheer; for there shall be no loss of any man's life among you, but of the ship. – Acts 27:22 KJV

As Paul was being taken to Rome, his ship was caught in a storm. Fear struck the crew as the ship was tossed around by the waves. Yet, Paul, with his quiet and peaceful demeanor, was able to calm the people on the ship.

John Wesley had a similar experience on his journey to America. On the ship he met a group of Moravian missionaries from Germany. These Moravian Christians had both a joy and a peace that Wesley did not possess. While they were traveling, they were caught in a violent storm that threatened to sink their ship. As the storm thrashed the ship, the Moravian believers began singing a psalm. At one point, the sea broke over the ship and split the mainsail into pieces. Panic spread among the other passengers as water poured over the deck, but the Germans remained calm and sang on. Afterwards Wesley spoke to the missionaries and asked them if they were afraid.

They answered, "I thank God, no."
"But were not your women and children afraid?"
Again they answered, "No; our women and children are not afraid to die."

Wesley had never experienced such calm assurance and peaceful faith. Their testimony shook him more than the storm; and Wesley came to realize that there was something still missing in his life.

Many times in your life you will face violent storms. But, if you accept Christ into your heart, you can have the same faith that Paul and the Moravian missionaries had.

~ Jeremy Grabiner

October 13

Rouse!

Passengers and crew roused from their apathy, and put forth all possible exertion to save their lives... Every effort within their power must be put forth to avert destruction; for God helps those only who help themselves. – Sketches from the Life of Paul, pg. 267

Have you ever observed the birds? Matthew 6:26 says, "Look at the birds of the air; they do not sow or reap or store away in barns, and yet your heavenly Father feeds them" (NIV). God indeed takes care of the birds. He gives them food to eat, feathers on their backs, and reasons to sing. But if you have ever watched a bird eat, you may have noticed that his food doesn't just fall out of the sky. The birds have to search for their food, build their own nests, and use their wings when danger comes near.

When Paul was traveling to Rome, he encountered a dreadful storm. An angel appeared to him and told him that there was to be a shipwreck, but that no lives would be lost. In the midst of this storm, God could have picked up that ship and moved it to a part of the sea that was not stormy, or He could have just spoken the word and the storm would have ceased. The people could have just sat back and lived on through a deadly storm just like that. But He allowed their ship to be wrecked for a reason. He wanted to save their souls. When Paul delivered the angel's message to them, everyone "roused from their apathy" and did everything in their power to make it to safety. God kept His promise and did what they could not.

Jesus is coming soon—very soon. If you are just sitting around thinking that He will save you, think again. He *will* save you if you ask Him to. He yearns to take you home with Him. He is extending the gift of salvation to you. Are you doing everything in your power to avert destruction?

~ Melissa Butler

October 14

Fear Not

Fear not, Paul; thou must be brought before Caesar; and, lo, God hath given thee all them that sail with thee. Wherefore, sirs, be of good cheer; for I believe God, that it shall be even as it was told me.
– Acts 27:24, 25 KJV

In 1853, when young Hudson Taylor was making his first voyage to China, his vessel was delayed near New Guinea because the winds had ceased. A rapid current was carrying the ship toward some reefs, and the situation was becoming dangerous. Even the sailors using a longboat could not row the vessel out of the current.

"We have done everything that can be done," said the captain to Taylor.

But Taylor replied, "No, there is one thing we have not done yet."

There were three other believers on the ship, and Taylor suggested that each retire to his own cabin and pray for a breeze. They did, and while he was at prayer, Taylor received confidence from God that the desperately needed wind would be sent. He went up on deck and suggested to the first officer, an unbeliever, that he let down the mainsail because a breeze was on its way. The man refused, but then they saw the corner of the sail begin to stir. The breeze had come! They let down the sail and in a short time were on their way!

God promised to preserve Paul, and he did. So Paul could say in confidence, "Fear not." Do we believe God will do what He says, when He says He will? "Faith is to believe what we do not see, and the reward of faith is to see what we believe."

~ Jourdain Smith

October 15

A Time for Action

A rain having come on, the whole company were drenched and shivering, and the islanders kindled an immense fire of brushwood, and welcomed them all to its grateful warmth. Paul was among the most active in collecting fuel. – Sketches from the Life of Paul, pg. 270

Though soaked to the skin, Paul worked to provide for the comforts of his fellow travelers. He sought to care for the urgent needs of the people. This was not the moment for him to preach an evangelistic sermon; this was a time for action. In whatever he found to do, even if it was the simple matter of gathering firewood, Paul did it with all his energy. Just as the wood must be gathered before the fire can burn, so the heart must be prepared before it can burn with conviction and love.

I too must put all of my focus into my work. There are many souls who could be reached if I would first lay a foundation of friendship, just as Paul met the ship-crew's needs. The most important thing though is that I take action. This is a call to be active and not passive. There are people who need to experience the love of God shining through me. I must not sit by idly, expecting someone else to take action. I must arise. I must reach out and touch lives. I must make a difference for God.

You, like Paul, are to be active. Don't wait for someone else to act. Care for the needs of those around you, preparing pathways to their hearts. Remember, you are responsible for those to whom you had an opportunity to witness (Ezekiel 33:6). The things you do may save someone else's life. This is a call to action!

~ Buddy Taylor

October 16

Your Influence

The Lord wrought through them in a remarkable manner, and for Paul's sake the entire company were treated with great kindness.
– Sketches from the Life of Paul, pg. 271

Soaked and exhausted, Paul floated in the sea. For the last fourteen days, he had wrestled with the tempest. The wind blew with its fullest fury, and the high waves determined to sink the ship. The crew knew that their situation was hopeless; there was nothing they could do to save themselves. Nevertheless, they still tried to save the ship. However, conditions grew worse all the time. The crew became discouraged. But, just as they were about to give up, Paul spoke words of assurance saying that it was God's will for them to be saved.

Why did God save them? He could have allowed them to die. God chose not to let everyone die because Paul pleaded that they all might be saved. If Paul had not interceded in behalf of the crew, they might have been lost.

Think about it. The lives of the crew were in Paul's hands. Did you know that your influence has similar power? You can influence a person for good or evil. To some degree, you have the power to decide the eternal destiny of others. But, guess what? You have a choice to make. Are you going to let your influence be molded by unbelieving people around you? Or will you choose to have an uplifting influence on them? Remember, you might be the only view of Jesus that others see.

~ David Chang

Above the Clouds

His hopes of winning many souls to the truth at Rome seemed destined to be disappointed. – Sketches from the Life of Paul, pg. 273

Have you ever imagined an experience before it actually takes place? What happens when you actually get to the situation? For me at least, my imagination's portrait of something usually stands in contrast with reality. Sometimes the reality I look forward to surpasses my wildest imaginations. On the other hand, I all too often am disappointed when I expect one thing but then get another.

Paul experienced both of these feelings as he entered Rome. For years he had longed to witness in Rome, and now he was there. But instead of a joyous meeting with fellow Christians, he was led toward the metropolis of the world as an add-on to one of the many chain-gangs that would pass through the gates of Rome en route to the dreaded prison. Disappointment crept into Paul's heart, and like storm clouds on a brilliant day, stripped the joy from a disciple who had been guided so far by God. But soon, Jesus would chase away the gloom enveloping the apostle, because Paul had not been led that far for nothing. "Suddenly a cry of joy is heard, and a man springs out from the passing throng and falls upon the prisoner's neck, embracing him with tears and rejoicing, as a son would welcome a long-absent father. Again and again is the scene repeated" (*Sketches from the Life of Paul*, pg. 273).

Above the clouds on that day was a risen Son that would shine through. Heaven never lets its followers down, and the reunion experienced by the brethren that day surpassed all of Paul's expectations.

~ Robby Folkenberg

October 18

20/20 Vision

With eyes made keen by loving expectation, many discern in the chained captive the one who spoke to them the words of life at Corinth, at Philippi, or at Ephesus. – Sketches from the Life of Paul, pg. 273

I'm sure that at some point in your life you have had your eyes checked. An optometrist in a white coat demanded your entire medical history and shone a bright light into your eyes. Then he made you stand in front of a chart and make a fool out of yourself trying to read the tiny letters. I remember getting my eyes checked and standing at the end of a long hall, trying to read the chart on the far wall. They say that 20/20 vision is perfect. I don't remember how I did on my eye test, but it probably wasn't perfect.

Unfortunately, I'm not the only one without perfect vision. Most of the Jews in Christ's day were practically blind. For hundreds of years, Jewish scholars had studied the prophecies about the coming Messiah, and every Jewish mother hoped that her son would be this Deliverer. But when the Messiah actually came, they didn't see Him. They constantly looked for Him at the top of the chart; they expected Him to come as a BIG letter, but He didn't. He came as a tiny letter, at the bottom of society and hardly noticeable; and the Jews' eyes were too bad to see Him.

But, a few did see. Their eyes had been "made keen by loving expectation" for a Messiah who would deliver them, not only from earthly oppressors, but also from the heavy yoke of sin. They had 20/20 vision and instantly recognized in the bleeding, dying form of a derided Galilean the Savior of the world.

Satan wants all of us to be spiritually blind. He will use anything to obscure our view of the Savior. But God is more powerful than Satan, and will give you spiritual 20/20 vision if you will ask Him. Have you had an "eye" checkup lately?

~ Cara Dewsberry

October 19

Love One Another

Owe no one anything, except to love one another, for the one who loves his neighbor has fulfilled the law. – Romans 13:8 NET

Many years ago, a man was walking down a busy street in New York City when he saw a young black gentleman walking along carrying two heavy suitcases. Immediately his heart prompted him to help. He put his hand kindly on the man's shoulder and said, "That's pretty heavy, brother, isn't it? Here, let me take one; I'm going your way." There was no use protesting, and so they walked along together.

The big-hearted man learned that his new-found friend was walking from the railway station to a hotel several blocks away because he couldn't afford a taxi, and that fact made his kind deed all the sweeter. He arrived at the hotel before he learned that the black gentleman was Booker T. Washington, who later became the founder of the Tuskegee Institute. And who was the big-hearted man who carried one of the suitcases? He was Theodore Roosevelt, who later became the President of the United States.

I have seen from my own experience that in order to become great we must first learn to serve. So, just look around you and faithfully carry out the helpful little things you find to do for others.

~ Rebecca Luchak

October 20

Hard-Core Testing

My grace is sufficient for thee: for my strength is made perfect in weakness. Most gladly therefore will I rather glory in my infirmities, that the power of Christ may rest upon me. – 2 Corinthians 12:9 KJV

While on tour with Fountainview Academy, I had an allergic reaction to a medication that I had been taking. One of the first symptoms I experienced was itchiness from head to toe. Then I started having severe muscle and joint pain. As things continued to worsen, my parents decided it would be best for me to leave the tour and come home to get proper care. While at home I started to get better, but very slowly! Doing the smallest things would make the reaction get worse. For instance, I went on a walk one evening with my parents, and when I got back, my ankle was so swollen that I couldn't walk on it. During this challenging time I was in intense pain almost constantly, even when I wasn't doing anything. At night I couldn't sleep because of the pain and would lie awake for hours, crying. It didn't make sense to me why everyone else could be having so much fun on tour, while I was at home almost bed-ridden and in constant pain.

There were times when I would doubt God and His promises. That's when I would get discouraged and depressed. But then, I would remember the promise that God would only allow to happen what I could handle. I wanted God to just heal me right away, but He had other plans. He wanted me to have patience and learn total dependence on Him. Even when to me it looked like things were out of control, He knew what was happening and wanted me to learn some precious lessons that otherwise I wouldn't have learned.

When brought into a trying experience like mine, remember that God is always in control. Things may not make sense at the moment, but someday in heaven we will understand. God's strength is "made perfect in weakness"; I am a living testimony of that. Trust Him with your life, and rest in the knowledge that His power is available to you.

~ Becky Brousson

October 21

Encouragement

Few realize the significance of those words of Luke, that when Paul saw his brethren, "he thanked God and took courage."... The cloud of sadness that had rested upon his spirit had been swept away.
– Sketches from the Life of Paul, pg. 274

When Bruce Johnston was seven, his father was killed in a brawl at the local bar. Bruce's family was very poor, so he had to work to help to support his mother and sisters. In fifth grade, his teacher told him he would never amount to anything, and he failed fifth grade. The first day of school the following year, his sixth grade teacher greeted him with a smile, complimented him on his new clothes and told him, "You're a fine young man! You're going to do well, and we're going to have a wonderful school year." That year was a turning point in young Bruce's life. He determined that he would be an encourager. As a pastor, college teacher, and administrator, he encouraged thousands throughout his lifetime all because of one teacher who had encouraged him.

Paul's life was much like Bruce's. He went through trials and persecution on every hand. It caused him grief and much distress when there was strife between believers; and sometimes he felt his work might be in vain. But when he walked down the Via Appia on his way to Rome, many Christians recognized him and, ignoring his chains, ran up to embrace him. He had visited them and written many letters of encouragement to them. Now it was their turn to encourage him. His "cloud of sadness" was swept away.

Maybe some weary soul will cross your path today. Just one word of encouragement or a smile will make their day a little brighter and their step a little lighter.

~ Melissa Butler

October 22

Happy

The cloud of sadness that had rested upon his spirit had been swept away. – Sketches from the Life of Paul, pg. 274

There once was a king who owned all the land as far as the eye could see. He had several castles and ruled his land with an iron fist. But, no matter how much he had, he was still a very miserable man.

One day he told one of his servants, "Go from one horizon to the other, find the happiest man on earth and bring me his shirt. Once I have the happiest man's shirt, I will be able to be happy myself. Do not return without that shirt or you will be beheaded."

The servant set out about his mission. As the king waited and waited, he became impatient. Finally, after many months of searching, the servant returned. Noticing the servant's hands were empty the king became very angry. He told the servant that he had one minute to explain why he had disobeyed his orders before he was to be beheaded.

With tears in his eyes, the servant looked to the king and said, "Master, I did as you said: I searched from horizon to horizon looking for the happiest man on earth, and I finally found him."
So the king asked, "Why didn't you bring me the shirt of this man?"
The servant replied, "Master, the happiest man on earth did not own a shirt."

There is little in this life that will make you truly happy. You must depend on God to make you happy and meet your needs. When a need arises in your life, trust God to supply for you according to His riches. When you put your trust in God, the clouds of sadness are sure to be swept away.

~ Jeremy Grabiner

October 23

Is It Worth It?

He felt that his labors had not been in vain. – Sketches from the Life of Paul, pg. 274

It was late at night when Jesus walked to the garden of Gethsemane. However, this was not a normal visit. His purpose was to prepare to be the Redeemer of this world. Can you imagine that the King of the Universe came down to be your Redeemer? Though this is hard to imagine, it did happen. However, before He died to take away our sins, He had to face a big question, "Is it worth it?"

Jesus has an amazing relationship with His Father. They are so close that the Bible says they are one. Can you imagine being so close to someone that your thoughts and actions are the same? That's how it is with Jesus and His Father. But, there in Gethsemane, sin was about to separate them. Was it worth it to be separated from His Father to save a rebellious race?

Furthermore, Jesus couldn't see beyond death. It was only by faith that He knew the Father would raise Him. If there was any sin found in Him, God could not raise Him from the dead. Would He risk His eternal life? Even if He *did* die for mankind, there was a possibility that all might reject that gift. Was His work in vain? No, through Him thousands of lives will be saved.

At times, I can relate to this. When I do a work for God, sometimes I question, "Is this really worth my effort?" In my eyes the situation may look hopeless. However, if I leave my work up to God, just as Jesus fully trusted in His Father, He will use my efforts to glorify His name. So, the next time you ask, "Is it worth it?" remember that if you are doing God's will, your labors will not be in vain.

~ David Chang

October 24

Abundantly Repaid

Although his Christian life had been a succession of trials, sufferings, and disappointments, he felt in that hour abundantly repaid.
– Sketches from the Life of Paul, pg. 274

Have you ever been afraid to risk your own life to save someone who was in danger?

A man was walking home from work one night, and for some reason he decided to take a different route home than what he normally took. Along the way, he was passing by some bushes when he heard scuffling noises, and intuitively he knew that someone was being kidnapped. The man decided that he would want someone to help him if he were in trouble, so he darted through the bushes and attacked the kidnapper. The kidnapper freed himself from the man's grasp and ran away. After the kidnapper escaped, a little girl's voice cried "Daddy?" The man in risking his own life to save another had unknowingly saved his own daughter; and what he had gone through for her didn't matter anymore because, in that hour, he felt abundantly repaid.

How do you think the dad would have felt if he hadn't attacked the kidnapper and had found out later that it was his own daughter whom he could have saved? Paul never worried about his own life; he knew that God would take care of him, and whatever trials he went through were from God's hand. His main focus was on helping and encouraging others, and the reward for doing that was worth any pain and suffering he had to endure.

If you keep a close connection with God and focus on others before yourself, you won't have to worry about what might happen to you. Although it may not be obvious right away, the final reward you will get for helping others is worth far more than all the pain and suffering you had to go through.

~ Jennifer Atkins

October 25

Forgetting What Is Behind

…Forgetting those things which are behind and reaching forth unto those things which are before… – Philippians 3:13, 14 KJV

    Snowmobiling is one of my favorite activities to do in the winter, with all the speed and mobility in the snow. One day I was pulling my brother on his skies around our house and up and down the road. Every once in a while, for safety's sake, I would turn around to see if he was still there, just to make sure he hadn't run into a tree or something. So, as I was going around the house I turned my head quickly to look back. Just as I was turning my head forward again, I saw our camping trailer coming up right in front of me. I slammed on the brakes to try to stop the snowmobile; though I squeezed the brakes with all my might, I wasn't able to stop the snowmobile from crashing into the trailer. After the snowmobile came to a stop, we could see that the snowmobile skis had gone right into the trailer. Luckily, they had not gone all the way through, and we were able to patch the hole fairly easily.

    It's the same way with our Christian walk. If we turn from beholding Christ for even half a second, we will crash into something, and our spiritual life will need to be repaired. In Paul's life we see that he didn't always keep on the path, but with God's help, he got back up and kept on going. I want to encourage you, that when you are tempted to look back, and even if you fall off the trail, don't be discouraged; ask for forgiveness, get back up and keep going.

~ Joey Heagy

October 26

Confidence

Trust in the LORD with all thine heart; and lean not unto thine own understanding. – Proverbs 3:5 KJV

Close to where I live there is a duck pond and a street nearby that ducks frequently cross to get to the pond. It is interesting to watch how the ducks cross the street. When they cross, they do so with confidence that everything will be okay. The ducks are only focused on the other side of the street, and they do not let anything else distract them.

If God cares enough to protect the ducks, then how much more does He care about us? God cares for us more than we can imagine. But, it's our choice to trust that He will take care of us. If we trust God, we will be able to walk the streets of life that are crowded with worries and difficulties with confidence, just like those ducks can. Also, just as the ducks only focus on the other side of the street, we need to focus only on God's promises, not the other things that may distract us along the way. The closer we draw towards Jesus, the more confidence we have; however, the farther we get from Him the more lost and confused we get.

When you place your faith in God, you will hear His voice speaking to you, "Fear not, for I have redeemed you; I have summoned you by name; you are mine. When you pass through the waters, I will be with you; and when you pass through the rivers, they will not sweep over you. When you walk through the fire, you will not be burned; the flames will not set you ablaze" (Isaiah 43:1, 2 NIV).

~ Jeremy Grabiner

October 27

In Love

He showed that religion does not consist in rites and ceremonies, creeds and theories. If it did, the natural man could understand it by investigation, as he understands worldly things. Paul taught that religion is a practical, saving energy, a principle wholly from God, a personal experience of God's renewing power upon the soul.
– Sketches from the Life of Paul, pg. 276

There are many religions in the world today: Christianity, Catholicism, Hinduism, Buddhism, Islam, Spiritualism, and many others. Each religion has a unique set of theories and traditions. And each one is worshipping something and trying to find the way to immortality. But religion isn't just going to church or being baptized. These things are undoubtedly a very important part, but true religion is a "saving energy," "a principle," a "personal experience" with God. To be saved, we must have a personal relationship with the Savior.

"If I have the gift of prophecy and can fathom all mysteries and all knowledge, and if I have a faith that can move mountains, but have not love, I am nothing. If I give all I possess to the poor and surrender my body to the flames, but have not love, I gain nothing" (1 Corinthians 13:2,3 NIV). All of these deeds are good things, but if you don't have love, they are useless. When you are in love with God, things like helping the poor and keeping the commandments will be things that you want to do because you love Him. But right doing is not what saves us, for then we would be able to understand salvation. Salvation is a mystery, something that we will be studying throughout eternity and yet will never fully understand. God is truly incredible—have you fallen in love with Him?

~ Melissa Butler

October 28

Saving Energy

Paul taught that religion is a practical, saving energy, a principle wholly from God, a personal experience of God's renewing power upon the soul. – Sketches from the Life of Paul, pg. 276

When my parents upgraded their first computer to one hundred megabytes of memory, they were thrilled! Later, they were amazed when they actually were able to have a gigabyte of memory. Today, we're talking terabytes and beyond! How can so much memory be crammed into such a small space? There is so much about technology that is beyond us.

My Pathfinder director was a telephone lineman, so we asked him some questions about telephone technology. How can a person on one side of the earth speak and instantly be heard by a person on the other side of the world? How can hundreds of millions of people around the world make phone calls at the same time? He tried to explain about fiber optics, signals bouncing off of satellites, and such, but finally admitted that even the experts don't know exactly why and how it all works perfectly; it just does.

There is no way of clearly explaining exactly how the saving energy from God works. It is a technology entirely outside of man's ability to understand. But, we can experience it if we accept Christ. The same God, who created all of the laws of nature that humans are tapping into, has created the spiritual laws. There is a real Power Source that renews our souls and gives us power, strength, and a peace that "surpasses all understanding" (Philippians 4:7 NKJV). I want to invite you to accept Christ as your Savior and experience His saving grace today.

~ Joey Heagy

October 29

Renewed

Paul taught that religion is...a personal experience of God's renewing power upon the soul. – Sketches from the Life of Paul, pg. 276

Rrrrrrrrrrrrring! My alarm clock rudely awakens me from my exhausted sleep. After dragging myself out of bed and accomplishing a few preliminary tasks, I sit down at my desk and open my Bible. *Boy, I'm just not in the mood!* I think to myself. *Why do I feel so "unspiritual"?* Even though I don't really want to, I decide to talk to God anyway. "Dear Jesus, I need a new heart. To be honest with You, my sinful nature is so strong right now that I don't even feel like spending time with You. But I don't want to be like this; please renew me by Your Spirit. Amen." Having prayed this prayer, I begin to read. Before long, I notice that something is wonderfully different. God is answering my prayer! He is implanting within my heart the desire to know Him better and a willingness to follow His plan. He is helping me to experience His "renewing power upon the soul."

True religion transforms; it rejuvenates the spiritual life. It is not something you wear when you go to church; it is not something you inherit from your parents. Instead, religion is a personal experience of God's power to save even the worst sinner.

Are you experiencing true religion? Is your soul being renewed by the power of the Holy Spirit? Just as King David pleaded with God to experience this kind of religion, you, too, can pray: "Create in me a clean heart, O God. Renew a right spirit within me" (Psalm 51:10 NLT).

~ Jonathan Sharley

October 30

Relationship

To apprehend Christ by faith, to have a spiritual knowledge of him, was more to be desired than a personal acquaintance with him as he appeared on earth. – Sketches from the Life of Paul, pg. 277

Paul was a brilliant and gifted Pharisee, the most intelligent scholar of the nation. He was well respected and rich. From the world's point of view, he had everything; he was a successful man. Though prior to his conversion, he seemed to have it all, he was never happy because his relationship with God wasn't right. In his youth, Paul was taught under a rabbi who followed the traditions of men. Consequently, his relationship with God had been superficial. He came to know traditions very well, but he never knew God. However, God did not give up on him. Instead, God revealed Himself to Paul.

Often times, we find our spiritual lives revolving around tradition. We tend to obliterate God from our thoughts and at the end of the day, we mindlessly pray, "Dear God, thank you for giving me a wonderful day and please forgive my sins. Amen." This happens day after day as if we are chanting to some idol! God wants to talk to us, not to our shallow rituals. Paul's life was transformed when he realized the King of the Universe came down just to know him, and that every time he sinned, he was crucifying the Savior who came to save him. When Paul realized this, his relationship with God became more intimate. No longer did he cling to his traditions; instead, he communed with God as a friend.

That same God who died for Paul died for you too. You are the apple of His eye. He watches you day and night hoping that you will talk to Him. God wants to hear how you are doing, what your struggles are, and what frustrates you. Next time you pray, don't chant; talk to Him and really get to know Him. If you do that, He will truly transform you.

~ David Chang

October 31

The Communion

The communion with Christ which Paul now enjoyed, was more intimate and more enduring than a mere earthly and human companionship. – Sketches from the Life of Paul, pg. 277

I've often wished that I could have been one of the disciples. Just think how wonderful it would be to learn at the feet of Jesus and witness His miracle-working power. I've been tempted to think that I would have a closer relationship with Christ if I had been a disciple. But Paul was just about as close to Jesus as anyone could ever get, and he didn't know Jesus while He was on this earth. The only glimpse he had of Christ was during their encounter on the Damascus Road.

If Paul had such a close relationship with God without being with Him, I can as well. You see, God is with us every moment of our day, even though we may not see Him. I often forget how near He is, but we can talk to Him whenever we need to, and He's never too busy to listen. He can talk to us through a variety of ways, especially through Scripture. Something that never ceases to amaze me is how much He wants to have a communion with me that is closer than anything here on earth. It's deeper than just being with Him. He wants to really know me, and He's genuinely interested in everything about me. He loves me and wants to be my best friend.

I have often heard the words, "I wish I could see Jesus and be with Him." It will be incredible to be in His presence, but something more amazing is the relationship we can have with Him right now. You don't have to wait until Heaven to have "communion with Christ."

~ Melissa Butler

November 1

More than an Acquaintance

To apprehend Christ by faith, to have a spiritual knowledge of him, was more to be desired than a personal acquaintance with him as he appeared on earth. The communion with Christ which Paul now enjoyed, was more intimate and more enduring than a mere earthly and human companionship. – Sketches from the Life of Paul, pg. 277

Paul walked with God, not physically, but spiritually—for he was not a disciple while Christ was on earth. His life was a constant communion with the Father. To Paul, Christ was more than a friend: He was his Savior. He had radically transformed Paul's life, and as a result, Paul became a channel of God's truth and love. God caused the light of His righteousness to shine through Paul into the darkness of ritual and superstition. God is still the same today.

It is true that Jesus wants to be our friend. His desire, however, is much deeper than just a friendship. He wants to create in us a new heart, to give us His righteousness. This is something that we of ourselves cannot do. We need a Savior. As I recognize this need and seek to come into close communion with Christ, I too can receive God's salvation. It is like the slave who experiences the indescribable joy of freedom. His hands are stretched up to the open sky in thankfulness; He is a new man, a free man.

God wants to make you free, but you need more than just an acquaintance with Him. He will take you to new levels in your experience with Him if you will follow. Walk as Paul walked, in the footsteps of Christ. Invite Him to be more than a friend to you. Then, with Christ as your Savior, your friendship will endure throughout eternity.

~ Buddy Taylor

November 2

Rivalry

They were determined that he should move no faster than they.
– Sketches from the Life of Paul, pg. 279

Once there was an eagle, which could out fly another, and the other did not like it. The latter saw a hunter one day, and said to him, "I wish you would bring down that eagle."

The hunter replied, "I would if I had some feathers to put into the arrow." With that said, the eagle pulled a feather out of his wing. The arrow was shot, but it missed the rival eagle; it was flying too high. The envious eagle yanked out more feathers for the arrows, and kept pulling them out until he lost so many that he was not able to fly anymore. Then the hunter turned around and killed him.

While the Jews of Rome were strong believers in the Law and the Prophets, there was a big difference between them and Paul. The apostle Paul had been led and taught by the Holy Spirit. The fellow Jews did not like this. Instead of learning the truth as Paul preached it, envy consumed them as they "studied only to find something to sustain themselves and condemn him" (*Sketches from the Life of Paul,* pg. 279).

Jealousy plants the seed of comparison, and we end up reaping the fruit of rivalry. As the fire of rivalry consumes our relationships with others, we tend to attempt to hurt those we envy. Just like the Roman Jews and the eagle, we become jealous of those that "move faster than we do." We envy those who can out fly us. But, in the end, we only destroy ourselves.

~ David Ortiz

November 3

The Truth Will Always Triumph

The truth always involves a cross. Those who will not believe, oppose and deride those who do believe. The fact that its presentation creates a storm of opposition is no evidence against the truth. The prophets and apostles imperiled their lives because they would conscientiously obey God. And our Savior declares that "all that would live godly in Christ Jesus shall suffer persecution." This is the Christian's legacy.
– Sketches from the Life of Paul, pg. 279

John Wycliffe lay on his bed, ill with a deadly disease. After years of avoiding the angry church members who were trying to stop the translation of the Bible into English, he was now confined to a bed, unable to finish the translation. It seemed as if the enemy would triumph at last, even after all his hard work. Needless to say, he was very discouraged.

To make matters worse, the very friars and church members who had been trying to stop him picked this time to visit him, hoping to discourage him further. "You're going to die!" they told him. "We'll get rid of you for sure, now," they taunted. "You know, this is your chance to take back everything you have said about us and the Pope!"

Wycliffe then asked an attendant to prop him up on his pillow before replying, "I will not die, but live to finish my work and declare again the evil deeds of the friars."

Sometimes, it seems that the truth will lose the battle, and evil will triumph. It seems that everything is going wrong, and no matter how hard we try, we can't make a difference. But really, hard trials only mean that Satan sees you are trying to do right, and he is desperately trying to mess up God's plan by getting you to do wrong. Have no fear. Truth will always triumph, just as it says in Romans 8:28, "All things work together for good to them that love God, to them who are the called according to His purpose" (KJV).

~ Dave White

November 4

Little Is Much When God Is In It

Many, in their pride and ignorance, forget that lowly things are mighty. – Sketches from the Life of Paul, pg. 283

This year, Fountainview went on a filming tour to California and Utah. I wasn't in all of the songs we filmed, and some days I didn't feel that I was very important. The last day we were in Utah we had a concert at the park. I sang only a few songs in the whole concert. My thoughts wandered to one of our earlier concerts in which one of my classmates had sung a song called "Little Is Much." The words to this song are as follows:

In the harvest field now ripened, there's a work for all to do.
Hark; the voice of God is calling, to the harvest calling you.

Does the place you're called to labor seem so small and little known?
It is great if God is in it, and He'll not forget His own.

When the conflict here is ended and our race on earth is run,
He will say, if we are faithful, "Welcome home, my child, well done."

CHORUS: Little is much when God is in it, labor not for wealth or fame. There's a crown and you can win it, if you go in Jesus' name.

Every word touched my heart. While I may wish I was a better musician, God knows it's better for me to do little things because I may become boastful. While I was in the park, I had an opportunity to talk to the bystanders during all the songs I was not singing or playing in. They were all touched by the music and could see something different in the students. When I walked away from the concert that evening, I felt that I had done much more in that concert than in any other. I knew that God was in the little that I had done.

~ Melody Hyde

November 5

The Path of Duty

Many, even of those who profess to believe the solemn truths for this time, feel but little moral responsibility. When they see that the path of duty is beset with perplexities and trials, they choose a way for themselves, where there is less effort needed; where there are fewer risks to run, fewer dangers to meet. By selfishly shunning responsibilities, they increase the burdens of the faithful workers, and at the same time separate themselves from God, and forfeit the reward they might have won. – Sketches from the Life of Paul, pg. 284

Lately, I have been attempting to make plans for my future, but something just keeps getting in the way: me. I want to go to college, but I can't quite decide what to take or which college to go to. I'm tempted to think it won't be worth going to college if I take something I'm not sure I want to do. Then recently, I was encouraged to go to an evangelism college. Oh no, I thought, evangelism is not for me! The last time I spoke in public, I nearly fainted! But then my thoughts turned to what God would have me do. After some prayer, I came across the quote above, and it seemed as if it were written just for me. College may be terrifying, preaching an evangelistic series may be daunting, and knocking on strangers' doors may still trigger butterflies in my stomach, but if that is my "path of duty," then I must go. If God is calling me to something that is uncomfortable, then I must forget about myself and what I can or can't do and simply trust in God's plan for me. When I said, "Lord, I can't do it," Jesus said, "My grace is sufficient for you, for My strength is made perfect in weakness" (2 Corinthians 12:9 NKJV).

God is constantly putting responsibilities in our path to test us and help us grow. But, often we take one look at them and try to find an easier path. Jonah tried that too, but running away from God's plan is not very smart. Today, when you are tempted to think God's task for you is impossible, surrender your will to Him, step out of your comfort zone, and let God work through you.

~ Melissa Butler

November 6

Forgive and Forget

He [Paul] therefore decided that Onesimus should at once return to his master... It was a severe test for this servant to thus deliver himself up to the master he had wronged; but he had been truly converted, and, painful as it was, he did not shrink from this duty. – Sketches from the Life of Paul pg. 285

Onesimus squinted as he surveyed the plantation below. It had been less than a year since, veiled by the shadows of night, he had stood on this same hilltop to take one last glimpse of his master's land before vanishing into the shadows. Now, as he made his way down the hill and onto the main road leading to his master's home, Onesimus couldn't help but wonder at what he might meet with, even after his master read the letter that Paul had sent with him. How could anyone forgive a slave who not only ran away, but also stole a large sum of money?

Deep in thought, Onesimus made his way toward his master's large house. As he drew near it, a wave of uneasiness swept over him. What if he was sent to the gallows or to a dungeon cell to live out his life in pure agony? His anxiety continued to grow as he neared the door. Reaching it, he knocked and then kneeled down to await his fate.

All of us have faced the same situation as Onesimus' master faced when he opened that door: What to do with someone who has wronged us? When Peter asked Jesus how many times he should forgive someone Jesus replied, "I tell you, not seven times, but seventy-seven times" (Mathew 18:22 KJV). Peter thought he was being lenient by forgiving someone seven times, but Jesus has made it clear that we should freely forgive no matter how many times someone wrongs us.

~ Brad Donesky

November 7

Making Things Right

It was a severe test for this servant to thus deliver himself up to the master he had wronged; but he had been converted, and, painful as it was, he did not shrink from this duty. – Sketches from the Life of Paul, pg. 285

George Eastman was the inventor of Kodak cameras and roll film. As a kid, George loved to play ball. When their homework was done, he and his friends would gather in a vacant lot nearby and play. One day, while he and his friends were playing, a boy named Hobart swung with all his might and hit the ball right through the neighbor lady's window. "Oh no! Let's get out of here!" a friend named Ben yelled. "Wait!" cried Jimmy, "We have to get that ball back; it's the only one we have!"

"Ok," George said, "I'll go with you, Hobart. Come on." They proceeded to walk over to the house they had just damaged. As they neared the door, an old lady opened the door and, smiling, asked if the ball was theirs. They then explained that it was and apologized about the window, expressing how sorry they were to have broken it. But, to their surprise, the lady quickly brushed it off by saying, "I can't get out anymore, and I love to watch you boys play. Run along now and finish your game."

You know, sometimes we won't apologize because we're afraid of the consequences. Or, we think the person we wronged might put us down and make us look bad. It is embarrassing, but God wants us to apologize for the wrongs we've done, because that's what we would want others to do for us. After you're finished, even if you have to make restitution, you'll feel better, because you did what was right in God's eyes.

~ Dave White

November 8

Him Instead of Me

How fitting an illustration of the love of Christ toward the repenting sinner! As the servant who had defrauded his master had nothing with which to make restitution, so the sinner who has robbed God of years of service has no means of canceling the debt; Jesus interposes between the sinner and the just wrath of God, and says, I will pay the debt. Let the sinner be spared the punishment of his guilt. I will suffer in his stead. – Sketches from the Life of Paul, pg. 287

I don't remember what our crime was, but we were guilty. My brother, sister, and I had done something that deserved a spanking. We didn't get very many spankings, but this time we knew it was coming!

Being the oldest, my sister went into my parent's bedroom first and the door was closed. There was silence for several minutes; then my brother and I heard the sound of the spanking. We winced, knowing we would be there shortly. However, there was no cry from our sister. In a couple of minutes the door opened and she came out smiling. *Wow, quick recovery!*, I thought.

I was next. Hesitatingly, I went into the bedroom. My dad asked me to sit beside him. We discussed the issue that was resulting in this punishment, and then my dad prayed with me. He then asked me to bend over his knee. I knew what was coming and gritted my teeth for the outcome. I heard the sound of the spanking, but didn't feel anything. My dad was actually spanking his own leg, taking my punishment (and he admitted that it really did hurt!).

When my spanking was done, he talked with me about it and explained that this is what Jesus has done for us. We are guilty, but He bore our guilt and with His stripes we are healed. I don't remember much about any other spanking I got, but the one that didn't hurt me stands out in my memory because it showed me the impact of Christ's love for me in taking the punishment for my sins.

~ Joey Heagy

November 9

Paid in Full

I will pay the debt. Let the sinner be spared the punishment of his guilt. I will suffer in his stead. – Sketches from the Life of Paul, pg. 287

Imagine with me that you were in debt and owed someone $75,000, and that you were required to make payments every month of $750. However, one day you received a letter in the mail informing you that your debt had been paid in full, and there was no need for you to continue making payments.

You could not believe your eyes—someone would do that for you! Deep inside you knew that you could never repay the kindness that person had shown you, and there was no way that you could fully express your thankfulness.

Well believe it or not, Jesus did this just for you! He paid the debt of your sin, freeing you from your punishment. And he suffered in your stead! What a wonderful debt to be freed from!

Now, think with me, this is a much greater debt than a debt of money. It is a debt of our eternal life, and Jesus has paid it all! This makes me realize the importance of taking this gift seriously. God has done everything for us, so why don't we express our gratefulness in giving our lives to Him?

~ Melody Hyde

November 10

Same Status

They have been washed in the same blood, quickened by the same Spirit; they are made one in Christ Jesus. – Sketches from the Life of Paul, pg. 289

"Red and yellow, black and white; all are precious in His sight." I'm sure you have heard these words before. You've probably seen someone else being made fun of, heard racist remarks, and witnessed people being made to look inferior. Jesus, however, is no respecter of persons. A blemish or defect does not make a person any less valuable to Christ.

Late one afternoon, a little boy peered into a pet shop window. There was a sign that read, "Puppies for Sale". Since all little boys love puppies, he ran in with his piggy bank and dumped it on the counter. The store owner sadly told the boy he was lacking nine dollars and seventeen cents. The little boy ran home and for the next week worked incessantly. Finally, the day came, and he went to get his puppy. He pointed to a small pup in the back with a gimp leg. The owner replied, "No, son, that dog will never run like the others. He's just a mistake."

"Yes," replied the boy. "I want THAT one!"
"Son, I don't want you to end up disappointed. But, if you insist, I'll give him to you for free."
"NO mister! He is just as good as the others. I worked for him, and I WILL pay for him." With that the boy lifted up his pant leg to reveal a large brace. He also had a leg that didn't function properly. "I want him. He's really like me. I understand him."That day the boy walked away with his puppy joyfully licking his face.

Jesus did the same thing for you and me. He picked us up out of the dumpster and carried us home. He paid for us regardless of our status, our infirmities, and our filthy condition. You, I, and every other creature are the property of Jesus. We are all children of the King.

~ Veronica Nudd

November 11

Unashamed

They were not ashamed of their faith. – Sketches from the Life of Paul, pg. 291

Paul's first visit to Rome was as a prisoner living in a rented house, a privilege granted him by the chief guard of the prison. Nevertheless, Paul took the opportunity to share the truth with all who came into his dwelling. Chained to a guard, yet allowed the freedom of visitors, Paul's every effort was to bring souls into the kingdom. Aside from studying the Word of God, Paul was found writing letters of encouragement and guidance to the growing churches of Asia.

Paul's labours resulted in the saving of many souls, even in the infamous Nero's household. These barbarous men saw the light and accepted it. However, it did not stop there. These men, the servants of a wicked king, were not afraid to share the truth. These men, in the court of the greatest king of that time, were beacons of light to a lost world. "They were not ashamed of their faith."

God is looking to His church today and is searching for fearless witnesses for Him. He has a work for such people: to go into the entire world and share Him and the message of salvation. Persecution will befall such men and women, but truth is dearer to them than their own comfort. Sharing it is their goal, even at the very loss of their lives.

God is looking for such people today. Are you willing to be one of them?

~ Douglas Schappert

November 12

A Workout for Others

It was not by the sermons of Paul, but by his bonds, that the attention of the court had been attracted to Christianity. – Sketches From the Life of Paul, pg. 292

Soviet cosmonaut Yuri Romanenko returned to earth on December 29, 1987, after 326 days in space orbit. This world, or should I say, out of this world record could not have been accomplished without a certain spacesuit. Zero gravity experienced outside the atmosphere relaxes bodies far too much, and previous cosmonauts had to undergo intensive therapy to revive their weakened hearts and atrophied muscles. To counteract these negative and often harmful side effects, the Russian space program developed the "penguin suit," an exercise suit made basically of rubber bands. As Romanenko went through his cyber exercise each day, the suit applied constant tension to his muscles, giving him an extra workout.

In your spiritual workout, it's necessary to undergo tension as well. Without this, we become weak and are defeated when the devil attacks. Trials help us realize our need of God and draw us nearer to the one who can free us from our troubles. But Paul's bonds in Rome show us another aspect of tribulation. As he stood before the Roman court, defending himself and his faith, he was actually witnessing to the court-members themselves! This testimony should give us courage and resolve when we face difficulties. Trials not only draw us closer to God, but through our Christ-like handling of them, they point others to the Savior as well!

~ Robby Folkenberg

November 13

Our Impossibilities

It was not by sermons of Paul, but by his bonds, that the attention of the court had been attracted to Christianity. It was as a captive that he conquered rulers. – Sketches from the Life of Paul, pg. 292

In the least likely place, Paul witnessed to the least likely people. Though a prisoner in bonds, he reached the hearts of the Emperor's family, winning a great victory for truth. When all others saw only hopelessness and imminent death, God saw an opportunity worthy of Caesar's court. To an aged prisoner, this might have seemed to be the least promising moment to reach the wealthy and powerful. The gospel, though, wasn't about what Paul could do, but rather what God could do.

Just as Paul was a captive, we in our own strength are feeble. Our times of weakness, however, are God's times of strength.

One Sunday, I had a lengthy essay due the next day. But that afternoon there was an activity planned to help a neighbor clear land for his farm. Even though I needed to finish my essay, I decided to go because this man really needed help, and it was a one-day opportunity. When I got back, I had a good feeling inside and was so energized that I was able to sit down and write the rest of my essay that evening. What made it a victory for me was being able to tell people that, even though something was an impossibility to me, it was accomplished because God is greater than our circumstances.

Paul's power was not found in his own greatness, but in his willingness to submit to God's plan. If Paul had decided to give up hope because he couldn't see any opportunity to witness for God, then he would have been just another prisoner. But in God's hands, Paul became a conqueror. You too will face impossibilities. But remember, God did not put you in those situations so that you would fail. Rather, you are there so that His glory and power might be shown. Remember, God can see the end of every situation. Trust Him to see you through.

~ Buddy Taylor

November 14

Courageous or Not?

His courage and faith were a continual sermon. And by his example, other Christians were nerved to greater energy. – Sketches from the Life of Paul, pg. 293

It was a cold, rainy day and Vasco da Gama stood on the deck of his ship, wondering what to do. You see, just seconds before, the captain of his fleet had yelled across the wind-tossed sea that the crew would mutiny if they did not turn back. Their fleet was headed for India, but after weeks of sailing, the sailors were getting restless and wanted to turn back. Finally gathering his courage, da Gama yelled back to call all hands to his ship.

Once everyone was present, he told them, "If I agree to turn back to Portugal, you must sign a paper telling the king that you forced me to do this." The men quickly agreed and went to a cabin below deck to sign the paper. Then, while they were all in the room, da Gama, with the help of several loyal sailors, bound the men who were capable of sailing and locked them in chains. Then, throwing the compass and astrolabe into the sea, he stated, "We will now sail with God as our pilot."

Sometimes, we tend to follow the crowd and do everything they do just because we don't want to look bad. We promise ourselves that we won't go past a certain line or that we'll never do this or that, but then, when the crowd does it, we seem to go along just because of what they might think, not having the courage to stand up for what we believe. Next time you find yourself lowering your standards, remember Vasco da Gama's courage and put the King of the Universe first in your life.

~ Dave White

November 15

Seeing a Sermon

His courage and faith were a continual sermon. And by his example, other Christians were nerved to greater energy. – Sketches from the Life of Paul, pg. 293

We are told that we should live lives that portray Christ. But do we really do that? I wonder that about myself; after watching me for a day, would someone say, "That girl definitely loves Jesus"? Or would they have a hard time telling that I am a Christian?

Paul probably preached hundreds of sermons in his lifetime, some of them in very famous places such as Mar's Hill. But perhaps some of his most amazing sermons didn't use words: they were preached by the example of his life. This was especially true during the years he was in prison. People noticed Paul's behavior in adverse circumstances, and their hearts were impressed. How could an old man, doubtless suffering from physical ailments, endure imprisonment and mistreatment with uncomplaining cheerfulness? How could he show such love to his persecutors? Many who would never have gone to hear Paul preach a sermon were converted by seeing the love of God in the way he lived.

There is a song that says, "I'd rather see a sermon than hear one any day. I'd rather one would walk with me than try to show the way." Someone can *say* all kinds of wonderful and true things about God's love and Christianity, but people will often ignore or argue with words; however, when someone's life is radically changed by the truth, the power of God is displayed in an indisputable way.

I want people to be able to look at me and know that I have been with Christ. I want my life to be a continual sermon that glorifies Him and His power. What about you? What sermon is your life preaching?

~ Cara Dewsberry

November 16

A Higher Calling

When a servant of God is withdrawn from active duty, when his voice is no longer heard in encouragement and reproof, we, in our short-sighted judgment, often conclude that his usefulness is at an end. But the Lord does not so regard it. The mysterious providences over which we so often lament, are designed of God to accomplish a work which otherwise might never have been done. – Sketches from the Life of Paul, pg. 293

My Grandpa Shafer was a Christian psychologist, college professor, writer, and speaker. For many years, he traveled to different places giving spiritual seminars. He also was on numerous boards and committees and was highly respected by people. However, he contracted a disease that caused him to lose much of his memory. Due to blackouts and being unable to remember, he had to give up his practice and public outreach. Until her death, my grandma had to drive for him and help him do things he had always done for himself. Even though he had been in the community for a long time, he couldn't even remember old friends and colleagues.

But the Lord was not finished with him. As he recovered, he purchased a computer and took classes on how to use it. Though he is now in his upper eighties, God has given him the opportunity to continue to touch people through poems and articles he is able to produce on his computer. He spends much time in prayer and study and has started giving Bible studies on how to prepare for the last days. He also gives all the money he can to spreading the gospel through various ministries. He even went on a mission trip with my family and gave a few sermons. God is working through my grandpa and many others like him who might seem to be passed by for active service, but still are of great benefit to the Lord's work.

For those of us who still have our youth and full strength of life, let's give God our best. Many young people are allowing their lives to be consumed in worldly pleasures, but God has given us a much higher calling. We can learn a lot from our elders who are giving their all for Christ, even when their strength is diminished.

~ Joey Heagy

November 17

Don't Miss Your Opportunity

Never let us excuse ourselves from efforts to win souls to Christ, even in the most unpromising fields. – Sketches from the Life of Paul, pg. 295

Have you ever been in a situation where you could have witnessed to someone, but you decided not to because you didn't know what to say? That has happened to me too many times.

I was in California with my friend, walking through the mall, when lunch time came. So we began looking around for a place to eat, and we decided on the buffet. When we walked up to the cashier and paid, I started to leave but my friend handed the cashier her own personal copy of the book *Steps to Christ* and said, "I was wondering if you'd like to have this? It changed my life." The cashier took the book and thanked her. Then we left to get our food. A few minutes into our meal, my friend said, "I wonder if that lady's reading the book." So, she got up to take a look. When she came back to the table, she had a big smile on her face and told me that she was reading it, and suggested that we should have prayer for her at that moment. When we finished our meal, we walked past the cashier on our way out and told her thank you and to have a good day, and she picked up the book and said, "I'm reading it!" When my friend asked her if she liked it so far, she said she did.

If it hadn't been for my friend handing the cashier that book, we could have missed an opportunity to witness to her. It really made me stop to think of how many times I've had a chance to witness to someone but never said anything.

The next time you have a chance to witness to someone, take it, for you might be their only chance to hear a message from Heaven.

~ Jennifer Atkins

November 18

Follow the Leader!

No man can be so situated that he cannot obey God. There is too little faith with Christians of today. They are willing to work for Christ and his cause only when they themselves can see a prospect of favorable results. – Sketches from the Life of Paul, pg. 296

An old Scottish woman, on her way to sell thread, buttons, and shoestrings, came to an unmarked crossroad. She threw a stick into the air and went in the direction the stick pointed when it landed. After that day, she would do this regularly. One day, however, someone saw her tossing the stick up several times. "Why do you toss the stick more than once?" the curious person asked.

"Because," replied the woman, "it keeps pointing to the left, and I want to take the road on the right." Dutifully, she kept throwing the stick into the air until it pointed the way she wanted to go.

There are times when God's will seems to take us to places where we did not plan to go. Most of the time, we fight back; we want to control the steering wheel of our lives. We are reluctant to accept that if we follow God's will, even if it's not what we want, our lives will be safe. The best thing to do is to humble ourselves and to follow His lead.

Just like Henrietta Mears wrote, "I cannot give up my will; I must exercise it. I must will to obey. When God gives a command or a vision of truth, it is never a question of what He will do, but what we will do. To be successful in God's work is to fall in line with His will and to do it His way. All that is pleasing to Him is a success."

~ David Ortiz

November 19

Excuses, Excuses

No man can be so situated that he cannot obey God. There is too little faith with Christians of today… Could there be an excuse for disobedience, it would prove our heavenly Father unjust, in that he had given us conditions of salvation with which we could not comply.
– Sketches from the Life of Paul, pg. 296

Obedience. It's something our parents strove to teach us, the policemen endeavor to teach us, and God seeks to teach us. Obedience is difficult because we always seem to find excuses to justify what we want to do. When my parents punished me for eating a cookie, I explained that I was hungry. After my dad got a speeding ticket, you'd think he'd slow down, but there's always that slow car to pass, or an appointment to get to. And then there's sin. We have a way of categorizing sin into small sins and big sins. We may think that lying is a small sin and committing adultery is a big sin. But, this way of thinking is not right! "For whoever keeps the whole law and yet stumbles at just one point is guilty of breaking all of it" (James 2:10 NKJV). If you've sinned, you've sinned, and there is no excuse for disobedience.

But it's too hard, you say. Isn't it impossible to obey God in some situations? I should say not! "There is too little faith with Christians of today." You may think it's all right to eat pork when there is nothing else to eat, but how could you forget the children of Israel? God sent them manna from heaven when there was nothing else. He sent Elijah food from raven's mouths when there was nothing else. And when your cupboards and pockets are empty, He will do the same for you. There is never a time when it is impossible to obey God because He will always provide a way for you to follow Him.

~ Melissa Butler

November 20

What You Could Have Known

The Lord holds us responsible for the light shining upon our pathway.
– Sketches from the Life of Paul, pg. 296

    God has placed many opportunities in our lives that we fail to take advantage of. He has put many people with us that have offered soft correction or wise advice. But, we often puff up with pride and refuse to listen. We are told that we will be held responsible for what we could have known.

    Molly was about to turn twelve, so, she wanted to bake a cake herself and invite her friends over. She told mother that she wanted no help after she received the directions. So, her mom told her that she would have to run to the store to get the ingredients. She listed off the ingredients and proceeded to tell her daughter how to bake the cake. But Molly was so excited that she dashed out the door before her mom could finish her instructions. Her mom called out the door,

"Molly, wait!"
"No Mom, I don't have time! They will be here soon!"

    So, Molly's mom decided that she would let her do things her way. Molly came home and mixed the ingredients together. When she went to turn the oven on she realized that she didn't know what to set the temperature to. She estimated that four-hundred degrees would be just perfect. She also didn't know how long to let it bake, so she set the timer for one hour and twenty minutes and went about her business as usual, cleaning, slamming doors, and what not. When her friends arrived, she went to get the cake out. It was a lovely charcoal color and flat as a pancake. She stuck a fork in it, but couldn't pull it back out. She was so embarrassed and apologized to her friends. They ended up eating bagels with frosting. If Molly had only listened to the rest of her mother's instructions, the cake would have been a success. Instead, she heard what she wanted to and hurried to the store.

    We should grasp the light that we are able to obtain and not use selective hearing. Try looking and listening for the insights that God has made possible for you to receive.

~ Veronica Nudd

November 21

Eyes Are On You

A consistent Christian life will accomplish more good than could be accomplished by many sermons. – Sketches from the Life of Paul, pg. 299

Have you ever wanted to do something really important for God? Maybe you wish to be a missionary, a bible worker, or a pastor. Deep inside you may feel that these are the things that would be most pleasing to God.

Well, believe it or not, even though you feel this way, God wants you to be faithful in the little things in life before you plan to do something great. Though you may feel that great things are the only ways to reach others, those around you are usually more impressed with the way you live your daily life. That is when you are truly preaching.

Paul was the "real deal." He lived the life he preached, and God blessed his faithfulness. God could truly speak through him because He knew that Paul would live up to the message. Could God send His message though you?

If you really want to represent God, you shouldn't have to act differently in church or around Godly people. What this world needs are people who are consistently true Christians. Often times, people will preach one thing, but don't apply it to their own lives. How about we start living like Christ?

~ Melody Hyde

November 22

Glorifying the Father

Whether therefore ye eat, or drink, or whatsoever ye do, do all to the glory of God. – 1 Corinthians 10:31 KJV

There was once a little girl named Jenny Lind. She didn't think she was very pretty and thought of herself as "plain old Jenny." One day she was sitting near her window, watching a plain brown bird that was sitting on a branch nearby. "You're a lot like me," she said to the bird. "You're not very pretty, and neither am I. Just plain old Jenny—that's me. Do you ever wish you could be beautiful like the swallows?"

Then the little bird lifted its head toward heaven and started to sing a pretty song. At this, Jenny smiled and said, "Oh, little bird, your song is pretty! Look over this way and sing for me." But, to her dismay, the bird just kept singing at the sky. All of a sudden, she realized that it was singing to God. That's when she decided that she wanted to be like the little bird and use her voice to glorify God. Jenny became known as the "Swedish Nightingale," and was one of the most highly regarded singers of the 19th century.

We all have our moments when we feel insecure—believe me, I know! But all we have to do is remember what our purpose is here on earth: to be Jesus to someone who needs Him. Then, if we focus on helping others and glorifying God, our own shortcomings will fade, and we will become more and more secure in Him.

~ Dave White

November 23
Convictions that are Consistent

A consistent Christian life will accomplish more good than could be accomplished by many sermons. – Sketches from the Life of Paul, pg. 299

    This year Miss California, Carrie Prejean, was just one of the many girls who were contestants in the 2009 Miss USA pageant. She went from the top 10 to the top 5. Now was the time for the judges to ask her the decisive question that, if answered correctly, might make her Miss USA. The question was: "Vermont recently became the fourth state to legalize same sex marriage, do you think that every state should follow suit? Why or why not?" Carrie said she thinks that a marriage should be between a man and a woman. That's what she grew up knowing to be biblically right. This answer made the judge very upset. Because he was a homosexual, he thought she was discriminating against him and all other's who choose to live that lifestyle. Because she felt this way with strong conviction, Carrie was disqualified. Afterward, she was asked if she had the opportunity to do it all over again, would she change her position so that she could be Miss USA? "No!" she responded emphatically. She would not silence her convictions for popular opinion. She knew what she believed, and no matter what people might say, even winning the pageant would not change her mind. Carrie's story was broadcasted extensively. Her answer caused a lot of controversy. But she was able to share her faith through this experience, and she encouraged other teens to believe that peer pressure isn't something that you just have to give in to. Standing for what you believe is more important than anything this world can offer, even if it means missing out on being Miss USA.

    Carrie's life was more of a sermon to me than many sermons I have heard. Would I, if in the same situation, stand for what I believe? Is my life a continual sermon that doesn't depend on who I am with, what I am doing, or where I am? These are some questions I think we need to ask ourselves. Like Carrie, I want to live a consistent Christian life that is based on God's sure word, not erratic feelings, unstable emotions, or the desire for fame and fortune. What about you?

~ Becky Brousson

November 24

Spiritual Muscle

Extraordinary trials, endured though the grace of God, will give him a deeper experience and greater spiritual strength, as vigilance, patience, and fortitude are called into exercise.
– Sketches from the Life of Paul, pg. 300

God will send us trials to test our faith and dependence on Him. It is by coming through difficulties that we will build spiritual strength and sinew. "Strength increases with difficulties met and overcome" (*Sketches from the Life of Paul*, pg. 297). We will become strong in Christ if we endure the testing and proving of God. We are the spectacle for the whole universe. Every time we fail to endure trails with cheerfulness, we are lessening our spiritual strength. As we learn to trust Jesus and lay all at His feet, we will find true joy and contentment.

During a severe allergic reaction I experienced, I was not able to do very much, not even exercise. It was very hard for me, because naturally I am a very outgoing person, and I don't like being inactive. I love to exercise and workout. Because I was not able to use my body, I started losing a lot of strength. I couldn't lift anything heavy or even do any fast walking. But I was gaining something of far greater value. Something that going to the gym couldn't achieve. Since I had extra time on my hands, I was able to pray and read God's Word. I learned to trust and fully rely on Him for all my needs. On my own I would get frustrated and depressed. By claiming the power of Jesus and His promises, I had peace, joy, and contentment. As we endure the trials God sends our way, we will develop spiritual strength, and in the end we will receive the crown of life He has waiting for us.

~ Becky Brousson

November 25

Who's in Control?

There was no atrocity which he [Nero] would not perpetrate, no vile act to which he would not stoop. – Sketches from the Life of Paul, pg. 302

Throughout history, many world leaders have been controlled by Satan. Certain names such as Hitler, Stalin, and Nero come to mind. Nero, the Roman emperor who sentenced Paul to death, "was more debased in morals…and at the same time capable of more atrocious cruelty, than any ruler who had preceded him" (*Sketches from the Life of Paul*, pg. 301). Can you imagine being so filled with evil that you would be willing to commit absolutely *any* wicked deed? There was no limit to the evil that commanded Nero's actions.

As we live from day to day, we often indulge in small sins—nothing really "bad," of course. We compromise on little things; we wait until tomorrow to fully surrender to Jesus; we hang onto things that He has asked us to give up. But in so doing, we forget what the motivating force is. We forget who is actually behind such actions. When put in the light of what Satan is really about, we see these small sins for what they really are: rebellion against God's love. Do you want to obey even the most trivial wish of a power that controlled someone like Nero?

There is only one way to be safe from diabolic control: Place yourself totally under *God's* direction. His love for you is beyond measure. Jesus is infinitely more loving than the devil is evil. As you live in God's control, He will transform you into someone who has no limit in sharing His love with others.

~ Jonathan Sharley

November 26

The Devil's Handshake

In every noble mind he [Nero] inspired abhorrence and contempt.
– Sketches from the Life of Paul, pg. 302

Nero, Emperor of the Roman Empire during Paul's time, was one of the monsters of history. He stooped to unprecedented levels of vice, debauchery, and cruelty, even murdering his own mother and wife. Nero and his close associates lived such demoralizing lives that they hardly seemed human. Because he was called the "Divine Emperor," Nero was honored, feared, and worshiped. But, in every noble heart, the very thought of the satanic king "inspired abhorrence and contempt."

A businessman attending a work-related party noticed a stranger among the many fashionable guests. Eventually, he wandered over to the stranger and started to make small talk with him. After a few moments the businessman introduced himself:

"I'm Fred Jones, and it certainly is a pleasure talking with you."
The stranger smiled and, holding out his hand, replied, "Indeed, a pleasure. I'm the Devil."
"What?" cried the businessman springing back in shock and alarm.
"Come now," said the Devil, "why so jumpy? Shall we not shake hands?"
"Shake hands? Never! I'll never shake hands with the Devil," the man looked horrified.
"Why not? You've shaken hands with me before."
"I have not!"
"Ahh, but you have. Every time you listen to my voice suggesting subtle sins, every time you compromise principle, every time you choose to do what you know isn't right—then you shake my hand."

I'm afraid this story is true of me. I would never shake the Devil's hand outright, but I excuse the many times I give in to his "little" temptations. If I am a true Christian, I will hate and despise sin and Satan as much as the Roman people hated the evil Nero. I want God to give me hatred for sin and strength to gain the victory, so that I will never shake the Devil's hand again!

~ Cara Dewsberry

November 27

Don't Get Bitter

Having rejected the truth, they were filled with hatred against it, and sought to destroy its faithful advocate. – Sketches from the Life of Paul, pg. 305

Down through the ages there have always been people who have rejected God's truth, and most of them have grown bitter and hateful towards those who do accept it. Some of those who had been bitterly opposed to the work of Paul in Ephesus were part of a group of Jews who accused Paul of starting the fire in Rome and caused his second arrest.

The Jewish leaders rejected Christ and guess what happened? They became so filled with envy and hatred that they allowed Satan into their minds. They caused Christ's death and both of Paul's imprisonments.

It is going to be the same in the last days. There will be some who accept the truth wholeheartedly; then there will be others who accept it temporarily and later reject it, and finally there will be those who completely reject it. Those in the middle class are often the ones who grow the most hateful towards those who accept the truth. Do you know anyone who has grown bitter toward the truth even though they used to be a part of it? Are you starting to stray from the truth? We need to pray for those who have grown bitter towards the truth, and for ourselves that our relationships with God stay strong.

~ Amy Windels

November 28

Those Habits

It is no easy matter to overcome sinful habits and practices. The work can be accomplished only with the help of divine grace.
– Sketches from the Life of Paul, pg. 306

An elderly teacher took a walk through a forest with his pupil. Suddenly he stopped and pointed to four plants close at hand. The first was just beginning to peep above the ground, the second had rooted itself pretty well into the earth, and the third was a small shrub, while the fourth was a full-sized tree.

The tutor said to his young companion, "Pull up the first plant." The boy did so eagerly, using only his fingers.
"Now pull up the second." The youth obeyed but found the task more difficult.
"Do the same with the third," he urged. The boy had to use all his strength to uproot it.
"Now," said the instructor, "try your hand with the fourth." The pupil put his arms around the trunk of the tall tree but couldn't even shake its leaves. "This, my son, is just what happens with our bad habits. When they are young, we can remove them easily, but when they are old, it's hard to uproot them, though we pray and struggle ever so sincerely."

We all have old bad habits that we need to break and things we should surrender to Christ. I have seen in my own life that the only way to overcome these evil tendencies is by enlisting God's help. Without Him, I know I would struggle on and on with little success. But, with Jesus by my side, I can be victorious. 1 Corinthians 15:57 says, "But thanks be to God, who gives us the victory through our Lord Jesus Christ" (KJV). Don't get discouraged; God wants to help you "uproot" those bad habits. Won't you ask Him for help today?

~Rebecca Luchak

November 29

Seeking God's Direction

The work can be accomplished only with the help of divine grace; but many neglect to seek such help, and endeavor to bring down the standard to meet their deficiencies, instead of bringing themselves up to meet the standard of God. – Sketches from the life of Paul, pg. 306

When I was in Pathfinders, we played a game called "The Great Controversy." The Pathfinders and staff were divided into three groups. One group represented Christians; the second group represented the influence of God, and the third group the distractions of life. The "Christians" were blindfolded, and then without their knowledge, two destinations were chosen—one for eternal life and the other for destruction.

During the game, the good and bad "influences" tried to convince the "Christians" to listen to their voices and would try to lead them to their destination. However, when the "Christians" raised their hands to "pray," only the "good influences" could speak.

The lessons we learned from this game were profound. Those who "prayed" constantly were never lost. Those who listened to the voice of a counselor or other person they trusted, without "praying," often ended up at the wrong destination.

We are now in a very serious game of life. We know Satan has many bad influences out there. However, we also know that we can connect with a God who has far greater power and wisdom than Satan. How amazing it is that we so often neglect to seek God's help and try to do things on our own, listening to the voices of friends or doing what we think is best. Proverbs 16:25 says, "There is a way that seemeth right unto a man, but the end thereof are the ways of death" (KJV). We cannot trust our own inclinations of what is right. We must constantly be seeking God's direction.

~ Joey Heagy

November 30

Enduring Hardships

Behold, we count them happy which endure. Ye have heard of the patience of Job, and have seen the end of the Lord; that the Lord is very pitiful, and of tender mercy. – James 5:11 KJV

Helen Roseveare was born in 1925 in England. She became a Christian as a medical student at Cambridge University in 1945. Later, in 1953, she decided to become a medical missionary to the Belgian Congo. When she arrived, she met a young man named John Mangadima. He wanted her to teach him how to be a doctor, and in exchange, he taught her Swahili. In 1960, the Congo declared its independence, and soon there was a bitter civil war. In the midst of the chaos and lawlessness, Helen continued to work. In the following years she was beaten, raped, and captured by rebel Samba soldiers. When she was finally freed a few months later, she left for England. Terrified, she vowed never to go back to the Congo. However, two months after she returned to England she received a letter from John. He told her that her work was not finished. In faith, Helen returned, and in her last years on the mission field, she established the Evangelical Medical Center, which consisted of a hospital, a training college, and four bush clinics.

Your Christian walk will not always be a "walk in the park." But, if you cling to your hope in Jesus, He will reward your faithfulness. Are you going through rough times? Ask God to strengthen you, as you remain committed in Him.

~ Jeremy Grabiner

December 1

Friends Forever

But notwithstanding the difficulties, Onesiphorus searched for Paul until he found him...The fear of scorn, reproach, or persecution, was powerless to terrify this true-hearted Ephesian... – Sketches from the Life of Paul, pg. 309

Have you ever had a friend like Onesiphorus? Have you ever been a friend like Onesiphorus?

Shortly before his execution, as Paul sat confined in a dark dungeon, he had little contact with his friends. Many, who had once come to his aid, now left him; for it was life-threatening to associate oneself with the apostle. "To visit Paul now was...to visit one who was the object of universal hatred..." (*Sketches from the Life of Paul*, pg. 307).

But Onesiphorus was not concerned about the dangers of visiting Paul. Only one thing was on his mind: Paul was in trouble and could benefit from his encouragement. With this goal, he set out to find Paul among the throngs of those in captivity. He finally succeeded and brought much joy to the apostle.

Onesiphorus is a wonderful example of the kind of friend Jesus is. In *our* great time of need, He left Heaven to bring hope to a captive world. He did not let the imminent dangers of persecution stop His plans. In dying on the cross, Christ made it possible to be a friend of God throughout all eternity. He succeeded in His mission and brought much joy to those who accepted His friendship.

What kind of friend are you? Are you a friend to those around you as Onesiphorus was to Paul? Are you that kind of friend to Jesus?

~ Jonathan Sharley

December 2

Peace

While his enemies were vehemently urging their accusations, Paul preserved a quiet dignity; no shade of fear or anger disturbed the peaceful serenity that rested upon his countenance. – Sketches from the Life of Paul, pg. 313

Confusion and madness filled the crowds of people rushing forward to see Paul's trial. He was supposed to be the man who had burned their city, and they wanted to see his fate. However, something was different about him. He had no fear in his eyes. Even the judges were surprised. They had seen thousands of criminals, but no criminal had ever looked so self-possessed and peaceful. They searched Paul's face, but nowhere in his countenance were they able to find a trace of guilt. So, why was Paul so peaceful in the midst of his opponents? No one was beside him to encourage him, but he knew that the God, Who controls the universe and placed the stars in heaven was with him.

Most of us panic and fear when we meet trials. But, if we are Christians, why do we have so much fear? Wasn't Jesus calm when He was in the midst of the Jewish council? Jesus and Paul learned how to trust in God no matter what. They learned that God, Who created the earth in six days and formed man out of dust, is in control of our lives. He is by our side when we are tempted. Jesus says to us, "Why are ye so fearful? How is it that ye have no faith?" (Mark 4:40 KJV). Someday there will come a time when you have to present your faith before judges, and if you fear the trials you face right now, how are you going to have peace before judges? The reason why Paul was so peaceful was that he knew God was in control, and he could trust Him. So if you are facing hard times, pray, "God I believe you are in control, grant me your peace."

~ David Chang

December 3

The Perfect Picture

The keen eyes of the judges, accustomed as they were to read the countenances of their prisoners, searched the face of Paul for some hidden trace of crime, but in vain. – Sketches from the Life of Paul, pg. 313

Jesus was perfect; not one fault could be found in Him. His perfection was not like the apparent flawlessness seen in the priests at the time. They merely put on this "godliness," and anyone with a bit of investigation could sense a serious masquerade.

The challenge for us today comes when we try to be Christians. Jesus was truly transparent, but as we try to be like him, we're usually faced with the sad truth that sin still dwells in us. With some examination, those closest to us can see how imperfect we are. We will get rid of problems with our characters as we draw closer to God, but the problems that others do see in us are bound to get in the way of our witness—and we really do want to show others an unmarred picture of Christ!

By committing and recommitting our lives to Jesus, we allow Him to flow through us without our blemishes integrating with His perfection. Christ longs to cleanse us so we can glorify God more and more. After all, He lives to glorify His father as well! With Jesus' help, we, like Paul, will be able to stand tall in the face of those who examine us, knowing that they examine a perfect picture, a heart cleansed in the blood of Jesus.

~ Robby Folkenberg

December 4

Mission

As Paul gazed upon the throng before him,—Jews, Greeks, Romans, with strangers from many lands,—his soul was stirred with an intense desire for their salvation. – Sketches from the Life of Paul, pg. 314

It was a bright morning when Paul was brought before Nero. Was Paul nervous? Not at all, for he knew Jesus was with him, and he had nothing to fear. However, as he stood before the haughty emperor, he took a quick look at the audience. There were rich, poor, educated, and illiterate, but all of them were destitute of the Bread of Life. As Paul saw this, his heart was stirred for the people's salvation. He lost sight of the perilous plight that he was in. Instead, he fixed his eyes upon Jesus and started to present the gospel. As Paul was explaining the truth, everyone was captivated, and many began to see what Jesus had done for them. They wept in gratitude for such amazing grace. No longer were they heathen; they were children of God.

Today we read stories like this and wonder why God doesn't use us like He did Paul. The answer is that we are not faithful to the mission He gives us. Christians, as followers of Christ, come to know the mission of God by looking at what Jesus did. Jesus' mission was to seek and save the lost. This was what He lived for. Often times we make so much of our own plans that we leave God out of the picture. God loves His children, and He chose you to accomplish His work. Just look around you; there are people physically or spiritually suffering not too far from you. They need Christ, and you can show Him to them. Stop neglecting your duty. Reach out your hand and do the mission that Jesus calls you to do.

~ David Chang

December 5

Losing Sight of Self

As Paul gazed upon the throng before him,—Jews, Greeks, Romans, with strangers from many lands,—his soul was stirred with an intense desire for their salvation. He lost sight of the occasion, of the perils which surrounded him, of the terrible fate which seemed so near. – Sketches from the Life of Paul, pg. 314

As Paul stood in front of the emperor and many onlookers, you would think that he might be frightened or nervous. He was accused of lighting the fire that burned half of Rome and was called before Nero, the one who could decide whether he should live or die. Nero was infamous for being appallingly cruel and utterly heartless. Now, I get very nervous in front of three or more people. My knees start shaking, my hands start sweating, and my heart beats faster and faster until I feel quite faint. But, here is Paul, with a calm about him that amazes everyone in the room. He's facing certain death, and yet he's not worried or nervous or even thinking about it. He looks at Nero and the throng and loses "sight of the occasion." He forgets about the trial and the fate which is about to be his. All he is concerned about is their souls.

You see, Paul was leaning on Christ for his strength and not on himself. He was thinking of the spiritual world and eternal life instead of earthly matters. He wasn't afraid of death for he knew in Whom he believed, and he yearned that the souls in the crowd could be given a chance to believe as well. He well knew that in such a pagan city, those people may never have another chance. So, putting aside all trepidation and forgetting about his own peril, he introduced them to Jesus, their Savior.

Think about it. Are you more worried about what others think of you than what God thinks of you? Are you more concerned with your earthly status than your record in the heavenly books? The next time you feel like hanging on to self, zoom out a little and try to imagine the bigger picture as God sees it. Earthly things will grow dim, and you will find eternal matters of much greater importance.

~ Melissa Butler

December 6

Take a Look

He looked above all this, to Jesus, the Divine Intercessor, the Advocate pleading before the throne of God in behalf of sinful men. Earnestly he pointed his hearers to the great Sacrifice...– Sketches from the Life of Paul, pg. 314

To any "normal" human being, the scene would have appeared dismal and miserably hopeless. Here was an innocent man being tried in the judgment hall of a blood-thirsty, demon-possessed emperor. But Paul did not see his situation in this manner. He was not focused on the trials which surrounded him. He was looking somewhere else. His mind was fixed upon Jesus, who had sacrificed everything to save those with whom he was speaking. The courtroom was filled with spectators and rulers who were held in Satan's firm grasp. But as Paul addressed the audience that wished him dead, "his soul was stirred with an intense desire for their salvation" (Sketches from the Life of Paul, pg. 314). As he spoke of the infinite Sacrifice that had been made, he longed for them to be set free by the One who is now "pleading before the throne of God in behalf of sinful men." He desired that they would look to Jesus, just as he did.

The old hymn says it so perfectly:

"Turn your eyes upon Jesus;
Look full in His wonderful face,
And the things of earth will grow strangely dim,
In the light of His glory and grace"
(words by Helen H. Lemmel).

What are you looking at? Are you focused on the seeming hopelessness of your situation, or are you "looking unto Jesus" (Hebrews 12:2 KJV). If you truly gaze upon the Savior, you will be inspired to point others—even those who wish you harm—to the Source of salvation.

~ Jonathan Sharley

December 7

Canute the Humble

His words are like a shout of victory above the roar of the battle. The cause of truth to which he has devoted his life, he makes appear as the only cause that can never fail. – Sketches from the Life of Paul, pg. 315

A certain king, named Canute, was out riding one day, along with several of his advisors. As they rode along a sandy beach, the king told them of some problems he was facing in England and how he wished he knew what to do. "Don't worry," an advisor stated, "You're the King of England; you can do whatever you want; all power is yours. You even rule land and sea!"

"You say I rule land and sea?" asked the king.

"Yes, of course," stated the advisor.

At that the king dismounted his horse and walked toward the waves. "What are you doing?" inquired his advisors. But, without answering, he strode toward the waves, commanding them to halt and not come any closer. Of course, the waves broke around his feet just the same as if he hadn't said anything at all. He tried again.

"Halt, don't come any further!" he cried, but to no avail. At that moment, his advisors reached him and pulled him back, telling him he could have drowned. Then the king answered, "Don't you see, I wanted to show you that there was a limit to my power." He then told his advisors not to talk of him being "all-powerful" anymore.

Do you ever feel like taking glory for something you didn't do? Maybe someone complimented you on a job well done, when you didn't actually do it, and you just decided to accept it anyways. Or maybe you exaggerated something you did to make it look better. You know, sometimes we don't think of this as being too bad, it's just a "little white lie"; it won't hurt anybody, and nobody will ever know. But really, God can see everything we do, and by doing these things, we are breaking His commandments. Next time you feel tempted to say or accept something false; remember that God hears every word. Don't make Him sad.

~ Dave White

December 8

Are You Sure?

...For I know whom I have believed and am persuaded that He is able to keep what I have committed to Him until that Day.
– 2 Timothy 1:12 NKJV

Paul exhibited a trust in his Savior that is rarely found in people today. His life was sustained by an assurance in Jesus and His saving power. This abiding peace allowed him to experience the harshest conditions and the sharpest persecutions without worry. Even the thought of death did not faze him! Knowing that he had received the gift of eternal life, he was "ready to give up life itself...for the good of others" (Sketches from the Life of Paul, pg. 312). This rock-solid confidence is what God longs for each one of us to have.

But how can we have this peace? How can we, like Paul, be sure of our salvation? First of all, we must realize that there is nothing that we could ever do to *earn* everlasting life. "Salvation is not a reward for the good things we have done" (Ephesians 2:9 NLT). On the contrary, "the free gift of God is eternal life through Christ" (Romans 6:23 NLT). Salvation is something that God gives us, even though we do not deserve it.

When you realize that you desperately need a Savior, when you sincerely confess your sins to Him, when you choose to follow His will—ask God for this free gift. "...whatever you ask for in prayer, believe that you have received it, and it will be yours" (Mark 11:24 NIV). When you believe that God has given you salvation, you receive it. What a foreign concept this is! Nevertheless, it is true! "Do not wait to *feel* that you are made whole, but say, 'I believe it; it *is* so, not because I feel it, but because God has promised'" (*Steps to Christ*, pg. 51).

In this manner, your assurance will strengthen until you have the confidence and peace that Paul had.

~ Jonathan Sharley

December 9

One Moment

For a moment, Heaven had been opened before him by the words of Paul, and its peace and purity had appeared desirable. That moment the invitation of mercy was extended even to the guilty and hardened Nero. But only for a moment...Not another ray of light was ever to penetrate the dense darkness that enveloped him. – Sketches from the Life of Paul, pg. 316

Nero was a very wicked man, whose atrocities and cruelty have seldom been surpassed. But contrary to logic, wicked people are not automatically lost. I believe every person has a chance to accept Christ as his Savior. Some may have several chances, but everyone has at least one moment of decision.

It may take you a moment to decide what to wear for the day or maybe a moment to answer a question on a test. Moments make up our hours, days, years, and lives. Have you ever stopped to think how important one moment is? One moment can mean eternal life or eternal death. You can accept Christ in a moment or reject Him just as quickly.

Nero, no doubt, had been given opportunities before and missed them. As Paul pleaded with him for his life, Nero faced his last "ray of light." He pictured Heaven as desirable and right then could have been saved. Think of it! God was reaching out to Nero, and for a moment, Nero felt like reaching back. "But only for a moment." Immediately, he sent Paul back to his prison cell, and fell back into the deep darkness. His last moment of opportunity was gone.

It's taken you many moments to read this. Do you see Heaven as desirable? Do you see God stretching out His hand of mercy to you right now? He is. Will you accept Him, this moment?

~ Melissa Butler

December 10

The Hard Way

[Nero cried] "I am lost! I am lost!" He had not, like the faithful Paul, a powerful, compassionate God to rely upon in his hour of peril.
– Sketches from the Life of Paul, pg. 317

The Roman people had finally tired of Nero's vice and cruelty and had risen up in rebellion. The fear-crazed tyrant could hear the confused ruckus of rioting and insurrection in the streets and knew that his days were numbered. I wonder if, in that moment of fearful despair, the emperor remembered the serenity of Paul at his trial. Oh, to have the same peace as he! But Nero had rejected the offered mercy, and now he had no refuge in which to hide from the storm.

In *Christiana* (the sequel to *Pilgrim's Progress*), Christian's son, Matthew, asks one of the damsels of the House Beautiful a question: Is it harder to be saved or harder to be lost? She responds that both are easier and harder. So, how can this be? Being saved seems harder because we must deny ourselves and battle against sin in this life; but it is really easier because Jesus will be there to help us, and in the world to come, we will enjoy unending peace and happiness. Being lost seems easier because we don't really have to do anything. We can just breeze through life following our carnal desires and enjoying the pleasures of this world. But in reality, "the way of transgressors is hard" (Proverbs 13:15 KJV) because they spend their lives fighting against the impressions of the Spirit, and in the end, they must face the just reward for their sinful lives—eternal death and separation from God.

If you, like Nero, choose "ease" in this world, you will lose the reward to come and will be told by God, "I never knew you: depart from me" (Matthew 7:23 KJV). But, if you choose the "hard" way, taking up your cross and following Christ, you will hear the loving welcome, "Well done, good and faithful servant…enter thou into the joy of thy Lord" (Matthew 25:23 KJV). What will you choose?

~ Cara Dewsberry

December 11

Sadia's Protector

The angel of the LORD encampeth round about them that fear him, and delivereth them. – Psalm 34:7 KJV

Sadia Sultana was a Muslim student. One day, she read a Christian pamphlet in her dorm room and decided to become a Christian. Her father was an Islamic ruler, so she expected to lose her inheritance because of her conversion. The reaction she got from her family was not what she had expected. When she told her father that she had become a Christian and that she had changed her name to Faith, he exploded with rage. Her father and brothers stripped her naked and tied her to a chair fixed with a metal plate with which they planned to electrocute her. Before they killed her, she asked for her Bible to be placed in her lap. They agreed, saying that her religion still would not be able to protect her. She was able to touch a corner of the Bible and felt a sudden peace, as though someone was with her.

They plugged the cord into the socket, but nothing happened. They tried four times with various cables, but it was as though the electricity refused to flow. Frustrated, her father yelled, "You are no longer my daughter." He then threw her out into the street, naked. She ran through the streets, humiliated and in pain, to her friend's house. The people stared at her with curiosity.

The next day, her friend asked the neighbors what they had thought when they saw Faith running through the street naked. "What are you talking about?" they asked. "The girl had a wonderful white dress on. We asked ourselves why someone so beautifully clothed had to run through the streets."

God had hidden Sadia's nakedness from the people and covered her with a beautiful white dress. This true story is living proof that we serve a God who still protects His servants. Are you His servant? If you are, then He will protect you.

~ Jeremy Grabiner

December 12

Mercy

God in his infinite mercy bears long with the transgressors of his law.
– Sketches from the Life of Paul, pg. 318

Paul, during the last days of his life, was facing the "king of the world," Nero. During his last trial, the apostle stood as God's representative. His words exhibited the happiness of being a son of God. Paul delivered to his audience the great gospel truths. "The gospel message found its way to the minds and hearts of many who would never have listened to it but for the imprisonment of Paul" (*Sketches from the Life of Paul*, pg. 315).

As Paul kept speaking, Nero started to listen to the truth. Finally, he saw what a blunder his whole life was. That moment, God extended an invitation of mercy to the sinful, cruel Nero. In those moments, "Heaven had been opened before him by the words of Paul, and its peace and purity had appeared desirable" (*Sketches from the Life of Paul*, pg. 315).

Unfortunately, Nero's heart ignored God's mercy. He ordered that Paul be taken back to his dungeon, and as soon as Paul left the judgment hall, so did the mercy of God.

God has oceans of mercy. He delights in showing this mercy and compassion. Even the stone-hearted Nero was shown God's mercy, no matter how cruel and dark his soul was. God offers His mercy to those that are repentant. The only thing that separates us from His unending mercy and love is our unwillingness to accept His invitation.

~ David Ortiz

December 13

Love Towards All

To hate and reprove sin, and at the same time to manifest pity and tenderness for the sinner, is a difficult attainment. – Sketches from the Life of Paul, pg. 321

As Jesus was dying on the cross for the sins of all, He still reached out to His mother. His mother had sinned of course, and in a sense Jesus was suffering right then because of His sinful mother. Here Jesus gives us an incredible example as well as a mandate. What is clear is that Jesus hated sin—He paid the ultimate price to have it exterminated forever! But, Jesus loved sinners. That's why he spent so long on earth. He ministered to the people for over thirty years because he loved and cared about them. Even on the cross, Jesus extended love towards the sinner.

I love apples! The crisp, flavorful, tangy, yet oh-so-sweet morsels brighten my day and satisfy my appetite. Yet, when a worm-infested apple approaches my mouth, I turn away in disgust! Do I now not appreciate those Granny Smiths? No, I am repulsed by the worms found within.

All too often, we shun sinners because of the sin in them, forgetting that they are still children of God, no matter how tainted they are. Now, I'm not advocating spending excessive amounts of time with sinners without caution and reserve. A rotten apple spoils the whole barrel. Instead, at least recognize those in sin as God's children, and Jesus will help you show pity and tenderness towards them all.

~ Robby Folkenberg

December 14

A Clearer Light

The more earnest our own efforts to attain to holiness of heart and life, the more acute will be our perception of sin, and the more decided our disapproval of any deviation from right. – Sketches from the Life of Paul, pg. 321

To attain holiness is no trivial matter. There must be a constant seeking after God, a constant desire to know His will more clearly. Holiness is essential if we are to honor the temple of God—our hearts and lives. We have become too laid back, and the fight that we should be winning seems a failure. If we are to perceive the arts of the enemy, then we must awaken and arise.

My life has recently been awakened from the delusive grasp sin had on me. Until recently, sin had invaded my mind without my knowledge. I did not see sin for what it was. As my relationship with God strengthened, however, it was as if my eyes were opened for the first time. It wasn't that my thoughts and actions hadn't been counted as sin; I had just not known the One who died for my sin. Suddenly, choices that had always been a struggle became a clear no, and decisions that had always been yes began to be doubtful in my mind. One such example is how I viewed the way I spent my time on Sabbath. I had always thought that since the Sabbath was made for man, that as long as I enjoyed my Sabbath, I could do whatever I wanted. Now, though, my time spent on Sabbath has become less about me and more about a friendship with my Creator. I now see the edges of the narrow path in a clearer light.

If you have lost sight of the path, return to where you last saw the light. If you have lost sight of the edge, ask God for clearer light. As you seek to attain holiness, God promises that His light will shine brighter and brighter around you, making it clear to see the path. Your perceptions will be quickened. Don't stop pressing forward. The battle for your soul is still raging.

~ Buddy Taylor

December 15

The Ivory Horn

Let him that thinketh he standeth take heed lest he fall.
– 1 Corinthians 10:12 KJV

    Roland, the finest knight in Charlemagne's army, owned a prized possession. This possession was an ivory horn, which had belonged to Charlemagne's grandfather and had been given to Roland as a token of appreciation for his great courage and valor. "If you're ever in trouble," Charlemagne had told him, "blow your horn, and I will come to your rescue."

    One day, the time came when Roland did need his horn. He and one hundred knights were traveling over the Pyrenees Mountains as the rear guard for Charlemagne's army when, suddenly, one thousand Saracens surrounded them. "Quick, blow your horn," a friend named Oliver urged. But Roland quickly dismissed the idea and replied that he was completely capable of winning the battle on his own.

    After about half of his men had fallen, he finally raised the horn and reluctantly blew a long blast. Charlemagne heard the sound and immediately turned his troops around and headed back through the pass; but it was too late. By the time he got there and scattered the Saracens, only a few knights were still alive. Roland was found among the fallen with the ivory horn still in his hand.

    How many times are you and I like Roland? We think that we are strong enough to handle Satan and his temptations, but really, he is far stronger than we are, and we end up losing the battle. Then, when we realize there's no hope, we blow on the "ivory horn" of prayer as a last resort. But sometimes it's too late, and we have to reap the consequences of our decision. Next time you're in a battle, use the "ivory horn" of prayer before it's too late.

~ Dave White

December 16

A Penny for Your Thoughts

In his sermon on the mount he showed how its requirements extend beyond the outward acts, and take cognizance of the thoughts and intents of the heart. That law, obeyed, will lead men to deny ungodliness and worldly lusts, and to live "soberly, righteously, and godly, in this present world." – Sketches from the Life of Paul, pg. 323, 324

When I was younger, I used to presume that I could just think whatever I wanted to. But as I have grown older, I have realized that our thoughts are something that we have to really take seriously. Thoughts turn into actions. The more you think about something, the more you want to do it. I had an experience once that illustrates this. I saw a yellow shirt in a store that I really liked. Everyday after that, I thought about it more and more, until I went and bought it. If I had told myself I didn't really need it, then I wouldn't have bought it. But, as I daydreamed about the shirt more and more, my thoughts turned into actually purchasing it.

You know, if we are constantly thinking about someone or something, inevitably we are going to gravitate towards what we are thinking about. We must spend time communing with God and ask Him to control our thoughts; then it will be easier for us to live "soberly, righteously, and godly in this present world." Nowadays, it's so easy to forget about God in our everyday activities because we are just so busy. But, if we purposely take time to spend with Him everyday and think pure thoughts, God will help us. Just because we can put on a good front while around others, doesn't mean anything. God can read our thoughts and He knows the very intent of our hearts; we can't fool Him. In the end, it will only be to Him that we must give an account. Try letting Him help you control your thoughts today; He's just waiting for you to ask.

~ Becky Brousson

December 17

Sabbath

These teachers trample under their feet the fourth commandment, and instead of the day which God has blessed and sanctified, they honor a day which he has not commanded, and upon which he did not rest.
– Sketches from the Life of Paul, pg. 324

God made the world in six days, and the seventh day He hallowed. God rested from His work on the seventh day because He wanted to spend time with us. God specifically designed that man should lay aside all his worries and get to know God on the Sabbath. However, Satan perverted the "holiday" that God made. Instead of worshipping on Saturday, Satan deceived man into worshipping on Sunday. Thus, man threw out the day that God hallowed and set up a new day to rest. This was an open rebellion against God, and Satan laughed in victory.

Exodus 31:16, 17 says, "Wherefore the children of Israel shall keep the Sabbath, to observe the Sabbath throughout their generations, for a perpetual covenant. It is a sign between me and the children of Israel for ever" (KJV). If Sabbath is a sign of the relationship between God and man, then keeping it signifies that you are Child of God! Furthermore, near the close of probation, everyone's destiny will be tested on whether or not they will keep the Sabbath. So, the Sabbath that God hallowed is not just a day of rest; it is also the test that judges the world. This does not mean that everyone that hasn't kept Sabbath will be lost. Only those that live near the close of probation will be tested on the issue of the Sabbath.

Sabbath is a day God has set apart to get to know us, and all He asks of us is to lay aside our work and spend time with Him. It doesn't mean that you should only study the Bible. Jesus healed on Sabbath. You can learn about God through witnessing, prayer, nature, and Scripture. But remember, for one day a week, lay aside all your worries and spend time with Jesus.

~ David Chang

December 18

Preach the Word

With the growing contempt for God's holy law, there is an increasing distaste for religion, an increase of pride, love of pleasure, disobedience to parents, and self-indulgence; and thoughtful minds everywhere anxiously inquire, What can be done to correct these alarming evils? The answer is found in Paul's exhortation to Timothy: "Preach the word." – Sketches from the Life of Paul, pg. 324

We live in an age of intensity, one of increasing ungodliness and evil. It seems there are more atheists, pleasure-seekers, and disobedient children than ever before. Even though it may appear that there is nothing to correct these evils, there is a solution. We must "preach the word." God's word has the power to change lives, and in order to correct these evils, we must preach the word.

Paul's counsel could be referring to huge evangelistic efforts or TV ministries (which are very important), but I think it's referring to our daily living. We must be in a spirit of evangelism. Wherever we go, we must be looking for opportunities to share the wonderful words of life.

If your influence changes only one person, you have changed the world. Don't ever think that there is nothing you can do to lessen the suffering on this earth. Even if you only introduce hope to one person, you have lessened suffering in the world. You can't feed every hungry child in Africa, but you can feed one hungry homeless child living down the street. You can't preach to the continent of Asia, but you can share the word on the bus or to a co-worker. As you go throughout your day, look for opportunities to make our world a better place.

~ Melissa Butler

December 19

Not Ashamed

Be not thou therefore ashamed of the testimony of our Lord, nor of me his prisoner: but be thou partaker of the afflictions of the gospel according to the power of God. – 2 Timothy 1:8 KJV

Hugh Lattimer once preached a sermon before King Henry VIII. King Henry was displeased by the boldness of the sermon and ordered Lattimer to preach again on the following Sunday and apologize for the offence he had given. The next Sunday, Hugh began his sermon by telling himself: "Hugh Lattimer, dost thou know before whom thou are this day to speak? To the high and mighty monarch, the king's most excellent majesty, who can take away thy life, if thou offendest. Therefore, take heed that thou speakest not a word that may displease. But then consider well, Hugh, dost thou not know from whence thou comest—upon Whose message thou are sent? Even by the great and mighty God, Who is all-present and Who beholdeth all thy ways and Who is able to cast thy soul into hell! Therefore, take care that thou deliverest thy message faithfully." He then preached the same sermon he had preached the preceding Sunday with considerably more energy.

Hugh Lattimer was not ashamed of what he preached, and he was willing to risk his life for it. So many times I lack the courage to stand up for what I believe in. I cower in a corner because I am afraid of being ridiculed. However, Paul tells us "For God hath not given us the spirit of fear; but of power, and of love, and of a sound mind" (2 Timothy 1:7 KJV). Accepting this spirit from God will give you the power to stand no matter what situation you are in.

~ Jeremy Grabiner

December 20

Amazing Grace

Moreover the law entered that the offence might abound. But where sin abounded, grace abounded much more. – Romans 5:20 NKJV

One day, while evangelist Billy Graham was driving through a small southern town he was stopped by a policeman and charged with speeding. Graham admitted his guilt, and was told by the officer that he would have to appear in court.

When the court date arrived the judge asked, "Guilty, or not guilty?" When Graham pleaded guilty, the judge replied, "That'll be ten dollars—a dollar for every mile you went over the limit." Suddenly, the judge recognized the famous minister. "You have violated the law," He began. "The fine must be paid—but I am going to pay it for you." He took a ten-dollar bill from his own wallet, attached it to the ticket, and then took Graham out to a restaurant and bought him dinner! "That," said Mr. Graham, "is how God treats repentant sinners!"

John Newton, an ex-sea captain who had been highly involved in the African slave trade to England, was extremely sorrowful because of his involvement in selling others into slavery. His sins seemed to be a great load pressing him down. But when he experienced God's forgiveness, a huge load of guilt fell from his shoulders and he was free. In his joy, he wrote the inspired song "Amazing Grace," which has touched many lives over the years.

We are all guilty under God's law and have fallen short of His salvation. But there is hope for the repentant heart. All you need to do is ask for God's forgiveness, and He will replace your guilt with His peace and joy.

~ Rebecca Luchak

December 21

No Question

God has declared His will, and it is absolute madness for men to change or even question that which has gone out of His lips.
– Sketches from the Life of Paul, pg. 325

Have you ever questioned God's will? Perhaps you have argued against your parents wishes. It almost always ends up for the worse. It takes much effort to surrender your will. But, being stubborn and resistant can have tragic consequences.

There was a couple with six children who were their dearest possessions. They lived in a two-story house in a quaint little neighborhood in Charlottetown, New Hampshire.

One day the parents came back from a trip to the grocery store, and found the house in flames. There were no firemen in those days, so the father ran over to the window where the children were crying. They were two stories up, but the father yelled for them to jump. Each child leaped out with unquestioning faith and landed safely in their father's arms. But, the last little boy was too afraid. He didn't know if his father was right. What if he failed to catch him? The house was too engulfed in flames for the father to go in and get his little boy. He begged and pleaded for his little boy to jump, but the child couldn't bring himself to jump. He wanted to jump, yet he stood by the window with a desperate struggle in his mind. The little boy could only think for so long before the smoke and flames stole his life. If only he had listened to his father. If only he had jumped on first impulse and not stopped to question.

Questioning leaves room for doubt. It gives Satan a foot in the door to plant seeds of uncertainty in our gullible minds. Following Jesus without a question only leads to happiness. Take God at His word and don't let Satan have the chance to make you reconsider.

~ Veronica Nudd

December 22

Looking to the Cross

He clung to the cross of Christ as the only guarantee of success.
– Sketches from the Life of Paul, pg. 326

Often we look to others for affirmation, wanting them to cheer us on so that we know we're doing a great job. It is easy to doubt whether or not we're successful if people are telling us different things. This has shown me that I need to base my identity on something that is always stable. It is hard to fully realize, but when we are insecure, we will always want to do what other people tell us to do. This may lead us into doing things we really don't want to. But, our desire to fit in often leads us to do them anyways.

Norma-Jean was an amazing young lady with many talents. When she went to Hollywood and started singing and acting, her producers changed her name to Marilyn Monroe. Whatever it was they wanted her to do, she did, just to keep up her appearance with the public. This path she was taking just kept going downhill. She ended up overdosing on pills, quickly ending her short, miserable life.

When we look to Christ for His approval and seek to have Him as our role model, He will bring us true success. Trying to fit in only leads to unhappiness; but when we look to Jesus and strive to be like Him, we will be happy with who we are.

~ Melody Hyde

December 23

A Few Good Men

Cultivated, refined, sanctified, self-sacrificing men are needed; men who will not shun trial and responsibility, but who will lift the burdens wherever they may find them; men who are brave, who are true; men who have Christ formed within them, and who, with lips touched with holy fire, "will preach the word" amid the thousands who are preaching fables. – Sketches from the Life of Paul, pg. 326

During World War II, the famous English Prime Minister, Winston Churchill, called together labor leaders to enlist their services for coal production. At the end of his presentation, he asked them to imagine a parade celebrating the British victory at the close of the war.

First, he said, the sailors that dominated the sea would come. Then the soldiers that fought in Africa would march in. Later, the dashing pilots would arrive. Last of all, he said, a long line of sweat-stained, soot-streaked men in miner's caps would approach the celebration. Someone would call from the crowd,
"And where were you during the critical days of our struggle?"
The answer would be exclaimed from ten thousand throats, "We were deep in the earth with our faces to the coal."

Not all the jobs in the church will bring the glamour and prominence that you want. But the people who truly help the church accomplish its mission, are those who have their "faces to the coal." God has opened the enlistment lines for His heavenly army. Are you willing to go "against the grain, and work without applause"? ("A Few Good Men" by Barry and Suzanne Jennings).

~ David Ortiz

December 24

Newness of Life

Except a man be born again, he cannot see the kingdom of God.
– John 3:3 KJV

In his book, An Anthropologist on Mars, neurologist Oliver Sacks tells about Virgil, a man who had been blind from early childhood. When he was fifty, Virgil underwent surgery and was given the gift of sight. Nevertheless, Virgil and Dr. Sacks found out, having the physical capacity for sight is not the same as seeing.

Virgil's first experiences with sight were confusing. He was able to make out colors and movements, but arranging them into a coherent picture was more difficult. Over time, he learned to identify various objects, but his habits and his behaviors were still those of a blind man. Dr. Sacks asserts, "One must die as a blind person to be born again as a seeing person. It is the interim, the limbo…that is so terrible."

Dying to self and leaving our old habits behind can be demanding at times. We must have, like Virgil, a completely new life. A cup made out of dirt cannot hold clean water for an extended period of time, because the dirt will eventually mix with the water. Being "born-again" is not only a mere observation of new life in Christ; it is a change in identity. If we have a half-hearted change, the result may be worse than what we had before. We must have a fully committed change. Will you accept the new life Christ offers you today?

~ Jourdain Smith

December 25

Purchase of Blood

Take heed therefore unto yourselves, and to all the flock, over the which the Holy Ghost hath made you overseers, to feed the church of God, which he hath purchased with his own blood.
– Acts 20:28 KJV

Christ purchased our fallen race with His very own blood. He gave us the inestimable gift of being able to choose between life and death. When we teach others about Christ, it is of great importance that we realize that we are speaking to the purchase of the blood of God.

We are to share Christ with others, but how can we do this if we don't live like He did? Our earthly calling is to be spiritual mirrors that take the Divine Light, which has shone upon us, and beam it upon others. The only way we can prove ourselves worthy of this calling is through a life of devotion, purity, and godly conversation.

As we endeavor to do the work that we have to do, it is inevitable that we will be persecuted and despised by men. God needs faithful workers who are not afraid to face these consequences. If we endeavor to accomplish our goals regardless of what people think, we will find a great reward waiting for us in the end.

~ Leighton Sjoren

December 26

Spread the Banner

As the faithful, toil-worn standard-bearers are offering up their lives for the truth's sake, who will come forward to take their places?
– Sketches from the Life of Paul, pg. 327

When I think universal, I think Coca-Cola. Wherever I've gone in the world, whether it is India or Tanzania, there are bound to be soda bottles, usually glass, with the Coca-Cola emblem or name somewhere on them. According to one source, 97% of the world has heard of Coca-Cola, 72% have seen a can of Coca-cola, and 51% have tasted a can of calorie-loaded Coca-Cola! Unbelievable, considering that Coca-Cola was founded fairly recently, in 1886! There must have been some extreme marketing strategies!

Now, I'm not suggesting we should be marketing the Gospel like Coca-Cola markets soft drinks, but just imagine if the church was like the Coca-Cola Company. By now, we could be in heaven, because we would have spread the Good News over the entire earth, fulfilling the great marketing plan of Matthew 28! Why is it that the gospel, after over 2,000 years of circulation, hasn't reached every kindred, tongue, and nation?

I feel responsible for this problem. As a young person, I haven't stepped up to the plate and taken this good news to the world! Revelation 3 says that the last day church will be lukewarm. But, this is no excuse for young people like me, because if we don't catch the flame, the fire will die! Whether young or old, the standard needs to be held high so the world can "see that the Lord is good" (Psalm 34:8 KJV)!

~ Robby Folkenberg

December 27

Heed the Call

As the faithful, toil-worn standard-bearers are offering up their lives for the truth's sake, who will come forward to take their places?
– Sketches from the Life of Paul, pg. 327

During the Revolutionary War, men were constantly being wounded and killed. In the midst of this chaos, William Hays faithfully fought at his post, firing the cannon at the opposing side. But one day, Mr. Hays was hit by enemy fire and was no longer able to continue fighting. His wife, Mary Hays McCauly (also known as Molly Pitcher), treated his wounds, but she didn't stop there. Not wanting her husband's noble efforts to die out, she decided to carry on the fight herself. She had seen him fire the cannon before and, thus, knew what to do. Although she was certainly not the most skilled or trained person on the battle field, she was able to take up the fight where her husband had left off.

On the spiritual battle field, many have been wounded in action. Countless more have given up their lives for the cause of Christ. Because the battle is so intense and the casualties so frequent, there is a constant need for additional recruits.

Will you heed the call to join the ranks of our strong Commander, Jesus Christ? This is no small thing; this war is very real—much more so than we realize. Are you willing to devote your entire self to the war effort, even in the possibility of death? Will you carry on the fight for which the martyrs so nobly gave their lives?

As we march on to ultimate victory, we will soon be able to say, "I have fought the good fight, I have finished the race, and I have remained faithful. And now the prize awaits me—the crown of righteousness, which the Lord…will give me on the day of his return" (2 Timothy 4:7, 8 NLT).

~ Jonathan Sharley

December 28

Faithful Youth

Will our young men accept the holy trust at the hand of their fathers? Are they now preparing to fill the vacancies made by the death of the faithful? Will the apostle's charge be heeded, the call to duty be heard, amid the incitements to selfishness and ambition which allure the youth? – Sketches from the Life of Paul, pg. 327

In the American Revolution, as the war continued, the British found that there was a big difference if they were fighting against a group of militia or the trained American army. When they advanced on the militia, the men would scatter and run at the first charge. However, the more trained and committed soldiers would stand their ground as long as they were able, even when they were outmatched. The British were the best trained army in the world at that time, and even when they marched in straight lines across a field directly into gunfire they kept their discipline. When a soldier fell, the one behind stepped in to take his place.

God needs the young to be training to be faithful soldiers for Him. We are to become an army of youth, rightly trained. The training and discipline we gain now in learning to follow Jesus in the smaller things of life, while we are sheltered in our "training camps," learning from Godly teachers, will be of tremendous assistance to us as we face the bigger battles of life in the future.

We are a generation that has the honor of being on the front lines of the final conflict in the Great Controversy as it comes to a dramatic conclusion. We don't want to be like the militia, who had a desire to stand for their country, but hadn't taken the time to gain the discipline they needed. So let's stand up and become that army, fighting against the forces of darkness and sin that are in this world.

~ Joey Heagy

December 29

Looking Back

The apostle was looking into the great beyond, not with uncertainty or in dread, but with joyful hope and longing expectation.
– Sketches from the Life of Paul, pg. 331

"I have fought the good fight, I have finished the race, I have kept the faith" (2 Timothy 4:7 NKJV). Paul expresses these words as he glimpses back into his life. He's happy to say that he has no regrets about it. But he is not standing on the champion's podium; he is imprisoned in a cold, damp cell awaiting his execution. Even though a horrible death awaits him, the fact that his life and ministry had not been in vain gives him hope for his impending future.

I have looked back at my life, and unfortunately, I have done regrettable things. I have started to see that on many occasions, I have wasted my time. In my life, I do not have the close-knit relationship that God and the apostle Paul shared. Paul's life has also taught me that my life had its lowest moments when I was furthest away from God. Paul's faithfulness to God has inspired me to change. It has helped me to realize that I must walk closer to my Savior.

Let us grow in Christ so that at the end of our labors, we will look back and say: "I have fought the good fight, I have finished the race, I have kept the faith. Finally, there is laid up for me the crown of righteousness, which the Lord, the righteous Judge, will give to me on that day, and not to me only but also to all who have loved His appearing" (verses 7, 8).

~ David Ortiz

December 30

Will You Trust Him?

And as the sword of the executioner descends, and the shadows of death gather about the martyr's soul, his latest thought springs forward, as will his earliest thought in the great awakening, to meet the Lifegiver who shall welcome him to the joy of the blest.
– Sketches from the Life of Paul, pg. 333

Inhumane torture is the best way to describe the steel factory in a federal prison of North Korea. The prisoners there worked around molten steel that exceeded 1,000 degrees Celsius. Though they worked 16 hours a day, they were given no food. Instead of telling them what to do, their taskmasters beat them until they understood their jobs. The prisoners' bodies were covered with lashes and were severely burned from the sparks that constantly flew out of the smelting furnaces. But guess what? These prisoners that were treated like animals were not hardened criminals, but Christians.

One day, the prison master gathered all the Christians together and screamed, "If any of you give up your faith, I will restore your freedom and make you rich and famous; all you have to do is step out of the crowd." After he spoke, there was dead silence. Nobody spoke or moved. In impatience, the prison master repeated the words. But the more he spoke, the more determined the Christians were not to move. The furious prison master started to beat them and curse the God they served. But, amid this persecution not one Christian compromised his faith. Their faith was strong, and they knew that if they died, their next sight would be of the coming of their Lord. When he was tired of beating them, the prison master ordered that buckets of molten iron be brought and poured over each prisoner. Instantaneously, their beaten bodies melted into liquid, and those who did not die were shot on the spot. In one day, all the workers from that steel factory died.

There will come a time when you will have to face death. But when it comes, you can say, "Though I walk through the valley of the shadow of death, I will fear no evil: for Thou art with me" (Psalms 23:4 KJV).

~ David Chang

December 31

Glorious Reward

Like a trumpet peal has his voice rung out through all the ages, nerving with his own courage thousands of witnesses for Christ, and wakening in thousands of sorrow-stricken hearts the echo of his own triumphant joy: "I am now ready to be offered, and the time of my departure is at hand. I have fought the good fight, I have finished my course, I have kept the faith. Henceforth there is laid up for me a crown of righteousness, which the Lord, the righteous Judge, shall give me at that day; and not to me only, but unto all them also that love His appearing." – Sketches from the Life of Paul, pg. 334

Oh, what a faith had the aged Paul! "Well nigh a score of centuries have passed since Paul the aged poured out his blood as a witness for the word of God and for the testimony of Christ" (*Sketches from the Life of Paul,* pg. 334). He regretted nothing in his life save the years spent persecuting the church of Christ. This apostle of God placed his entire life in the service of the Gospel. He gave himself, as a martyr, for Him in whom he had believed.

Luther, Huss, Wycliffe, Calvin, Simons: all these men also gave their lives for Christ. Nothing could separate them from Him in whom they believed. Faithful, even unto death, these preachers of truth stood in the strength of their risen Lord. Together with Paul, they leave this message: Be faithful to God!

Today, we stand on the brink of a life and death decision. Will we reject truth for a longer, easier life on this earth, only to die eternally? Or will we sacrifice our lives for the Lord, looking forward to that eternal crown of righteousness? The decision is yours alone. Time is short, and the Lord will soon return to reward the faithful.

Paul died looking forward to that crown of life. Are you looking forward to the Second Coming? My prayer is that you and I will be ready.

~ Douglas Schappert